Lauren Wright has written a timely and important book. A reality game show host is in the Oval Office amid speculation of other glitterati considering a challenge. Wright raises the critical question of whether the skills of celebrities have any relevance to those required for political leadership and governance. A Princeton University lecturer, she combines the rigorous research of an academic intellectual with a keen understanding of practical politics gleaned from her participation and earlier writings. This is a must read for anyone interested in political leadership today.

Albert R. Hunt, *former Washington Bureau Chief and Executive Editor of* The Wall Street Journal *and* Bloomberg News

It was perhaps inevitable that in a culture as obsessed with celebrity as ours, we would someday end up with one in the White House. Is Donald Trump an aberration and a corrective, or a sign of things to come? Lauren Wright explores how the world of politics and celebrity have become so intertwined, and where this may be taking us.

Karen Tumulty, *Columnist,* The Washington Post

Lauren Wright has written the opening salvo to the age of celebrity politics. Set within a historic framework, her study combines her own research, scholarly literature, and astute analysis to warn Americans of the very dangers the framers feared when they created the U.S. Constitution: demagoguery, ill-informed decision-making, and self-interested, autocratic rule. Who's to blame and what do we do about it? Read Wright's innovative, well-written and thought-provoking book to find out.

Stephen J. Wayne, *Georgetown University*

Donald Trump wasn't the first celebrity to win an election, and he won't be the last. Lauren Wright helps explain why celebrities run for office and why many voters will support them. Her conclusion is a troubling one: Celebrities have the tools to entertain voters, but not the tools to govern effectively. This is a timely and important book.

John Sides, *George Washington University*

STAR POWER

Are celebrity politics the spice of American public life or a pox on policy progress? This book identifies and measures the attributes of celebrities that make them well-equipped to win campaigns and yet poorly prepared to govern effectively. The framers of the U.S. Constitution worried about the propensity of an undereducated public to elect unqualified entertainers rather than fit characters to government positions. Celebrities have come to play an increasingly central role in the American political process as fundraisers, surrogates, and as candidates themselves, yet remain a sorely understudied topic in political science. Through a multimethod approach that includes qualitative analysis, novel public opinion surveys, and survey experiments, this book assesses whether Americans are more likely to vote for celebrities than well-known traditional politicians and the implications of these preferences for democracy in the U.S. Perfect for students, scholars, and interested citizens, *Star Power* looks at the contemporary American political landscape through new lenses of research as well as popular appeal.

Dr. Lauren A. Wright is a Lecturer in Politics and Public Affairs at Princeton University, where she teaches courses on The Presidency and Executive Power, Women and Politics, and Political Communication. Wright is also the author of *On Behalf of the President: Presidential Spouses and White House Communications Strategy Today* (Praeger, 2016). Wright is a contributor to *The Hill* and *The Huffington Post* and her writing has frequently appeared in *The Washington Post*. Her commentary has also been featured in *The Atlantic*, *The Chicago Tribune*, *The Denver Post*, *The Houston Chronicle*, *Newsweek*, *The New York Daily News*, *The San Francisco Chronicle*, *USA Today*, and *US News and World Report*. She is a frequent guest political analyst and has appeared on CNN, C-SPAN, Fox News, and MSNBC. Wright's research interests include presidential politics, public opinion, and public and private sector communications strategy. She currently serves as Strategic Communications Director at NV5 Global, Inc. (Nasdaq: NVEE) and is a board member of The White House Transition Project. Wright received a Ph.D. in Government from Georgetown University in 2014. Before that, she was a Field Representative for Meg Whitman's campaign for Governor of California.

MEDIA and POWER

Series Editor: David L. Paletz
www.routledge.com/Media-and-Power/book-series/MP

Media and Power is a series that publishes work uniting media studies with studies of power. This innovative and original series features books that challenge, even transcend, conventional disciplinary boundaries, construing both media and power in the broadest possible terms. At the same time, books in the series are designed to fit into several different types of college courses in political science, public policy, communication, journalism, media, history, film, sociology, anthropology, and cultural studies. Intended for the scholarly, text, and trade markets, the series should attract authors and inspire and provoke readers.

Published Books

Star Power: American Democracy in the Age of the Celebrity Candidate
Lauren A. Wright

Presidents and the Media: The Communicator in Chief
Stephen E. Frantzich

Politics in Popular Movies: Rhetorical Takes on Horror, War, Thriller, and Sci-Fi Films
John S. Nelson

Presidential Road Show: Public Leadership in an Era of Party Polarization and Media Fragmentation
Diane J. Heith

Media and Conflict: Escalating Evil
Cees Jan Hamelink

Evil and Silence
Richard Fleming

Sex and Violence: The Hollywood Censorship Wars
Tom Pollard

Art/Museums: International Relations Where We Least Expect It
Christine Sylvester

Netroots: Online Progressives and the Transformation of American Politics
Matthew R. Kerbel

Spinner in Chief: How Presidents Sell Their Policies and Themselves
Stephen J. Farnsworth

Age of Oprah: Cultural Icon for the Neoliberal Era
Janice Peck

Mousepads, Shoe Leather, and Hope: Lessons from the Howard Dean Campaign for the Future of Internet Politics
Zephyr Teachout and Thomas Streeter

STAR POWER

AMERICAN DEMOCRACY IN THE AGE OF THE CELEBRITY CANDIDATE

LAUREN A. WRIGHT

NEW YORK AND LONDON

First published 2020
by Routledge
52 Vanderbilt Avenue, New York, NY 10017

and by Routledge
2 Park Square, Milton Park, Abingdon, Oxon, OX14 4RN

Routledge is an imprint of the Taylor & Francis Group, an informa business

© 2020 Lauren A. Wright

The right of Lauren A. Wright to be identified as author of this work has been asserted by her in accordance with sections 77 and 78 of the Copyright, Designs and Patents Act 1988.

All rights reserved. No part of this book may be reprinted or reproduced or utilised in any form or by any electronic, mechanical, or other means, now known or hereafter invented, including photocopying and recording, or in any information storage or retrieval system, without permission in writing from the publishers.

Trademark notice: Product or corporate names may be trademarks or registered trademarks, and are used only for identification and explanation without intent to infringe.

Library of Congress Cataloging-in-Publication Data
A catalog record for this book has been requested

ISBN: 978-1-138-60394-3 (hbk)
ISBN: 978-1-138-60395-0 (pbk)
ISBN: 978-0-429-46879-7 (ebk)

Typeset in Galliard
by Apex CoVantage, LLC

For Steph

Contents

List of Illustrations		*x*
Preface		*xi*
Acknowledgments		*xv*
Chapter 1	A Short History of a Longstanding Obsession	1
Chapter 2	In Their Own Words: Why Celebrities Run	30
Chapter 3	Celebrities, They're Not Like Us	65
Chapter 4	Do Voters Prefer Celebrity Candidates to Politicians?	101
Chapter 5	The Death of U.S.?	119
Appendix		*137*
Index		*141*

Illustrations

Figures

3.1	Name Recognition, Open-Ended Responses	72
3.2	Name Recognition, Multiple Choice	73
3.3	Favorability	78
3.4	Relatability	82
3.5	Donald Trump at Trump Steaks Event	85
3.6	Twitter Followers	87
3.7	Google Search Results	93
4.1.A	Example of Democrat Paired Comparison	104
4.1.B	Example of Republican Paired Comparison	104
4.2	Candidate Selection Rates	105
4.3	Candidate Support by Celebrity Status, Democrats	110
4.4	Candidate Support by Celebrity Status, Republicans	110
4.5	Candidate Support by Celebrity Status and Gender	113
4.6	Candidate Support by Celebrity Status and Gender (Independents)	114

Table

A.1	Celebrity Runs for Elective Office	138

Preface

I remember the precise moment I realized Donald Trump might become President of the United States. I was watching television. Like every major news network, CNN provided wall-to-wall coverage of the 2016 Republican primary, and with so many candidates in the field early on, it was not uncommon for campaigns to hold events at the same time.[1] On this particular day, Donald Trump and Ben Carson scheduled competing rallies, but Trump was late to his. Full-screen coverage of the Carson rally quickly changed to a split-screen of an empty stage awaiting Trump at a campaign site, and Ben Carson's live remarks at his. Fair enough. Trump had already established himself as a ratings force to be reckoned with, and the network did not want to miss his entrance. But then something surprising happened. The network dropped coverage of Ben Carson's live rally altogether, and the cameras remained fixed on the empty stage at the Trump rally. A shrewd producer in a control room somewhere decided to ditch Carson, knowing, based on instinct, or perhaps experience, at that point, that an empty stage Trump would approach at no certain time was more interesting to viewers than Ben Carson speaking in real time. I was watching a live feed of a Trump podium with some flags behind it. And like millions of others, I was glued.

Donald Trump, as we know now, was the beneficiary of a disproportionate amount of media coverage throughout the 2016 election season.[2] Even after the race narrowed to two candidates, Trump was given hours of unfiltered coverage while Hillary Clinton sometimes struggled to get networks to air her speeches and appearances. Much has been written since then about the other reasons why a reality television star won the White House over a seasoned politician who had an experienced team and the most advanced tools at her disposal.

To Democrats, the story of the 2016 election is the story of Hillary Clinton's excruciating loss. In a speech in April 2017, Clinton said former FBI Director James Comey's inopportunely timed announcement that the agency was reopening the investigation into her email server was to blame. "If the election was two weeks before," she said, "I would be your president."[3] Others have pointed to Hillary Clinton's overconfidence in the rust belt states of Michigan, Ohio, and

Pennsylvania and her failure to spend an adequate amount of time campaigning there, while some have blamed her lack of an economic message for those losing their jobs to technology.

Political observers have also pointed to acute factors, like dysfunction within the campaign ranks and overreliance on the old Clinton guard that lost Hillary the Democratic primary in 2008. Finally, the failure of political methodology to predict the general election outcome, and public misinterpretation of this methodology, has its place in these discussions.[4] Most social scientists understand that a prediction that misses by 30,000 votes is not that bad in the first place. But the polling predicting Hillary's win was flawed in part because of social desirability bias. Many voters did not want to admit they were supporting a candidate who regularly spewed racist and sexist remarks, or that they simply were not comfortable with a woman president (the latter of which has been estimated to be as high as 26% of Americans).[5] More have asserted the bad polling caused Democrats to stay home, and that Hillary's internal polling was driven by data scientists who may have been too confident in their models.

Then there are the results deniers. "Don't act like there's some popular mandate for your message," said Jennifer Palmieri during a testy post-election exchange with team Trump. "He lost by two million votes."[6] To many people, Donald Trump did not even win the election.

Yet to Republicans, the story of 2016 is one of Donald Trump's brilliant victory. The Republican narrative is that Trump's team outsmarted the Democrats, choosing gut instinct over high-tech computer models—or that the Trump campaign's computer models were simply better. Some people emphasize that Trump reached out to the voters losing their coal mining and manufacturing jobs and assured them they would not be ignored in the future. That Trump visited working class voters in Michigan, Ohio, and Pennsylvania many times. He eased American anxiety about the growing threat of terrorism in the world and worries about illegal immigration, others say. He proffered a simple, memorable message the average person could understand. He took on political correctness and he said what people are afraid to say out loud. Or was he simply a better candidate than Hillary, not embroiled in secrets and scandals, a what-you-see-is-what-you-get kind of guy non-politicos could relate to, and a brash New Yorker that made the Northeastern elite feel at home?

Like most phenomena in American politics, there is no single explanation for the outcome. But one of the least common explanations is Trump's unique celebrity status, despite the central role it played in his victory. Donald Trump's presidency is both the result and the cause of the current media environment that propelled a reality television star into the White House. Like any decent Hollywood plotline, Trump's campaign entertained and held the attention of the media elite and the mass public. And yet now, years into the administration and many crises and fumbles later, many have started to underestimate Trump once again. Predictions of an epic loss in 2020, Trump's resignation, or even impeachment are tossed around the news circuit daily.

While the possibility remains that 2016 will prove to be the exception rather than the rule, since then, stars from music, movies, television, and business have come out of the woodwork to hint at their aspirations to run for elective office in 2020. Alec Baldwin, LeBron James, Kanye West, Kim Kardashian, Dwayne "The Rock" Johnson, Mark Zuckerberg, Mark Cuban, Oprah Winfrey, Katy Perry, Chris Rock, Will Smith, Bob Iger, Cynthia Nixon, and Caitlyn Jenner have all at least briefly mentioned the possibility. In the time is has taken to formulate this book, Cynthia Nixon announced a run for the Democratic nomination for Governor of New York, campaigned hard, and lost to incumbent Andrew Cuomo in mid-September. Kid Rock's Republican Senate bid in Michigan turned out to be a publicity stunt, but only after he received endorsements from former White House strategist Steve Bannon and a PAC affiliated with Senate Majority Leader Mitch McConnell.

Even in the age of President Trump, there are many people who see these names and dismiss the idea that celebrities can succeed in the arena of presidential politics. To those people, I offer the following reality check.

At 425 million, Selena Gomez, Taylor Swift, and Ariana Grande have more Instagram followers than there are people living in the United States of America.

Jump down a mere 20 slots on the list of most followed accounts, 18 of which belong to celebrities, and you will see that the 25 most followed celebrities on Instagram have more followers than there are people in China, India, and the United States combined. Now, of course there is a lot of overlap among these, as many social media users are not people. But this is the sobering state of the world we inhabit. Celebrities are different than the rest of us, and they are different than the average politician.

One of the greatest consequences of the emergence of social media is that it created a new way to quantify public attitudes toward, and the amount of attention paid to, certain things, people, places, and topics. And man, do people care about celebrities.

There has never been a time when the least serious people in society need to be taken more seriously. And that is the purpose of this book in a nutshell; to address the uncomfortable question of whether celebrities are more likely to win elections than traditional politicians, why this may be, and what this means for our democracy.

The thought that Kanye West might be more successful as a candidate for elective office than someone who has already held it is an understandably unsettling one for people who conceive of celebrities as fluffy fixtures of American pop culture; poor caricatures of American values at which the rest of the world pokes fun. But that does not change the fact that Kanye is beloved and passionately followed by millions of registered voters. Most politicians, even at the national level, are not. They should only hope a famous rapper has not decided to run against them.

Consider the following for a moment: What *is* the actual difference between the qualifications of Kanye West and Donald Trump to run for public office?

Both men are wealthy, having run billion-dollar business empires, and are fixtures of reality television. Neither had political experience, but often made outlandish public statements about politics. And both have a notorious ego, which many experts would say is almost requisite to becoming leader of the free world. They also share an arsenal of attributes that are highly correlated with electoral success and while these attributes are inherent to celebrity, they are difficult for politicians to acquire. I call these attributes the Seven Deadly Ins. Name recognition, favorability, outsider status, fundraising ability, media attention, a large and passionate following, and relatability are the factors that give celebrities a natural advantage over their more boring, less photogenic opponents. Yet it remains unclear how Donald Trump's presidency will shape the future involvement of celebrities in the electoral process.

If the Trump presidency continues to be marked by chaos, it could hurt the chances of celebrities running for office in the future who risk being associated with Trump in the minds of voters, but the opposite effect could also take hold. Witnessing the unsuccessful presidency of a fellow celebrity could entice celebrities into electoral politics who believe they can do a much better job than Trump and previously thought they were underqualified. The megalomaniacal nature of celebrities, combined with the very short political memory of Americans, is a precarious equation that deserves the serious attention it is granted herein.

Notes

1. Reisman, Sam. March 3, 2016. "Trump Gets Three Major News Networks to Broadcast Image of Empty Podium for 30 Minutes." Mediaite.com.
2. Confessore, Nicholas and Karen Yourish. March 15, 2016. "$2 Billion Worth of Free Media for Donald Trump." *The New York Times*.
3. Rucker, Philip. May 3, 2017. "'I Would be Your President': Clinton Blames Russia, FBI Chief for 2016 Election Loss." *The Washington Post*.
4. Westwood, Sean, Solomon Messing, and Yphtach Lelkes. "Projecting Confidence: How the Probabilistic Horse Race Confuses and Demobilizes the Public." February 2, 2018. Available at SSRN: https://ssrn.com/abstract=3117054.
5. Streb, Matthew et al. 2008. "Social Desirability Effects and Support for a Female President." *Public Opinion Quarterly* 72(1): 76–89.
6. Tumulty, Karen and Philip Rucker. December 1, 2016. "Shouting Match Erupts Between Clinton and Trump Aides." *The Washington Post*.

Acknowledgments

I am very thankful for every casual and professional conversation I have had throughout the process of writing this book. The book started as a conversation with my husband over dinner in Palo Alto, California in the summer of 2016 and it finished at Princeton University where we both teach in the Department of Politics and the Woodrow Wilson School. We have met many brilliant and kind people there. My students inspire me every day and their interest in my work on celebrities gives me hope that more people than the handful of friends and family mentioned here will read it. My husband Jonathan Mummolo sat with me for long tedious stretches as I toiled at this, trying to make the most of very few days to work on a very big project and maintain sanity. He is an amazing professor, researcher, editor, and partner. Thank you Jonathan. Sean Westwood at Dartmouth University is equal parts genius and generous. Thank you Sean for the survey collaboration and great ideas. Thank you also to Carole Claps, Meryl Moss, and John Willig for the strategic and moral support, to Ze'ev Sudry and Jennifer Knerr at Routledge, and to my mentor Stephen Wayne at Georgetown University for introducing me to Taylor & Francis. My mother, Katherine Wright, and sister, Stephanie Wright, are endless sources of encouragement and patient listeners. Your confidence in me is overwhelming and will always feel undeserved. Thank you. My father, Dickerson Wright, remains the best role model for hard work and self-determination anyone could have. When people ask me why I have never written a book with co-authors I respond with one of his favorite business proverbs: "I get along awfully well with myself." Thank you also to Avery Gordon, Chelsea Murphy, Christina Bruno, Areta Bendo, Alexis Vergos, Sandra Mummolo and Phyllis Reggio for all of your support.

Chapter 1

A Short History of a Longstanding Obsession

Roadmap

The increasing involvement of celebrities in the American political process reached a seeming crescendo in November 2016 when voters sent a reality television star with no political or military experience to the White House for the first time in history. But it did not stop there.

Dwayne "The Rock" Johnson announced his candidacy for President of the United States on the season finale of Saturday Night Live. Tom Hanks agreed to be his running mate. Caitlyn Jenner jumped into the mix not long after, telling CNN's Don Lemon, "I would look for a senatorial run."[1] Cynthia Nixon made a serious bid for Governor of New York. Kid Rock teased a run for United States Senate and a Super PAC backed by Mitch McConnell threw its support behind him. On his freshly launched campaign website, www.kidrockforsenate.com, the singer wrote "The democrats are 'shattin' their pantaloons' right now . . . and rightfully so! . . . it's game on mthrfkers."

Kid Rock's assertion is bothersome in many ways, but what most concerns me is its accuracy. Celebrities possess a multitude of attributes traditional politicians do not that amount to high levels of electability. As a GOP campaign operative recently mentioned, Kid Rock was polling only eight points behind Michigan Democrat Debbie Stabenow heading into the 2018 midterms.[2] Another poll projected that The Rock would beat Donald Trump in a hypothetical 2020 matchup by a five-point margin.[3] But celebrities lack the knowledge and experience we typically associate with effective governance.

This combination does not bode well for our republic. The founding fathers believed that Americans would elect 'fit characters' to represent them in government, responsible delegates who would prevent the socioeconomic clashes that ultimately destroy democracies. The problem is, of course, that Americans do not elect fit characters to positions of power. As scholars who study candidate quality and polarization have long noted, the difficulty of campaigning for and holding office prevents the most qualified people from running.[4] The result is a dysfunctional and highly polarized government, of which the Trump administration is arguably indicative.

Instead of keeping the tendency of voters to choose unqualified candidates in check, the media has exacerbated the problem by giving celebrities more airtime than ever to discuss current affairs and advertise their political aspirations. The broadcast and print journalists who bemoaned the election of Donald Trump after they facilitated his success have already gone so far as to promote the candidacy of Hollywood heavyweights. In response to The Rock and Tom Hanks's presidential announcement on SNL, *USA Today* said, "We would definitely be here for that."[5] *Vanity Fair* quipped, "Are we the only ones hoping this comedy becomes a reality?"[6]

Scholars, too, are complicit in the current state of our elections. Even with all the proper tools at hand to study the appeal celebrities have to the voting public, political scientists have not taken the topic seriously. Historians have been equally limp in their attempts to explain the powerful role of fame in our electoral process. "Celebrity is an ineffable quality," said Mark D. Upgrove in an interview with Kenneth Walsh.[7] That, it is most certainly not.

The same components of celebrity that drive television ratings contribute to their electability. They are identifiable, they are measurable, and this book is the first to estimate the effect these qualities have on vote choice.

The first attribute celebrities bring to electoral politics is name recognition. The idea that it is difficult to get people to vote for a name they do not recognize on a ballot makes common sense, and political science research has shown that high name recognition is a considerable advantage to candidates, particularly at the earliest stages of a campaign when numerous candidates are competing for attention.[8] This was certainly the case heading into the first Republican debate in August 2015. At 92% name recognition among Republicans, Donald Trump dominated a field of 16 of the nation's most prominent politicians. Even Jeb Bush, a well-liked former Governor of Florida with two former presidents in his family, had just 81% name recognition at the time. Trump's numbers also dwarfed those of Governors Rick Perry, Mike Huckabee, George Pataki and Senators Rand Paul and Marco Rubio. Former Hewlett Packard CEO Carly Fiorina and Ohio Governor John Kasich had just 39% and 35% name recognition, respectively.[9]

In addition to being more recognizable than traditional politicians, celebrities are more popular. Unlike politicians, who are in the business of publicizing controversial policy views and staking divisive partisan claims, celebrities operate in mostly apolitical spheres. Celebrities rise to prominence in the context of products and activities Americans of all political stripes know and love: music, movies, television, and sports.

Outsider status is a closely related attribute that is nearly impossible for traditional politicians to access but that celebrities have in spades. Celebrities are popular in part because they are not political insiders and therefore are not perceived to be responsible for the nation's current problems. Their station outside of the Washington swamp, as Donald Trump commonly characterizes it, not only relieves celebrities of this negative association, but makes it difficult for their opponents to dig up misdeeds and use their record against them. Since celebrities are not career politicians, their character is often judged by the standards to which entertainers adhere, or the lack thereof, rather than a stricter code of conduct we generally expect our government representatives to follow.

How many times has the outsider explanation been used by Trump's supporters to unburden him from the criticism that follows abhorrent behavior? "He's just new to this," House Speaker Paul Ryan has said of the president.[10] When tapes were released of Trump casually talking about sexually assaulting women in October of 2016, one of the main arguments Republicans made on Trump's behalf was that the tapes were old. In an op-ed written for *The Hill*, Ben Carson, who endorsed Trump after dropping out of his own race, said, "the incident happened ten years ago, well before Trump entered the political arena."[11]

Outsider status not only serves as a get-out-of-jail-free card for celebrities entering the political fray, but is perceived to be a positive trait. As former Clinton adviser Sidney Blumenthal wrote of Ronald Reagan, "he finessed the 'actor issue' by casting himself as a 'citizen-politician,' asserting his lack of qualification precisely as his salient qualification."[12]

The lack of qualifications most celebrities have to run for political office and govern also makes it easier for the general public to relate to them. Relatability is something traditional politicians spend time and resources attempting to achieve in vain. Being an elected official or wanting to run for office is not something most Americans have experienced, and the rigidity and formality of government jobs, not to mention the artificial packaging of campaigning, makes politicians seem even more distant. When politicians appear on television, they must simultaneously appease their base and avoid alienating people outside of it, a tightrope walk that ends up sounding robotic and rehearsed. Every statement is crafted just so.

Celebrities, by contrast, are native to television. Their livelihood depends on exceling at public performance. While this amounts to a considerable advantage over their less telegenic opponents in an age of ubiquitous media, celebrities are also excused when they stumble on the campaign trail. Gaffes that result from inexperience reinforce their outsider status, and enable voters to put themselves in a celebrity candidate's shoes. This particular artifact of relatability may be one of the more striking features of Donald Trump's candidacy and presidency. Underneath the president's inarticulate bumbling and embarrassing indiscretions is an imperfect person that reminds Americans of their own mistakes and makes them feel better about their moral shortcomings. Trump is not better than the average American. In many ways he is one.

Another way celebrities build relatability is through continuous public exposure. This is especially true of reality television stars, whose personal interactions and daily routines are documented and broadcasted to the world. These shows are a priceless political platform. Traditional politicians spend months on the campaign trail shaping a public persona with no guarantee it will stick or resonate in the minds of voters. Celebrities can skip this step. They have already spent years character-building. Donald Trump's tenure on *The Apprentice* gave millions of viewers valuable insight into the future president's personal strengths and weaknesses, his failures, and his successes.

Among all of these attributes, relatability is perhaps the most intriguing. It is a common misperception that Americans want to elect people that represent the best of society. Many would rather elect people who remind them of themselves. This is something Donald Trump understood intuitively heading into the 2016 election that countless elites missed. Trump also debunked the notion among historians that for presidential candidates to succeed, they must distinguish themselves from their competitors in positive ways. The first step, and therefore the more essential one, is attention-getting, by any means possible, even if it is negative. Campaign advertising studies have shown that although Americans say they detest negative ads when surveyed, they are actually more likely to watch them, remember them, and respond to them than positive ads in many cases.[13]

Relatability, however, is not the same as favorability. Familiarity with a person does not imply fondness, a notion exemplified by the president's historically low approval ratings. Yet by attaining fame, celebrities prove that they are interesting to the public and the media. Similarly to the way in which name recognition necessarily precedes favorability, public interest in the lives of celebrities begets media attention. Few would deny that most mainstream media outlets remained critical of Trump throughout the 2016 election, but constant coverage of his candidacy produced historically high ratings for news networks. Even as his administration struggles to minimize the negative cloud surrounding it, Trump continues to maximize public interest in himself and his presidency.[14]

In addition to tracking television ratings, counting social media followers can be a valuable tool to quantify public interest in traditional politicians and celebrities, especially because the number of people who get their news and information from social media is growing rapidly. Social media gives followers a chance to actively engage with their representatives and favorite celebrities, rather than passively reading or hearing about them. Research demonstrating how tweets and shares can predict vote choice, or even electoral outcomes, has only started to emerge. But one of the most foundational indications of a candidate's progress remains fundraising.

Donating to a campaign signals often signals a high level of commitment to a candidate because doing so requires more sacrifice and effort than liking a post on Facebook. The same goes for volunteering, which is perhaps the most time intensive signal of support for a candidate. Celebrities have been shown to be fairly effective at garnering volunteers, media attention, and financial support on behalf of candidates they have endorsed. One study in 2012 suggested that Oprah's endorsement of Barack Obama in early 2008 indirectly earned him more than one million votes in his favor.[15] On the eve of the voter registration deadline in her home state of Tennessee before the 2018 midterms, Taylor Swift took to Instagram to urge her fans to visit Vote.org and make their voices heard on November 6. Less than 48 hours after Swift's post, 169,000 people had registered to vote on the site, which credited the singer with drawing young people who might not have been aware of the deadline otherwise.[16] But little if any research has been published on whether celebrity candidates are more effective grassroots motivators and fundraisers than the traditional candidates they run against. What is clear from existing political science research is that while campaign donations do not give donors disproportionate influence over the decisions candidates make (e.g., a floor vote) they do give donors more personal access to candidates.[17] The public is exceedingly interested in meeting celebrities. They travel to see them, buy their products, and pay to watch them perform. This gives celebrities a natural fundraising advantage over traditional politicians.

The qualities and instincts celebrities have that make them successful in the political arena are the driving force behind the theory of this book. Even in the most prominent books about how the rich and famous shape our political culture, celebrity has been treated as an ethereal quality, something on which we cannot quite put a finger.

When I talk to people about this book, I often ask them exactly what they think makes a celebrity a celebrity. "It's the feeling you get when someone famous is in the room, like, chills," one woman told me. "It's not like being in the company of normal people." "Their eyes are brighter," another man said, "and their smiles are whiter." "They make you feel special." The chord celebrities strike with the voting public is a delicate and impressive one that elicits an emotional, irrational, gut-level response from their audience. It is a skill they require to survive in the entertainment industry that has been carefully honed over many years of practice, and it is a valuable tool for winning elections. Celebrities are familiar, yet inaccessible, real, yet godlike, criticized, yet revered. The pride and shame of our country.

This book is organized into three broad sections broken up into five chapters. Over the course of a historical chapter that provides background on the problems we face in American politics today, I introduce the central dilemma of the book: why are we electing celebrities to represent us in government if they are unsuited to do the work of governing?

The reason why we are electing celebrities is the overarching theme of the next section, which comprises two chapters of the book. Celebrities are campaigning machines, equipped with bells and whistles of which even the most promising politicians cannot avail themselves. These seven factors (i.e., name recognition, favorability, relatability, fundraising ability, media attention, outsider status, and built-in fans and followers) are dissected in Chapter 3. Chapter 3 also digs into the makings of these factors. For example, we have established that celebrities are popular, and we can quantify and track this, but what makes someone popular in the first place? And, central to our understanding of this topic, what makes celebrities want to run for office? This section of the book draws heavily on research from political science, communications, media and advertising studies, and psychology to address these questions. Chapter 4 tests whether people actually vote for celebrities over traditional politicians once factors like party ID, race, and gender are held constant. The tests are conducted in the form of survey experiments that are systematically introduced and explained.

The final section of the book integrates all of its findings to answer the following questions. What does this mean for our future? Where should we go from here? It is rare for a social scientist to make a prescription at the conclusion of a study, unless that prescription is for future research. Readers familiar with my research know it is impartial, self-aware, and rigorous. But the threat an emerging celebocracy presents to our values system, and the consequences of what has already taken place, outweigh the convenience of refusing to engage in normative debates. I'm jumping in head first, and I want readers to join me.

A Cultural Divide

It is no surprise that few political scientists have been willing to acknowledge the important and growing role celebrities have in American politics. It is difficult to devote serious attention to a topic if you find it silly at best and abhorrent at worst. The goals and priorities of political science are fundamentally out of sync with the world of celebrities and the study of them. Almost everything that political scientists stand for—deductive reasoning, slow, careful and painstaking research, well-defined processes, replication, on-average results—the entertainment industry avoids. Entertainers prioritize stories over facts, emotion over empirics, instincts over proof, youth and beauty over experience, and individuals over groups of people. To say entertainers and academics do not see eye to eye is an understatement. Perhaps Oprah demonstrated this phenomenon best in her speech about the ubiquity of sexual abuse and misconduct at the 2018 Golden Globes when she became the first black woman to receive the Cecil B. DeMille Award. In a statement my students might call a 'burn' of epic proportions, Oprah said:

> Each one of us in this room is celebrated for the stories that we tell. So I want tonight to express gratitude . . . to the women whose names we'll never know. They're domestic workers. And farm workers. They are working in factories and they work in restaurants and they're in academia, and engineering, and science . . .[18]

In other words, nobody cares about what you academics (and engineers and scientists and domestic and factory workers) do. You are irrelevant. You are invisible. The fruits of your labor will never be seen or appreciated unless we, celebrities, acknowledge them. When I interviewed former Clinton White House advisor Sidney Blumenthal for my first book about presidential spouses—another underestimated group that turns out to be an unmatched source of political power—he summed up the first lady version of this disconnect quite well. "Political scientists don't take first ladies seriously," I said, recounting the difficulty I had getting buy-in for the idea of an empirical study of first ladies in graduate school. My professors were worried I would not be perceived as a serious scholar. "Well many people don't take political scientists very seriously," he retorted with a smile.[19] True.

No science, even a young science like political science, should be concerned with how others perceive it. To avoid the study of a topic because it does not sound serious or difficult is to abandon the scientific enterprise of the search for truth (or at least that which we cannot prove to be untrue). A scientist who engages in self-conscious topic selection is no wiser than an undergraduate student who chooses a pre-med major over philosophy or sociology because she thinks it makes her sound smart.

This is not to say that we should feel sorry for social scientists. Scholars can be brutal in their critiques of public figures. And much of this criticism, unfortunately, has nothing to do with scholarship. It is personal. Consider evaluations of our recent presidents. Oxford University Professor Richard Dawkins once said George W. Bush "isn't quite as stupid as he sounds, and heaven knows he can't be as stupid as he looks."[20] University of Virginia Professor Larry Sabato said just recently of the Trump administration, "Now we know where the cast of "Animal House" landed."[21] Senior Hoover Fellow Thomas Sowell has called Barack Obama "a truly great phony,"[22] and former Rutgers University and Montclair State University professor Kevin Allred, among much more insidious and violent things, has called Donald Trump "a f*cking joke."[23] If we consider President Obama an academic in his own right here (he spent several years as a Lecturer at the University of Chicago), his roast of Donald Trump at the 2011 White House Correspondents dinner also bears mentioning. Ironically, all of Obama's Trump jokes touched on the absurdity of then reality star Trump's aspirations to run for president.

> "All kidding aside, obviously, we all know about your credentials and breadth of experience," President Obama said. "For example, no, seriously, just recently in an episode of 'Celebrity Apprentice,' at the steakhouse, the men's cooking team did not impress the judges from Omaha Steaks. And there was a lot of blame to go around, but you, Mr. Trump, recognized that the real problem was a lack of leadership and so, ultimately, you didn't blame Little John or Meatloaf—you fired Gary Busey. And these are the kinds of decisions that would keep me up at night. Well-handled, sir. Well-handled."[24]

Even now, as President Trump sits in the Oval Office few thought he had a chance of ever occupying, social scientists are engaged in an active debate about whether the president is mentally ill, unintelligent, or both.[25] And the celebrity-turned-president has not warmed to the academic community either. As *The Washington Post* has reported, the president is skeptical of experts because "they can't see the forest for the trees" and finds his instincts to be "more accurate than guys who have studied it all the time."[26] And who can forget Trump's now infamous comment, "I know more about ISIS than the generals do. Believe me"?[27] In his controversial[28] book, *Fire and Fury*, Michael Wolff writes about the president's reading habits: "For anything that smacked of a classroom or of being lectured to—"professor" was one of his bad words, and he was proud of never going to class, never buying a textbook, never taking a note—he got up and left the room."[29] At a bare minimum, the way in which celebrities, academics, and politicians speak about each other often indicates a lack of understanding or respect for the other. That is a difficult starting place for an honest conversation.

Celebrities' conceptions of the American presidency as a highly prized yet attainable role have only been exacerbated by the election of an unexperienced reality TV star. Celebrities see Donald Trump as a reflection of the way politics works, rather than an exception to the rule. 'If *he* can do it, then I can too,' they think. In an interview with Bloomberg in 2017 about her potential political ambitions, Oprah explained this sentiment in no uncertain terms. "I thought, 'Oh, gee, I don't have the experience, I don't know enough.' And now I'm thinking 'Oh,'" she said.[30] On the same note, "Sex and the City" actress Cynthia Nixon recently said of her lack of experience to run for elective office, "Sometimes a little naiveté is exactly what is needed."[31]

Social scientists, in contrast to celebrities, are trained to conceive of the election of Trump as a single observation that is not necessarily representative of a new trend in American politics. In order to draw conclusions about the electability of celebrities, we need to examine other celebrities besides Trump, as well as non-celebrities. Unlike the entertainment industry—which is built on the premise that there is a special class of celebrated individuals in society who are unique in their appearance, personality, or ability to draw attention—social science assumes that people are more alike than they are different. By examining their common characteristics, behaviors, and attitudes, scientists can learn something about society as a whole.

Does It Matter Who Gets Elected?

The philosophical divide between scholars who study individuals versus those who study systems and social forces is alive and well *within* social science as well as outside it. Take one of the most basic debates in presidency studies for example. Scholars who study the 'personal' presidency look to the idiosyncratic qualities of individual presidents to explain political outcomes.³² They focus heavily on the psychology and character of individual presidents and candidates, their family background, career experience, and their talents and vices. 'Institutional' presidency scholars, instead, are concerned with the institutional context in which presidents operate and the laws and formal powers that restrict or enable their behavior. Taken to its extreme, the institutional perspective asserts that it does not matter who is President of the United States, because every president faces the same challenges and enjoys the same advantages inherent to the office. As presidency scholar Terry Moe says, "stop thinking of the presidents as people, and start thinking about them generically: as faceless, nameless, institutional actors whose behavior is an institutional product."³³

The downside of the institutional approach is that it risks trivializing the considerable unilateral powers presidents have, both over the military and international affairs and in the domestic policymaking and policy implementation process—powers that the framers of the U.S. Constitution believed should be in the hands of capable and responsible individuals, not masters of the "little arts of popularity," as Alexander Hamilton called celebrities.³⁴ In fact, the framers were so wary of the election of unqualified celebrities to the presidency—and the creation of a ruling class that resembled the European monarchies they rejected—that they designed the Executive Branch in a way that enables presidents to act swiftly and unitarily when necessary, but heavily restrains them in most cases.³⁵

The framers accomplished this by making the language in Article II of the Constitution outlining the powers and responsibilities of the president exceedingly vague, a compromise between Alexander Hamilton, who thought presidents ought to be able to make laws *and* enforce them, and James Madison, who insisted the president's powers must be stringently checked. It is this vagueness, both in the 'vesting clause' (executive power is entrusted only to the president) and especially in the 'take care' clause (the president shall take care that all laws be faithfully executed) of Article II that has allowed presidents to preserve and maximize their power throughout history.

It makes sense, then, that one would want the Commander-in-Chief to be an experienced, knowledgeable, and unselfish public servant. She must also be ambitious and determined, for the glamour of campaigning is not an informative preview of the drudgery of governing. Because of the way the three branches of American government are structured, and because of the complex, slow-moving, three-million-person bureaucracy that underlies the executive branch in particular, even the most talented politicians have trouble enacting change. That is how the framers intended it. Government institutions are biased toward the status quo, so it is not easy for an authoritarian or otherwise dangerous figure to enter office and make sweeping revisions to our laws. Another point for the institutionalists on the presidential scholarship scoreboard. But presidents have found another way around the institutional bonds that tie them, beyond constitutional interpretation.

In the mass media age, presidents can circumvent government intuitions entirely by appealing directly to the public.[36] Whether these public appeals generally succeed in their attempts to influence public opinion is questionable. Public opinion surveys taken directly after major televised presidential addresses do not paint a clear picture of whether Americans watched the speech closely or at all, or were influenced by the speech itself and not the news stories surrounding it. We also know that the particular messenger delivering the speech is exceedingly important, as is the specific political context in which it occurs, making the general effect of going public even more difficult to measure. As my survey experimental research on political surrogates shows, even when the same exact political message is delivered by different figures, responses to those messages vary substantially.

For example, in a series of survey experiments conducted from 2015 through 2017, I asked respondents to evaluate presidents and presidential candidates according to a variety of criteria after viewing the same speech excerpt attributed either to a president or a first lady. While the results varied considerably within and across administrations, in certain cases, respondents evaluated presidents and their policy agendas more positively when the message was attributed to a first lady, rather than the president himself. These results were particularly pronounced in the Bush administration. When survey respondents viewed the exact same education and foreign policy speeches randomly assigned to be attributed to Laura Bush instead of George W. Bush, President Bush was evaluated more positively on the way in which he handled foreign policy and education policy in general, how he handled No Child Left Behind and the U.S. war in Afghanistan specifically, and even on character and approval measures such as whether George W. Bush is intelligent, whether George W. Bush is a strong leader, and how George W. Bush handled his job as president.[37]

I observed similar variation across surrogates for Donald Trump, both on the campaign trail, and in the White House. Again, even after viewing the same generic speech excerpt praising Trump's leadership capabilities, respondents evaluated candidate Trump differently based on whether Melania Trump, Chris Christie, or Donald Trump himself was designated the speaker.[38] Particularly on issues of the candidate's character, including whether Donald Trump cares about people 'like me,' and whether Donald Trump is honest, Melania Trump appears to produce the most favorable impressions of her husband, especially among political Independents. A related survey experiment conducted in 2017 again randomly assigned respondents to see a speech excerpt praising Trump as a leader, this time attributing it to Melania Trump, Ivanka Trump, Mike Pence, or President Trump himself. Again, the person delivering the message matters very much, as does the audience receiving the message.[39] Melania Trump again proved to be the most effective presidential surrogate in this study, weakening the widespread impression that has circulated for some time about whether Ivanka Trump is "the real first lady."[40]

Presidential campaigns, of course, only amplify the extent to which presidents can circumvent formal institutions. The campaign trail is in many ways a complete departure from the confines of the White House, its precedents, and its watchdogs. Campaigns are extended sales pitches untethered by the realistic expectations presidents learn to have. Even the most sincere politicians make promises they cannot keep on the campaign trail. Elections are, quite literally, popularity contests.

I mention first ladies here not only because my study of them has important implications for studies of the effectiveness of presidential surrogates as communicators, but because findings surrounding the unique status first ladies occupy as highly visible political outsiders with personal and noncontroversial messages to share with the American public have useful applications to the study of celebrities in politics. Like the study of celebrities, the study of first ladies, though academically marginalized, falls squarely into the aforementioned school of the personal study of the presidency, rather than the institutional school. First ladies lack institutional power of any kind, save for an annual appropriation by Congress to fund their staff, which only came into existence in 1979, and some language that resulted from a court case filed in 1993 (*American Association of Physicians and Surgeons v. Hillary Rodham Clinton*), which deemed first ladies to be the functional equivalents of government employees when carrying out tasks on behalf of the president. Yet their widespread appeal and ability to garner attention and shape national conversation makes them very important presidential and campaign surrogates, much more important, even, than official members of the president's administration, such as vice presidents and secretaries of state. First ladies have soft power, not hard power, and that actually makes them more relatable, more appealing, and highly effective campaigners and messengers. That we need to take these figures seriously, even though they are not politicians, is something upon which all celebrity scholars, and most scholars of the personal presidency, can agree.

However my findings that suggest first ladies are effective at building political support for others, namely their husbands, directly contradict existing celebrity studies that largely find celebrity endorsements of candidates for elective office to be ineffective. Most celebrity scholars also find that celebrity advocacy on behalf of political issues and causes appears to fall flat. In other words, celebrity endorsements, especially for candidates for President of the U.S., are overhyped, and charitable organizations and initiatives that seek the help of celebrities to draw attention to humanitarian issues are wasting their time.[41] These conclusions seem to be fundamentally out of whack with the way American politics has unfolded before our very eyes. A reality television star, is, after all, is President of the United States, and many celebrities have successfully entered politics before him.

In order to dig into the existing celebrity scholarship and discuss its implications for the endeavor herein, it is important to establish a working definition of "celebrity" and a few other key words that will come up a lot in this book.

What Is a 'Celebrity' Anyway?

For the purposes of this book, a *celebrity* is a person who became famous in the broad context of the entertainment industry (including sports—a form of entertainment after all—and excluding politics—not a form of entertainment, no matter how much it looks it at times). 'Celebrity candidates' have *not* held elective office before. A *politician*, as in 'traditional politicians' or 'traditional candidates,' for the purpose of this book, is a person who *has* held elective office. Sometimes politicians become very famous after holding elective office, such as presidents, but they are *not* considered celebrities for the purpose of this book. Celebrity status will be assessed according to seven key attributes I outlined earlier in this chapter: name recognition, favorability, outsider status, relatability, social media following or fan base, fundraising ability, and ability to garner media attention. The term 'celebrity' in this book is at times used interchangeably with 'fame' and 'stardom.' Communication and media scholars who study celebrity may find this definition unsatisfying or overly specific, especially because conversations surrounding the term in the contemporary media environment have been so inconclusive in recent years that they have been described as a "crisis in terminology."[42] The challenge in defining the term, it seems to me, as a relative newcomer to the field of 'star studies,' is a result of the shift from the Old Hollywood period in which movie stars and celebrities could be treated as synonymous concepts, to the current media landscape in which fame and celebrity are much less precise terms. Here, as in the field of presidency studies, divisions are plentiful.

Some scholars, such as Barker (2003)[43] and Jermyn (2006)[44] characterize the aforementioned shift and widening of the definition of celebrity as a decline. Where there used to be an exclusive hierarchy of famous people, the top of which was occupied by film stars, there is now one giant elevated platform occupied by celebrities from many different areas of pop culture. Celebrities are musicians, writers, scripted and reality TV stars, the people who make movies and TV shows, broadcasters, athletes, politicians, and the people who comment on sports and politics. As David Schmid puts it, summarizing a point made by Giles (2000), "On one level, these two categories [fame and celebrity] seem as distinct as ever, fame remaining an honorific category with a long and glorious history, while celebrity seems a much more recent and debased category, usually because of its association with the mass media."[45] This phenomenon, in which the definition of celebrity has expanded to include stars from different industries, is often referred to as "liquid celebrity," stemming from Zygmund Bauman's concept of liquid modernity (2001).[46] Liquidity is an especially helpful concept to bear in mind when considering celebrity. Not only do celebrities now hail from a variety of industries, but their fame is fluid, rather than static. Celebrities can be more or less famous, suggesting a sliding scale rather than a binary definition of fame, and they may enter the limelight at certain times and then retreat at others. Celebrities can be more relevant or less relevant to the national conversation at a given point.

To help them navigate this variation in types and 'levels' of celebrity, scholars have turned to typologies of celebrities to try to understand their public behavior and impact. Many of these typologies center around the manner in which the celebrity became famous. Chris Rojek's categorization of celebrities is helpful here.[47] Rojek distinguishes between "achieved celebrity," in which fame results from talent and accolades, (e.g., Olympic athlete Bruce Jenner, now Caitlyn Jenner), "ascribed celebrity," in which celebrity status is inherited from one's family (e.g., O.J. Simpson attorney Robert Kardashian's family), and "attributed celebrity," in which fame simply follows from concentrated media coverage of the person (e.g., Snooki from the reality television show Jersey Shore, or Ken Bone, a friendly-seeming man in a bright red sweater who asked the 2016 presidential candidates a substantive question during the debates and was thrust into instant internet fame). Holmes (2005) argues that we have largely moved into the realm of attributed celebrity.[48]

Darrell West and John Orman (2003) created a similar typology of celebrity as it relates to politics, particularly relevant to my efforts here. West and Orman's four categories of celebrity include "legacies," which, not unlike Rojek's ascribed celebrity category, includes political figures with famous political families, such as the Kennedys or Bushes, "political newsworthies," which includes famous political operatives who frequently appear on television such as James Carville and George Stephanopoulos, "famed nonpoliticos," which includes both politicians who attained fame before running for elective office (e.g. astronaut John Glenn, or Ronald Reagan) and unelected individuals who use their fame to advocate for political causes (e.g. Jane Fonda and Charlton Heston), and finally "event celebrities" who become famous overnight due to a highly publicized tragedy.[49] West and Orman mention Sarah Brady, wife of former White House Press Secretary Jim Brady and a prominent gun control advocate, as an example of an event celebrity. The three American soldiers who thwarted an ISIS attack on a train heading to Paris in 2015 and portrayed themselves in a new Clint Eastwood movie immediately come to mind, as well as Sully Sullenberger, an airline pilot who successfully landed a plane of 155 people on the Hudson river in 2009.

The desire to organize and compartmentalize people and experiences into categories in an effort to make sense of the complex world is part of human nature. Scholars are not immune to these urges, and the result is typologies. But lumping people into groups can just as easily lead to stereotyping and inaccuracies as it can helpfully distill a complicated political phenomenon. The accuracy-simplicity tradeoff is a tricky one. If we examine the celebrity categories promulgated by existing scholarship, we see many examples of celebrities that fit into more than one category, or celebrities that do not perfectly fit any one category. They are not mutually exclusive or even independent. Take Rojek's category of achieved celebrity, for example. Here it is clear that athletes are an ideal fit for this category. No matter how famous an athlete's parents are, each individual athlete needs to excel based on his or her own merit to become well-known. But what if an athlete has both talent and famous parents? We will never know for sure, for instance, whether Barry Bonds benefited at least indirectly from Bobby Bonds's success and name in baseball (whether he had confidence in his natural ability, the best training as a child, or extra attention from scouts), or Ken Griffey Junior from Ken Griffey Senior, for that matter, Luke Walton and Bill Walton, or Peyton Manning, Eli Manning, and Archie Manning.[50] Sports, it seems, has just as many legacy stories as Hollywood or Washington, DC.

West and Orman's categorization of event celebrities and Rojek's of achieved celebrity suffer from a similar endogeneity issue (did the athlete make the celebrity or the celebrity the athlete), only they touch on a key issue in my investigation of whether celebrities are uniquely equipped to succeed in electoral politics: talent. The concept of "achieved" celebrity is so difficult to wrangle because being a celebrity, and reaching celebrity status, are skillsets in and of themselves. Being a celebrity and maintaining fame requires one to constantly cultivate a fan base, lobby on behalf of oneself, and sustain a positive public image. In this way, achieved and attributed celebrity overlap considerably. Media concentration more often results from a job well done than it does from happenstance. The highly skilled pilot portrayed in the movie 'Sully' and the military stars of 'The 15:17 to Paris' reflect that quite markedly.

Typologies often teach us more about the scholars who make the categories than the people and behaviors they are meant to explain. Scholars, as we established earlier, are not unbiased arbiters of the social world. And when the question at hand is one of the ability of celebrities to get elected and whether they are undermining democracy, it is very important that we understand exactly what their appeal is and what they are capable of. First ladies, as I continue to remind readers, face the same issue as celebrities in this regard. Typologies of first ladies, such as "traditional" vs. "modern" first ladies, "private" vs. "public" first ladies, and "active" vs. "passive" first ladies are created by historians in an attempt to simplify efforts to compare them, but are not based in empirics. They are based on subjective factors like personality, political knowledge and interest, or body language. When we count public appearances and speeches, though, and gauge the political influence of first ladies, we find these typologies to be quite uninformative, if not downright irresponsible. Just as Laura Bush was inaccurately deemed traditional, passive, and private by historians—despite the finding that she gave more public speeches than Hillary Clinton and was a more effective policy advocate—it would be premature to write off Kim Kardashian, Dwayne "The Rock" Johnson, or Donald Trump as attributed or legacy celebrities, rather than try to understand what qualities have propelled them into the spotlight in the first place.

One of the aspects of celebrity studies that makes the prospects for further development and improvement of the topic promising is that celebrity and its constituent parts can be readily measured. Name recognition is a close proxy for fame. We can ask about name recognition in public opinion surveys. We can also ask whether survey respondents perceive someone to be relatable, or "down to earth," or not, or whether a celebrity "cares about people like me." Popularity, measured through a feeling thermometer, is a standard public opinion survey question. Many fundraising statistics are public. Social media followers are countable. And whether or not someone has run for public office before is a useful indication of political outsider status.

I am not alone in my relatively practical definition of celebrity, however. Though scholars such as Turner et. al (2000) have argued that "celebrity is not a specific property of individuals" but is rather "constituted discursively, by the way in which the individual is represented," others find value in breaking celebrity down into components (as I do) in order to be able to distinguish between celebrities and non-celebrities, and in my case, measure the electability of celebrities compared to traditional politicians.[51] For example, Mark Harvey's definition of celebrity, based on Barrie Gunter's 2014 book, looks a bit like mine. A celebrity "is a person who has a high public profile, usually promoted by appearances in the mass media and they are consequently readily recognized by others . . . characterized by exceptional or extraordinary qualities in terms of their abilities, attractiveness, personalities, and lifestyles."[52,53] Harvey's differentiation between politicians and celebrities also supports the approach I take in my analysis. Harvey's need to separate the two categories stems from his goal of measuring the political influence of celebrities (for example, as issue advocates), which is distinct from, albeit closely related to, my objective of assessing whether Americans prefer celebrities as political candidates to politicians and what this means for democracy. The bluntness of his demarcation is very helpful and appreciated nonetheless. Harvey asserts:

> A celebrity is someone who is otherwise famous—usually involved in the media and entertainment industry. Celebrities who advocate on public issues or get involved in political organizing are not politicians. A politician is a public official who holds (or held) public office. Bono is a celebrity. George W. Bush is a politician.[54]

What About Famous Journalists? (And Other Gray Areas)

One question Harvey's definition leaves unanswered is the question of how to categorize journalists with high name recognition. Many reporters have gained notoriety sharing their insights on television and radio and have built a substantial following of readers and viewers in their own right. Many even host their own television shows. Thinking about the divide between entertainment and news here is helpful, especially because the competitive landscape of television news has given way to "infotainment" and "soft news," mediums through which viewers are exposed to political information incidentally or in the context of entertainment.

Soft news media, as Matthew Baum puts it, are in the business of packaging human drama as entertainment, and political stories, especially when they are sensationalized and dramatized, often meet these criteria.[55] Clearer examples of soft news include late night and daytime television shows that routinely feature political content and are hosted by comedians and actors, such as *The Tonight Show with Jimmy Fallon* (NBC), *Real Time with Bill Maher* (HBO), *The Talk* (CBS), and *The View* (ABC)—the last two of which even call their hosts "cast members." But scholars are divided on whether these soft news shows actually consistently garner the higher ratings they intended to capture since they were conceived. Traditional "hard" nightly network news broadcasts (e.g., CBS, NBC, ABC) still attract large audiences (Markus Prior estimated this hard-to-soft news audience ratio may be as high at 3-to-1, contrary to Baum's analysis) despite the fact that they are less likely to feature the made-for-TV partisan brawls that daytime and cable news shows (e.g., CNN, MSNBC, Fox News) feature.[56] In other words, considering whether a journalist is in the business of "hard" or "soft" news or appears on network or cable television may not completely answer the celebrity question.

There are some journalists that maintain they are not in the entertainment business but are instead strictly providers of information to the public. The print and broadcast journalists in the latter group tend to be the most hesitant to publicize their political leanings and engage in partisan debates, which is obviously eventually required for a celebrities seeking elective office. Most newsrooms have codes of conduct for their reporters that preclude them from getting involved in politics. The Society of Professional Journalists (SPJ) Ethics Committee makes this clear in their position paper on whether journalists should engage in political activity: "The simplest answer is "No." Don't do it. Don't get involved. Don't contribute money, don't work in a campaign, don't lobby, and especially, don't run for office yourself."[57]

Many journalists take these guidelines to the extreme, not only refraining from registering with a political party, but refraining from voting altogether. As stated by Mike Allen of Politico, "I'm part of a minority school of thought among journalists that we owe it to the people we cover, and to our readers, to remain agnostic about elections, even in private. I figure that if the news media serve as an (imperfect) umpire, neither team wants us taking a few swings." But not all journalists share this perspective, a standard of purity Allen's colleague John Harris calls "an old notion of neutrality and fair-minded presentation."[58] And one could argue that in order to have a successful journalism career in the fragmented new media environment, *especially* a career in broadcast journalism, some ability to command public attention and hold it is required. Others would argue that all television, no matter the content, is a form of entertainment.

Indeed, there is a new crop of broadcast journalists in particular who not only share their political views with the public, but openly advocate for one party over another and carefully curate an audience of partisan sympathizers. This group is especially relevant to my study, since cable news anchors who share their opinions and participate in intense on-air debate sessions have been able to build large, passionate audiences. In recent years, the most ideologically extreme cable news networks—Fox News on the right end of the spectrum and MSNBC on the left—have enjoyed the highest ratings, both during peak viewing hours and throughout the day.[59,60]

Contrary to their more reserved counterparts who anchor traditional news shows (e.g., Lester Holt, a registered Republican who hosts NBC's Nightly News broadcast, or Chris Wallace, a registered Democrat who hosts Fox News Sunday), the stars of prime time opinion-oriented cable news shows have become outspoken fixtures in the political arena.[61,62] Fox News host Laura Ingraham delivered a rousing speech endorsing Donald Trump at the Republican National Convention. Left-leaning MSNBC host Rachel Maddow has emphasized that MSNBC values hosts who are interesting characters who try to represent themselves as "real" people rather than those who aim to appeal to the median viewer.[63] Conservative broadcasters Alex Jones and Sean Hannity have defined themselves as entertainers. "I'm not a journalist, I'm a talk show host," said Fox News host Sean Hannity in 2016.[64] In the midst of a custody battle, Infowars host Alex Jones's lawyer made a similar comment about the conspiracy theorist's career: "He's playing a character . . . He is a performance artist."[65]

Unfortunately, whether journalists should be considered celebrities is still a gray area, even when we have clear-cut cases of entertainment journalism. There have also been very few cases of journalists running for elective office. What happens more often is that politicians become broadcasters. Similarly to actors, actresses, and athletes, there is a lot of variation in name recognition among journalists, as I will demonstrate later in this study. Some journalists are much more famous than others, so for pedagogical purposes it is sometimes helpful to point to obvious examples, as Harvey does in his definition of celebrity. Sean Hannity is a celebrity. Peter Baker is a journalist.

In the next section of this chapter, I will review the major findings of existing empirical research on celebrities and draw on several different disciplines in the social sciences and humanities in an effort to understand why Americans have an affinity for celebrities and whether they are inclined to vote for them. First, I will examine findings in the considerable body of research that has sought to address whether celebrities have political influence, including Harvey's. That is, are celebrities effective surrogates for other politicians (i.e., can they convince voters to support candidates for office other than themselves, through endorsements, high-profile campaign speeches, or otherwise)? Are celebrities effective advocates for political issues?

Existing Scholarship: Celebrities, Public Opinion, and Voting Behavior

What little empirical research does exist concerning the role of celebrities in contemporary politics sprouts from a fundamental normative concern in political science: how to get young people to vote. Declining and flat rates of participation and the gap in political knowledge across age groups have long been concerns of political scientists, as have declining rates of trust in government institutions. These combined issues are the subject of Stephen Bennet's 1997 article, "Why Young Americans Hate Politics, and What We Should Do About It."[66] Bennett provides a comprehensive summary of the contributing factors to the detachment young people feel from the political system, including their general distrust of politicians and government representatives, who they believe are self-serving and disingenuous, low rates of voter participation (only 35% of people under 30 years of age reported voting in 1994), disinterest in engaging in political discussions, and finally, different media consumption habits. Young people tend not to consume as much political news as their parents and grandparents, even when a variety of mediums are considered, such as newspapers, radio, and television. To this list, E.J. Dionne adds that professional politicians are alienating young people with ideological arguments from the 1960s which have no relevance to the serious and pragmatic issues faced by Americans today.[67]

Some of these phenomena have improved since the time in which Bennett was writing. In 2016, 49% of Millennials (voters aged 18–35 in 2016) reported voting in the general election, a slight decrease from 50% in 2008, what Pew calls the "high-water mark" for Millennial voting behavior, and a slight increase from 46.4% in 2012.[68] Millennials account for a growing proportion of the U.S. electorate (69.2 million eligible voters), almost equal to the Baby Boomers (69.7 million eligible voters), and they are now the largest living generation.[69]

Information technology optimists also point to the rapidly changing news media environment in their arguments that young people are not "newsless" or even averse to reading newspapers. Instead, young people are getting their news online. In 2015, 69% of Millennials reported getting news daily, and young Americans regularly got election news from national newspapers at equal or greater rates than their elders in 2016.[70,71] But pessimists observing the current technology landscape do not agree that the availability of political information and news online will lead to increased rates of political knowledge and engagement. Instead, the internet enables people to access their preferred media—entertainment media—more easily and more quickly. In other words, more choices do not necessarily mean better choices. Young people still prefer entertainment over politics.[72]

Trust in government institutions, including the news media, is also at an all-time low. Only 18% of Americans today say that they trust the government in Washington, DC to do what is right "just about always" (3%) or "most of the time" (15%). This figure is even worse among young Americans, only 15% of whom have trust in the government to do what is right.[73]

Prior empirical research on the role of celebrities in politics is focused on the ability of celebrities to influence public opinion of politicians and policy issues. It is no surprise then, that one of the key demographics in which these studies are interested is young voters. In their study of whether celebrity endorsements can influence first-time voters, Natalie Wood and Kenneth Herbst propose two avenues through which celebrities can influence youth votes (in their study, voters ages 18–24), opinion leadership, and influence of subjective norms. Since young voters are the most inexperienced and unknowledgeable when it comes to voting and politics, they may be particularly susceptible to the influence of elites as well as the people around them. Lacking information and exposure to political debates, young voters are more likely to pick up on the actions of celebrity surrogates through the mass media and entertainment media than they may be traditional politicians. That is, celebrity endorsers not only function to draw attention to the political candidates for whom they advocate, but to shape the image of those candidates in a positive manner. Celebrities are a source of inspiration to many young people, and can influence the "hipness" of a candidate that might otherwise be perceived to be boring or out of touch.[74] By surveying a convenience sample of 506 students in 2004 which asked students which forces motivated them to vote the most, including, community events arranged or attended by celebrities, advertising campaigns containing celebrities, or personal and family relationships, the authors found that students were much less likely to cite celebrity endorsements and events as drivers of their voting decisions than the opinion of family and friends.

Another notable study conducted in 2004 using similar methods finds almost the opposite. Erica Austin et al. surveyed a convenience sample of 305 college students in order to gauge their receptiveness to celebrity endorsement efforts and whether the involvement of celebrities in political campaigns made students more or less complacent about politics. Similarly to Wood and Herbst, Austin et al. focus their analysis on whether celebrities can combat political disaffection among voters aged 18–25, and they ask survey respondents whether they "have liked the get-out-the-vote promotions celebrities have been doing" and whether they "admire the celebrities who have been promoting voting or candidates." However, through a multiple regression analysis, the authors instead found a negative relationship between receptivity to celebrity endorsements and political complacency, and a positive relationship between receptivity to celebrity endorsements and self-efficacy. According to Austin et al., the young voters who were most open to (and perhaps most influenced by) celebrity involvement in political campaigns had more positive views of their own role in the American political system and were the least complacent. Austin et. al conclude that celebrity-endorsed GOTV campaigns can help persuade young voters to participate in elections and have positive implications for civic engagement.[75]

A more recent study by Craig Garthwaite and Timothy Moore examines celebrity endorsements more closely. While Wood and Herbst and Austin et al. address the question of the "general" influence of celebrities, in other words, whether celebrities are effective at getting out the vote, or garnering support for candidates in general through endorsements, Garthwaite and Moore attempt to measure the effect of one very high profile endorsement of a presidential candidate by a celebrity in 2008: Oprah Winfrey's endorsement of Barack Obama. To accomplish this, the authors estimate the effect of Oprah Winfrey's endorsement of Obama on Obama's vote share, and the effect of Winfrey's endorsement on voter participation. Garthwaite and Moore again use multiple regression in order to generate predictions of the vote share Obama would have received with and without Winfrey's endorsement. They leverage circulation of Oprah's magazine to locate the highest concentrations of her fans. The authors find that support for Obama in the highest magazine circulation area was much higher after Oprah's endorsement than it would have been otherwise. Specifically, they estimate that Oprah's endorsement was responsible for more than one million votes for Obama, increased the campaign contributions Obama received, and increased the overall level of voter participation.[76] Garthwaite and Moore, do, however, qualify their findings. They note that their estimates of the 'Oprah effect' should be viewed as an upper bound for celebrity influence. Oprah is a celebrity of unmatched popularity and recognition.

The level of fame and favorability celebrities possess clearly affects their ability to shape public opinion, and the level of political engagement and age of voters also matters a great deal. So too, does the political context in which these campaigns take place. Academic researchers in the UK have attempted to answer similar questions about the role of entertainers in their own democratic system. Inthorn and Street suggest that "the weaker, more decentralized U.S. party system may be more hospitable to celebrity politics than the UK's more centralized party and electoral system."[77] For example, in their article "If Kate voted Conservative, would you?" Ekant Veer et al. leverage a factorial design survey experiment to compare the effect of celebrity vs. non-celebrity endorsers on political party vote choice and the endorsers themselves. Similarly to research in the U.S., celebrity endorsers, on average, were found to be more likable and more familiar than the non-celebrity endorsers. And celebrity endorsers were shown to be influential over vote choice among low-engagement, low-knowledge voters. However, this effect was negated among voters who actively engage in and think about politics.[78]

In a series of focus groups and in-depth interviews conducted with first-time voters in the UK, Inthorn and Street find support for the notion that celebrities can effectively connect citizens with a political cause, and that celebrities in general are discussed in much more positive terms than politicians, who the focus group participants found to be distrustful, inauthentic, and professionally motivated (in a bad way). The authors sum up their findings and this mechanism in a particularly useful way:

> . . . the young citizens we spoke to responded positively to the general idea of celebrity politics because they saw it as an alternative to formal government . . . What gives celebrities like Eminem the advantage over an elected politician is public access to his private life. The young citizens we spoke

to look for authentic politics, and they use the private personas of political actors as markers of authenticity and genuine commitment to a cause.[79]

One of the most fascinating advantages enjoyed by celebrities that appears repeatedly in celebrity studies literature is that voters—particularly young people—appear to be skeptical of the true motives of traditional politicians, and thus view the political advocacy efforts of politicians as non-genuine attempts to sell themselves to voters or convince voters of a particular policy position. However, voters do not seem to evaluate celebrities who are trying to sell something, whether it is a product or a political candidate or cause, in the same way, even though advertising is a big part of a celebrity's professional duties. For this reason, it is valuable to look at studies in marketing and advertising, which generally show that celebrity endorsements of commercial products have a positive impact on consumer perceptions and attention.

Somdutta Biswas et al. found in their study of consumer attitudes in India and the United States that there is a moderate positive impact of celebrity endorsements on attention and exposure of consumers to product advertisements.[80] Like celebrity endorsements of politicians, celebrity endorsements of products are thought to draw more attention to advertisements for products than would have been garnered otherwise, make ads more memorable and credible, and make products appear to be more glamorous and appealing. Biswas et al. also caution that increased attention to and attitudes toward products endorsed by celebrities does not necessarily translate to the ultimate choice of the consumer to buy the product. This is an important point. Even if the research on the relationship between political endorsements and evaluations of candidates and parties was conclusive, most studies do not purport a direct connection between celebrity endorsements and vote choice (perhaps with the exception of Garthwaite and Moore's Oprah study).

So what happens to the effect of a celebrity product endorsement, if a celebrity becomes unpopular, or loses some of her fame? Clinton Amos, Gary Holmes and David Strutton address this question in their study of the moderating forces that determine the effectiveness of celebrity endorsements. The variables in which Amos et al. are most interested include celebrity performance (i.e., the level of achievement a celebrity has reached in her career), negative information (about the celebrity herself), celebrity credibility, celebrity expertise, celebrity trustworthiness, celebrity attractiveness, celebrity familiarity, celebrity likability, and the fit between a celebrity and the product she endorses. While the authors find trustworthiness, expertise, and attractiveness to be the most important variables in a celebrity's influence over perceptions of the brand, consumer intention to purchase the product, attitude toward the advertisement, believability of the advertisement, and how memorable and recognizable the product is, they also found that negative information about a celebrity endorser—because celebrities become so closely associated with the products they sell—can have powerful negative effects on perceptions of the product.⁸¹ This finding has logical and important implications for politics. While we know that negative information about a celebrity (or a candidate for that matter) can lower opinion of the person to whom the bad behavior is ascribed, it is unclear whether negative information about a celebrity could influence opinion of the politicians they endorse. This is akin to the idea in the celebrity studies and interest groups literature that celebrity or interest group endorsement of a candidate can actually contribute to votes for the opposing candidate or party.⁸²

Is 'Celebrity' a New Phenomenon?

Even among the most cited historians, there is considerable debate about whether the study of celebrity is extricable from the history of the mass media and the emergence of social media. To some scholars, fame as we know it is a product of the contemporary media environment. And the current media environment has become so saturated, with hundreds of television channels, publications, and websites competing for public attention, that more opportunities have arisen to make more people famous for more reasons. In order to compete against providers of pure entertainment, broadcast journalists, for example, have shortened soundbites, emphasized conflict and horserace-style election coverage, and provided more analysis than straight description. They have also, in many cases, shared information with their audiences about their personal lives, beliefs and experiences. By increasingly inserting themselves into news broadcasts and exercising more autonomy over the way in which news is presented, some journalists have themselves attained a degree of fame that would meet many scholars' definition of 'celebrity.' Joshua Gamson has a very good way of summarizing this process: "Changes in the organization, availability, and visibility of fame technologies have pushed certain themes to the forefront and tangles the two stories—fame as rise to greatness and fame as artificial production—in particular, curious unions.⁸³

Put a different way, Chris Rojek says, ". . . we now live in the age of the pseudo-event, with the result that the line between fact and fiction, reality and illusion has been erased . . . Once we recognize attributed celebrity as a category, we disarm the argument that the line between reality and illusion has been erased."⁸⁴ Recall our conversation earlier in this chapter about definitions of celebrity. Once again, both authors emphasize the shift from achieved to attributed celebrity and the extent to which attributed celebrity requires concentrated media exposure.

The same authors, however, acknowledge that achieved celebrity pre-dated the mass media age. The notion that celebrities of any kind, whether achieved or attributed, have been around at least since the times of Ancient Greece, tells us that the media is not the only force that contributes to fame. There is something larger going on here about human nature and the desires that we have to elevate certain people over others, take an interest in them and what they say, and even to hand them political power. Lapham writes in his book:

> The wish for kings is an old an old and familiar wish, as well known in medieval Europe as ancient Mesopotamia. The ancient Greeks assigned trace elements of the divine to trees and winds and stones . . . The modern Americans assign similar powers . . . to individuals blessed with the aura of celebrity.[85]

In this sense, it does not matter what we do to attempt to change the way the media operates—a media apparatus which Lewis Lapham excoriates for acting as a lapdog rather than a watchdog of elites including celebrities—because humans have always had a need to promote themselves and be known, and also to idolize ideal types of people or tear them down.

Psychology offers helpful insights here. In his book *Illusions of Immortality: A Psychology of Fame and Celebrity*, David Giles puts forth an important concept. Though the widely circled labels of achieved and attributed celebrity imply that one kind of celebrity has been around forever and is more socially acceptable or deserved (achieved) and one is bad, undeserved, and reflects poorly on modern society (attributed), what celebrity status almost universally involves is the lifting of behavioral constraints.[86] That is to say, although it is tempting to reduce the earliest celebrities, for example, from Greek mythology, to infallible gods and human heroes, even achieved celebrities make mistakes and behave distastefully. Celebrities are permitted to behave in ways a normal person would not or could not. They are in many ways reflective of our worst tendencies as human beings rather than our best ones.

There is perhaps no better example of the longstanding interaction between celebrity and politics than the military career of Alexander the Great (born in 356 BC), who Leo Braudy calls the first famous person. "Alexander the Great ostentatiously imitated Achilles among other gods and heroes; Julius Caesar mourned that he had not done as much as Alexander, and the Wichita murderer said he was moved by the same force as Jack the Ripper," writes Braudy.[87] Alexander III of Macedonia created the name Alexander the Great for himself through constant and skillful self-promotion.[88] He mythologized himself by comparing his achievements to those of well-known gods and heroes and honed public perceptions of himself. Alexander encouraged the dissemination of tales of his positive qualities: generosity, charm, boundless energy, and his brilliance as a military strategist and warrior, but historians have suggested that he also found it difficult to control his angry impulses given how much attention and adulation he received. He often ordered his political opponents killed, and was responsible for more than one massacre of his own Greek subjects.[89]

Equally, if not a more, image conscious political leader was Julius Caesar (born 100 BC). In her book *Caesar: A Life in Western Culture*, Maria Wyke describes Caesar as the most famous of all the Romans. We know that not only because of ancient writings about him, but from his own writing, in which he creates a portrait of himself as an unprecedentedly charismatic, talented, sophisticated, strong, focused, and magnetic leader. Caesar is closely associated with the extravagant triumphs that he staged to celebrate military victories as well as the awards and honors he bestowed upon himself, but his own commentary on the war in Gaul and other conflicts revealed that Caesar even talked about himself in the third person, as Wyke notes, "a separable entity whose reputation can be favorably manipulated, polished, and inflated." Wyke further notes, "The Roman general and dictator constantly cultivated a public image for himself that was larger than life in order to arouse admiration, and therefore, increase his political authority, and also to achieve a lasting recognition (or *fama*) for those great deeds of state."[90] In one of Caesar's last and yet most image-conscious acts, after being stabbed 23 times by his colleagues in the Senate, Caesar adjusted his toga to cover up his face.[91]

Other scholars identify the 16th and 17th centuries as the bedrock of our conception of celebrity today. The widespread dissemination of images through new technology in printing and engraving, or "faces," as Gamson and Braudy write, increased the prevalence with which "the wise, the artistic, the holy, and the powerful" were widely depicted as examples of contemporary heroism.[92] The dissemination of images of "great men" (typically political leaders, like George Washington in the U.S.) through written accounts, as well as oral accounts, statues, children's schoolbooks, and monuments continued through the 18th and 19th centuries, but they were accompanied by images of people who were not famous for their skills or leadership capabilities. As Rojek writes, the range of famous people included "bigots, forgers, criminals, whores, balladeers, and thinkers."[93] Professional photography and journalism evolved to the point where "publicity stunts" were already common, as were the public spectacles orchestrated by showman-publicists like P.T. Barnum. Barnum's first successful attempt to promote a person by provoking and fooling the press, Gamson writes, was a former slave, Joice Heth, who Barnum alleged was George Washington's nurse and 161 years old. The full evolution from achieved to attributed celebrity, one could argue, had taken place. Fame was no longer necessarily, as Socrates once wrote, "the perfume of heroic deeds." "As celebrity became systematized in the early twentieth century," Gamson notes, "the leisure-time business of the "show" was, not surprisingly, its primary arena: famous people as entertainment and entertainers as famous people."[94]

At the same time as the press and the definition of celebrity were transforming in the U.S., the framers of the Constitution were debating what form of American government would best serve to preserve the union. The Federalist, a series of papers published in by Alexander Hamilton, James Madison, and John Jay in support of the 1787 Constitution, and constitutional republicanism as a form of government, is one of the best examples of the early fears the founding fathers had of the combined intoxicating quality of fame, the natural human desire to acquire power and garner distinction, and the irrevocable freedom of American citizens to elect their own government representatives. The central problem Madison and Hamilton debated was one of human nature, which they, and other founders, viewed as deeply flawed. Benjamin Franklin once wrote in a letter to Joseph Priestly in 1783:

> Men . . . are more easily provoked than reconciled, more disposed to do Mischief to each other than make Reparation, much more easily deceived than undeceived, and having more Pride and even Pleasure in killing than begetting one another; for without a Blush, they assemble in great Armies . . . to destroy, and when they've killed as many as they can, they exaggerate the Number to augment the fancied Glory . . .[95]

Madison and Hamilton worried that as long as citizens were free to make their own choices and cast their own votes, they would be susceptible to self-destruction. Madison says in Federalist 10, "As long as the reason of man continues fallible, and he is at liberty to exercise it . . . As long as the connection subsists between his reason and his self-love, his opinions and his passions will have a reciprocal influence on each other; and the former will be objects to which the latter attach themselves."[96] Madison continues later, "It is in vain to say that enlightened statesmen will be able to adjust these clashing interests and render them all subservient to the public good. Enlightened statesmen will not always be at the helm."[97] The people who would be at the helm, Madison feared, would be those who rise to power on the tides of popularity (Federalist 51) and then betray the interests of the people. As Hamilton put it in Federalist 68, "Talents for low intrigue, and the little arts of popularity, may alone suffice to elevate a man to the first honors in a single state; but it will require other talents, and a different kind of merit, to establish him in the esteem and confidence of the whole Union."[98] It is not a stretch to say that even Hamilton on his most pessimistic day might not have been able to fully imagine the extent to which the tides of popularity carried the current President of the United States into power.

Not only do deeply flawed human beings get to select their representatives, they have the opportunity to run for public office. Madison writes in Federalist 51 that the greatest difficulty in framing a government that is governed by imperfect men over imperfect men is that "you must first enable the government to control the governed; and in the next place oblige it to control itself."[99] It is not sufficient to examine the reasons celebrities might appeal to voters as political candidates, but what drives them to seek office in the first place. In the next chapter, I examine several cases of successful bids for public office by very famous people, including Ronald Reagan, Jesse Ventura, Arnold Schwarzenegger, Al Franken, and Donald Trump, and how their victories are interrelated. By examining each of their autobiographies, I gain valuable answers to the following questions: Why do celebrities see themselves as fit to govern? How do they explain their victories in their own words?

Notes

1. Zaru, Deena. August 14, 2017. "Caitlyn Jenner Latest Celebrity to Float Run for Office." CNN.
2. Breiner, Andrew. August 1, 2017. "Poll Shows Kid Rock as Republican Front-Runner, 8 Points Behind Stabenow." Roll Call.
3. Jerkovich, Katie. May 16, 2017. "Latest Polling Shows 'The Rock' Leads Trump in 2020 Matchup." The Daily Caller.
4. Hall, Andrew. 2016. *Who Wants to Run? How the Devaluing of Political Office Drives Polarization*. Book Manuscript.
5. Jensen, Erin. May 21, 2017. "'SNL': Dwayne Johnson, Tom Hanks 'Partner' for 2020 Presidential Race." USA Today.
6. Robinson, Joanna. May 21, 2017. "S.N.L.: Watch The Rock and Tom Hanks Announce They're Running for Office." Vanity Fair.
7. Walsh, Kenneth. 2015. *Celebrity in Chief: A History of the Presidents and the Culture of Stardom*. Boulder, CO: Paradigm. Page 2.
8. Kam, Cindy and Elizabeth Zechmeister. 2013. "Name Recognition and Candidate Support." *American Journal of Political Science* 57(4): 971–986.
9. Gass, Nick. July 24, 2015. "Trump Dominates GOP Field in Name ID." *Politico*.
10. Raymond, Adam. June 8, 2017. "Paul Ryan's Excuse for Trump: He's 'Just New to This.'" *New York Magazine*.
11. Carson, Ben. October 8, 2016. "Op-Ed: Dr. Ben Carson on the Donald Trump Video." *The Hill*.
12. Walsh, Kenneth. 2017. *Celebrity in Chief: A History of Presidents and the Culture of Stardom*. New York, NY: Routledge. Page 47.
13. Iyengar, Shanto. 2015. *Media Politics*. New York, NY: W.W. Norton.
14. Steinburg, Brian and Cynthia Littleton. June 13, 2017. "Cable News Wars: Inside the Unprecedented Battle for Viewers in the Trump Era." *Variety*.
15. Garthwaite, Craig and Timothy Moore. 2008. "Can Celebrity Endorsements Affect Political Outcomes? Evidence From the 2008 US Democratic Presidential Primary." *Journal of Law, Economics, and Organization* 29(2): 355–384.
16. Wang, Amy B. October 9, 2018. "Taylor Swift's Endorsement of Democrats Is Followed by a Spike in Voter Registration." *The Washington Post*.
17. Hall, Richard and Frank Wayman. 1990. "Buying Time: Moneyed Interests and the Mobilization of Bias in Congressional Committees." *American Political Science Review* 84(3): 797–820.
18. January 10, 2018. "Read Oprah Winfrey's Rousing Golden Globes Speech." *CNN.com*.
19. Interview with Sidney Blumenthal. June 13, 2014. Washington, DC.
20. Engel, Joel. May 26, 2003. "Too Smart To Be So Dumb." The Weekly Standard.
21. Sabato, Larry (@LarrySabato). "Now We Know Where the Cast of "Animal House" Landed. The Drinking Games in this Key White House Office Are the Least of It." March 30, 2018. 9:50 AM. Tweet.
22. Sowell, Thomas. August 27, 2013. "A Truly Great Phony." Townhall.
23. O'Reilly, Andrew. February 8, 2018. "Apologetic Prof Is Just Latest Academic to Inflame with Talk of Trump's Death." Fox News.
24. Wang, Amy B. February 28, 2017. "'It Was Fantastic': Trump Denies that 2011 White House Correspondents' Dinner Spurred Presidential Bid." The Washington Post.
25. Barklay, Eliza and Brian Resnick. January 19, 2018. "Donald Trump's Fitness for Office Isn't a Medical Question." Vox.
26. Fisher, Marc. July 17, 2016. "Donald Trump Doesn't Read Much. Being President Probably Wouldn't Change That." *The Washington Post*.

27. Blake, Aaron. October 4, 2016. "19 Things Donald Trump Knows Better than Anyone Else, According to Donald Trump." *The Washington Post.*

28. Certain stories and details about the president and other White House staff members in Michael Wolff's book have been questioned and debunked since its publication, but the president's reading habits have been widely discussed and corroborated. See Politifact's "A Fact-Checker's Guide to Michael Wolff's 'Fire and Fury: Inside the Trump White House'" (Angie Drobnic Holan, 2018) for a near-comprehensive list.

29. Klein, Ezra. January 9, 2018. "Beyond the Gossip, Michael Wolff's Fire and Fury Reveals a President in Crisis." Vox.

30. Blake, Aaron. September 29, 2017. "Oprah Just Teased a Run for President in 2020—Again." The Washington Post.

31. Wright, Lauren. March 27, 2018. "Cynthia Nixon Is No Donald Trump." The Hill.

32. Howell, William G. 2017. *An American Presidency: Institutional Foundations of Executive Politics.* Boston, MA: Pearson.

33. Edwards, George C. III, John Howard Kessel, and Bert Rockman, eds. *Researching the Presidency: Vital Questions, New Approaches.* Pittsburgh, PA: University of Pittsburgh Press. Page 379.

34. Alexander Hamilton. 1961. Federalist 68. Clinton Rossiter's edited version of The Federalist Papers (New York, NY: Penguin Group, Page 412).

35. Following Richard Neustadt (*Presidential Power and the Modern Presidents*, 1990, New York, NY: Free Press, Page 3), the use of the male gender throughout this book is justified historically but not prospectively when referring to a president. When used as a synonym for human beings it is outmoded. For that reason, I use "she" as a general pronoun referring to a person of any gender, or a hypothetical president throughout the book.

36. Kernell, Samuel. 2003. Going Public: New Strategies of Presidential Leadership. Washington, DC: CQ Press. Also see George Edwards, On Deaf Ears (2003, Yale University Press) and Fred Greenstein (The Presidential Difference, 2001, Princeton University Press).

37. Wright, Lauren. 2016. On Behalf of the President: Presidential Spouses and White House Communications Strategy Today. Santa Barbara, CA: Praeger. Pages 127 and 128.

38. Wright, Lauren. March 30, 2016. "Here's Evidence that Melania Trump Could Actually Boost Donald Trump's Popularity." The Washington Post.

39. Wright, Lauren. April 7, 2017. "Is Ivanka Trump an Effective Ambassador for Her Father's Presidency? It Depends on the Audience." The Washington Post.

40. Frei, Matt. October 1, 2017. "Ivanka Trump: America's Real First Lady?" CBC.com. Also see Saturday Night Live (NBC) Season 43, Episode 15 for skit entitled 'First Lady' in which Ivanka Trump is portrayed to fulfill all of the traditional duties associated with First Ladies of the US.

41. These findings are echoed in several well-known academic studies of celebrity endorsements and celebrities and advertising which will be discussed in depth and individually cited in the section that follows. They include Austin et al. (2008), Amos et al. (2015), Garthwaite and Moore (2012), Thrall et al. (2008), and Wood and Herbst (2007).

42. Holmes, Su. 2005. "Starring . . . Dyer?: Re-visiting Star Studies and Contemporary Celebrity Culture." *Westminster Papers in Communication and Culture* 2(2): 6–21. Page 9.

43. Barker, Martin and Thomas Austin, eds. 2003. Contemporary Hollywood Stardom. London: Arnold.

44. Jermyn, Deborah. "'Bringing Out the * in You'" In eds. Su Holmes and Sean Redmond. 2006. *Framing Celebrity.* New York, NY: Routledge.

45. Schmid, David. "Idols of Destruction" In eds. Su Holmes and Sean Redmond. 2006. *Framing Celebrity.* New York, NY: Routledge.

46. Redmond, Sean. 2010. "Avatar Obama in the Age of Liquid Celebrity." *Celebrity Studies* 1(1): 81–95.

47. Rojeck, Chris. 2001. *Celebrity*. London: Reaktion Books.
48. Holmes, Su. 2005. "Starring . . . Dyer?: Re-visiting Star Studies and Contemporary Celebrity Culture." *Westminster Papers in Communication and Culture* 2(2): 6–21. Page 11.
49. West, Darrell and John Orman. 2003. Celebrity Politics. Washington, DC: Pearson.
50. Jussim, Matthew. May 18, 2017. "27 Celebrities and Athletes Who Followed in their Fathers' Footsteps." Men's Fitness.
51. Turner, Graeme, Francis Bonner, and P. David Marshall. 2000. *Fame Games*. Cambridge: Cambridge University Press.
52. Gunter, Barrie. 2014. *Celebrity Capital: Assessing the Value of Fame*. New York, NY: Bloomsbury Academic.
53. Harvey, Mark. 2017. *Celebrity Influence*. Lawrence, KS: University of Kansas Press. Page 18.
54. Ibid. Page 20.
55. Baum, Matthew. 2002. "Sex, Lies, and War: How Soft News Brings Foreign Policy to the Inattentive Public." *American Political Science Review* 96 (1): 91–109.
56. Prior, Markus. 2003. "Any Good News in Soft News?" *Political Communication* 20: 149–171.
57. Brown, Fred. "SPJ Ethics Committee Position Papers: Political Involvement." www.SPJ.org.
58. Vandehei, Jim, John F. Harris, and Mike Allen. 2008. "Should Journalists Vote? Yes, No, Sometimes." *Politico*.
59. Mitchell, Amy et al. 2014. "Political Polarization and Media Habits." Pew Research.
60. Otterson, Joe. December 12, 2017. "Cable News Ratings: MSNBC Posts Big Percentage Gains, Fox News Stays Number One, CNN Sets Records." *Variety*.
61. Darcy, Oliver. October 20, 2017. "Fox News Host Chris Wallace Slams Network Colleagues for Attacks on the Press." *CNN*.
62. Miller, Zeke. September 20, 2016. "Donald Trump Called Debate Moderator Lester Holt a Democrat. He's Actually a Republican." *Time*.
63. Adler, Margot. October 23, 2008. "Rachel Maddow: Sassy, Acerbic And—Yes—Liberal." *NPR*.
64. Marans, Daniel. April 14, 2016. "Sean Hannity: I'm Not a Journalist. I'm a Talk Show Host." *The Huffington Post*.
65. Rhodan, Maya. April 17, 2017. "President Trump's Favorite Conspiracy Theorist Is Just 'Playing a Character,' His Lawyer Says." *Time*.
66. Bennett, Stephen. 1997. "Why Young Americans Hate Politics, and What We Should Do About It." PS: Political Science and Politics 30(1): 47–53.
67. See Gladdis Smith's book review in *Foreign Affairs* magazine. Dionne, Eugene Joseph Jr. 1991. *Why Americans Hate Politics*. New York, NY: Simon and Schuster.
68. Fry, Richard. July 31, 2017. "Millennials and Gen Xers Outvoted Boomers and Older Generations in 2016 Election." *Pew Research*.
69. Fry, Richard. May 16, 2016. "Millennials Match Baby Boomers as Largest Generation in U.S. Electorate, But Will They Vote?" *Pew Research*.
70. Media Insight Project. March 16, 2015. "How Millennials Get News: Inside the Habits of America's First Digital Generation." Published online by the American Press Institute.
71. Barthel, Michael and Jeffrey Gottfried. February 17, 2017. "For Election News, Young People Turned to Some National Papers More than Their Elders." Pew Research.
72. Iyengar, Shanto. 2007. *Media Politics: A Citizen's Guide*. New York, NY: W.W. Norton. Chapter 3.
73. Pew Research Center. May 3, 2017. "Public Trust in Government: 1958–2017."
74. Wood, Natalie and Kenneth Herbst. 2007. "Political Star Power and Political Parties: Does Celebrity Endorsement Win First-Time Votes?" *Journal of Political Marketing* 6(2–3): 141–158.

75. Austin, Erica Weintraub, Rebecca Van de Vord, Bruce Pinkleton, andEvan Epstein. 2008. "Celebrity Endorsements and Their Potential to Motivate Young Voters." *Mass Communication and Society* 11(1): 420–436.
76. Garthwaite, Craig and Timothy Moore. 2012. "Can Celebrity Endorsements Affect Political Outcomes? Evidence From the 2008 US Democratic Presidential Primary." *The Journal of Law, Economics, & Organization* 29(2): 355–384.
77. Inthorn, Sanna and John Street. 2011. "'Simon Cowell for Prime Minster?'? Young Citizens' Attitudes Towards Celebrity Politics." *Media, Culture & Society* 33(3): 479–489.
78. Veer, Ekant, Ilda Becirovic and Brett Martin. 2010. "If Kate Voted Conservative, would You?" *Eurpoean Journal of Marketing* 44(3–4): 436–450.
79. Inthorn and Street 2011, Page 486 and 487.
80. Biswas, Mahmood Hussain and Kathleen O'Donnell. 2009. "Celebrity Endorsements in Advertisements and Consumer Perceptions: A Cross-Cultural Study." *Journal of Global Marketing* 22(2): 121–137.
81. Amos, Clinton and Gary Holmes and David Strutton. 2015. "Exploring the Relationship Between Celebrity Endorser Effects and Advertising Effectiveness." *International Journal of Advertising* 27(2): 209–234.
82. Wood and Herbst 2007, Page 147
83. Gamson, Joshua. 1994. *Claims to Fame*. Los Angeles, CA: University of California Press. Page 17.
84. Rojeck, Chris. 2001. *Celebrity*. London, UK: Reaktion Books. Pages 18–19.
85. Quoted in Neimark, Jill. May 1, 1995. "The Culture of Celebrity." *Psychology Today*.
86. Giles, David. 2000. *Illusions of Immortality: A Psychology of Fame and Celebrity*. London, UK: Macmillan Press.
87. Braudy, Leo. 1986. *The Frenzy of the Renown*. New York, NY: Vintage Books. Pages 3–4.
88. Gamson 1994.
89. See Wood, Michael. 1997. *In the Footsteps of Alexander The Great*. Berkeley, CA: University of California Press and Bosworth, Albert Bryan. 1996. *Alexander in the East*. Oxford, UK: Oxford University Press.
90. Wyke, Maria. 2008. *Caesar: A Life in Western Culture*. Chicago, IL: University of Chicago Press. Pages 1–9.
91. Goldsworthy, Adrian. 2014. *Augustus*. New Haven, CT: Yale University Press. Page 466.
92. Braudy, Leo. 1986. *The Frenzy of the Renown: Fame and Its History*. New York, NY: Oxford University Press. As quoted and paraphrased in Gamson 1994, Page 17.
93. Rojek 2001, Page 19.
94. Gamson 1994, Page 23
95. Schoenbrun, David. 1976. *Triumph in Paris: The Exploits of Benjamin Franklin*. New York, NY: Harper & Row. Page 387.
96. All excerpts from Clinton Rossiter's edited version of The Federalist Papers published by Signet Classics (New York, NY) in 2003. Page 73.
97. Ibid, Page 75.
98. Ibid, Page 412.
99. Ibid, Page 319.

CHAPTER 2

IN THEIR OWN WORDS
WHY CELEBRITIES RUN

A Note on Political Memoirs

Memoirs and autobiographies of politicians remain virtually untapped resources in qualitative political science research. Scholars have understandable concerns with using memoirs to gain insight into the decision-making processes of American leaders. Relying on politicians' personal interpretations of historical events in order to understand them is surely unadvisable. Political memoirs are not as much representations of what actually happened, or what a politician actually thought, during key moments of a campaign or while in office, for instance, as they are representations of what politicians want us to believe happened at those times. They are carefully curated vehicles that elected officials use to positively influence their own legacies.

Hillary Clinton's memoir about the 2016 campaign, for example, is aptly named *What Happened*. The book has been criticized for the extent to which it places the blame of a losing presidential campaign not on Hillary Clinton herself, but on the broader sociopolitical context that Clinton believes worked against her, including the bias of voters and media organizations against female candidates. Memoirs of presidents and presidential candidates, indeed, are rosy analyses of history, usually intended to favorably sway public opinion post-presidency or post-campaign. To continue the example above, we can see that Hillary Clinton wants her legacy to be a burden-free one, perhaps of a woman who tried her best to break the highest and hardest glass ceiling, but did not succeed because of sexism. Yet despite this positive bias, political communication scholars can rest assured there is an equally valuable insight to be gained from the memoirs of politicians: how politicians *want* to be seen, how they present themselves to the public, and what they imagine a favorable public image of them might look like.

It is important to remember that interviews with politicians, while they do not afford politicians as much time to craft and edit a public image as do books, bear many of the same weaknesses. In fact, every public appearance presidents make, everything they say, and everything they write lacks verifiable authenticity. What we know about presidents in many cases is precisely what they want us to know. The presidency is a public-facing job, and thus what we perceive is a carefully crafted image.

Luckily, celebrities, like presidents, are prolific memoir writers. Public interest in celebrities and their careers renders these books valuable and numerous. And similarly to politicians, what we glean from celebrity memoirs and interviews is what celebrities choose to publicly present. With these tradeoffs in mind, this chapter mines the memoirs and autobiographies of celebrities who have run for public office. The goal of memoir analysis in this case is to learn about celebrities' motivations for running for office and to clarify their perspectives on winning versus losing an election (or, at least, what celebrities want us to believe about their motivations for running, and what they want us to believe about the reasons they won or lost). This qualitative analysis from the perspective of celebrities themselves serves as a valuable contrast to the commentary of elites on why they run, win, and lose, and especially to the quantitative analysis in Chapters 3 and 4, which provides the most reliable evidence thus far of how voters think about celebrities, whether they prefer them to professional politicians as candidates, and whether the public portraits that celebrities proffer are successful. In this chapter, I examine the letters and memoirs of Roy Acuff, P.T. Barnum, Shirley Temple Black, Sonny Bono, Bill Bradley, Al Franken, Jack Kemp, Bob Mathias, Ronald Reagan, Jim Ryun, Arnold Schwarzenegger, Donald Trump, Upton Sinclair, Jesse Ventura and Gore Vidal.

Before Trump, There was Sinclair

84 years ago, a well-known public figure who with no professional political experience ran for Governor of California. An expert at gathering media attention, the candidate used his fame to make headlines in the years leading up to the election. When he was not teasing a run for statewide office himself, he engaged in provocative political debates from the sidelines of California politics, taking controversial stands on issues that did not consistently align with either political party, but tapped into the bubbling mistrust along class lines. In 1934, he decided to run as a Democrat and announced his candidacy in earnest. His timing was impeccable, for the California Democratic Party at this time was plagued by deep divisions between its liberal and conservative factions. Party leadership failed to unite around an alternative contender. Armed with a catchy four-word slogan and a simple platform that voters and journalists could easily digest, the candidate won the Democratic

primary by 436,000 votes, easily beating eight establishment politicians who were too busy attacking each other or begging each other to drop out, for every one was certain he would win if the other would withdraw. The campaign was so contentious that reports abounded of families being torn apart by their support of different candidates and students being beaten up in playgrounds for wearing campaign buttons.

Sound Familiar?

That candidate was Upton Sinclair, the muckraking socialist journalist who gained widespread notoriety after writing *The Jungle*, which exposed the inhumane, unsanitary and dangerous conditions in meatpacking facilities. Sinclair's ideological unorthodoxy on issues ranging from psychic telepathy to civil liberties and his knack for self-promotion are not the only aspects of his campaign that were eerily similar to Donald Trump's presidential upset in 2016. Sinclair may have been an eloquent writer, but his books were never aimed at educated audiences. Although he lived a life of luxury in Beverly Hills, he understood the importance of appealing directly to the working class through accessible rhetoric. And he could make a point and teach a lesson without seeming like an elitist. Sinclair regularly asserted that he knew more about the economy than economists, (who he called fools), and that the only kind of economics that made sense were common sense, and that the government needed to do more to get people back to work. He only used his wealth and status to drive home the point that he was not beholden to campaign donors. "I have not taken one dollar with a string tied to it," Sinclair said.[1] He was much more comfortable in combat than cooperation, and he lead an all-out assault on the California media, which he later referred to as a "lie factory" that produced "a mess of falsehoods" and only reported "according to their prejudices."[2] How did he know they were lying for political purposes and not because they disliked him? They "were my friends," Sinclair said. He knew the system. Sinclair routinely called out specific news outlets, and even accused them of libel, writing of the powerful editor of *The Sacramento Bee*, *The Fresno Bee*, and *The Modesto Bee* in his memoir *I Candidate for Governor*:

> All right Mr. McClatchy! You think you have done your full duty because you have allowed me to deny the slanders in your columns—but with no retraction or apology from you—what I ask is, why, before publishing grave charges against a man's honor, not give the man a chance to say whether there is any basis of fact in them? The answer is, because you wanted to discredit the man, and you didn't care what means you used.[3]

Even after Sinclair lost the general election, he did not let up. He painted a picture of big California business criminally conspiring with trust lawyers in Los Angeles to steal the election from him by assailing his character and alleging that his voters were registered illegally. The "would-be Fascists," Sinclair huffs, who "engineered the "sham proceeding and perversion of our court process," and got themselves denounced in those scathing words by a Justice of the Supreme Court, are still part of the ruling gang of the State of California."[4]

Sinclair's ego, his obsession with his reputation, and what resembles paranoia also spills out in the pages of his memoir. He regularly refers to himself in the third person, as in "lying about Upton Sinclair"[5] or "stopping Sinclair"[6] and accuses the media of digging up embarrassing stories from his past and taking his written comments about sex out of context, all to build a case for his "very offensive personality." He speaks about his wildly successful campaign events, his effective rhetorical strategy of taking questions from the audience, the cheering people packed inside who would stand when he approached the platform and crowd around him afterward to shake his hand and touch him. Sinclair brags about his ability to spur his supporters into action, who agreed he was being treated unfairly by the media. In a mixed admission of his self-centered nature, Sinclair writes, "I have talked a lot about myself, and have changed my mind frequently—unlike *The Times*, which is fixated in its hate of every progressive idea."[7]

Around the same time Sinclair was considering a libel suit against *The San Francisco "Chronicle"* (quotes his) for doctoring a photograph of his house—his lawyer who Sinclair described as a man who "does not believe in seeking trouble" stopped him from filing one—Sinclair discusses "menacing developments" that he assures were corroborated by his friends. "There were strange men hanging around the place, I was being followed; our telephone wires were tapped" and he had received warnings about "gangsters from the East" coming to harm him.[8]

In addition to his gripe with the newspapers, Sinclair believes the film industry has conspired against him by refusing to make his books into movies, denouncing him in interviews (in one case, for being "unbalanced") and running newsreels throughout the election that did the same. "One of the great institutions of Southern California is the movies, and now I have to tell what they did to "stop Sinclair,"" he says.

> I don't think I am egotistical in saying that I have offered to the motion pictures industry some good opportunities. *King Coal, Jimmy Higgins, 100%, They Call Me Carpenter, Boston*—all these are motion picture scenarios ready made. There is only one thing wrong with them. They indict the profit system.[9]

Despite its prevalence, Sinclair and Trump's egomaniacal style of campaigning is not generalizable to celebrities. As Barack Obama said in a 2007 interview with ABC News, "If you don't have enough self-awareness to see the element of megalomania involved in thinking you should be president, then you probably should not be president. There is a slight madness to thinking you should be leader of the free world."[10] But most celebrities do not admit it, even if they are aware of it. What celebrities do instead is self-deprecate and play the part of the humble outsider. Or they make a big deal about how they were recruited to run by others and felt pressured to give in to public demands for their candidacy, as if they never had these aspirations themselves. Most of all, celebrities relate their existing professional skills to the skills they imagine are necessary for success in politics. Nowhere is this more prevalent than in the political campaigns of athletes, who draw countless parallels between teamwork and bipartisanship, physical suffering and training and the ordeal of campaigning, and the humility of having to learn something for the first time or spending overtime practicing.

Celebrity Athletes and the Rigors of Politicking

"Americans often attribute to successful athletes qualities that are unrelated to athletic performance," writes former U.S. Senator, NBA champion, and Olympic gold medalist Bill Bradley in his memoir *Time Present, Time Past*. "When reporters began questioning my friends about my nonathletic interests, they didn't just say I wanted to be a diplomat. They said I'd be secretary of state . . . Why write about jump shots if you could engage in hyperbolic speculation at little apparent cost to the athlete and great benefit in reader interest?"[11] As the celebrity athletes featured in this chapter attest, there is a lot of variation in the skills required to succeed at the highest levels of a professional sport. Former Olympians Jim Ryun (1,500 meter runner turned U.S. Congressman), Bob Mathias (Decathlete turned U.S Congressman), and Ben Nighthorse Campbell (Judo champion turned U.S. Senator) each emphasize the high tolerance for physical pain and suffering and extreme discipline that was required of them at a young age when they relate particular experiences to politics. Bob Mathias recalls "shivering in the cold rain, dog tired, soaked to the skin, staring at a pole vault bar as high as the Empire State Building" as a 17-year-old.[12] To test how much oxygen his body could process, 21-year-old Jim Ryun's physiologist would mount VO_2 testing equipment onto the hood of a pick-up truck traveling 15 miles an hour and ask Jim—who was also attached to the truck via a tube in his mouth and a clip plugging his nose—to run alongside it until he was exhausted.[13] Ben Nighthorse moved to Tokyo in 1960 to train for the Olympics, where new Judo students cleaned the toilets and the floors, washed the older students' uniforms, and were motivated with the crack of a bamboo stick across the back. "If you lost, you were required to shave your head. If you threw a guy down in training, someone would kick him in the head or the stomach to make him try harder," Nighthorse described.[14] Having endured experiences like these in order to win a contest in which each athlete proudly represented the United States of America, it is perhaps no surprise that a congressional campaign was no sweat to these stars. To many athletes, playing sports is exactly like campaigning, so much so that they thought the latter prepared them for the former. ". . . they both take courage," said Ryun of being an athlete and being a politician.[15]

I have always preferred moving to sitting still," writes Bill Bradley in his memoir. "For ten years after finishing college, I made by living by running around in short pants in drafty arenas across America, as a professional basketball player. The rhythm of the road—a drive, a flight, a performance, a hotel, a sleep, and a drive, a flight, a return—provided the framework through which I saw America and myself . . . For the past seventeen years, I have crisscrossed America as a politician, a United States Senator from New Jersey, following a familiar rhythm . . ."[16]

According to Arnold Schwarzenegger, "Just like bodybuilding, campaigning is all about reps, reps, reps."[17] Former NFL pro and famed Head Coach of the University of Nebraska Football team Tom Osborne likened campaigning to a much more grueling football recruiting season. "I remember talking with Vince Dooley, the former football coach at Georgia, who had run for Senate but abandoned his campaign," said Osborne. (See how common this is)? Osborne continues, "He told me that, for him, campaigning was like recruiting but seemed to go on forever. Recruiting was intense, but over fairly quickly."[18] Both Osborne and Jack Kemp, also a beloved former NFL player who became a successful politician, liken their former jobs as head coach and Quarterback, respectively, to being a leader in government. Osborne thought being Governor of Nebraska would be more like being a head football coach than his job as a U.S. Congressman—a central part of his decision to abandon his seat and run in 2006. It would allow him "to initiate agenda items and make a real difference in the state."[19] Like Osborne, Kemp saw countless parallels between football and politics: "quarterbacking as capitalism, the huddle as cooperative endeavor, booing as no big deal, the next play as the chance to win."[20] Moreover, as Bill Bradley notes, political campaigns were winner-take-all events in which a champion and a loser might only be one point apart. And campaigns are covered by the media exactly like sports events, so it is no surprise that these athlete candidates also had a degree of comfort and familiarity there: "What's the score today? Just how did you win this game? What's your strategy for tomorrow? How do you feel about where you are in the standings?"[21] Jim Ryun, whose 1996 congressional campaign slogan was "Run With Ryun" adds "As a successful athlete, I had become quite familiar with media interviews . . . at first, there were as many questions about my running career as there were about politics."[22] Professional wrestler turned actor Jesse Ventura was a record-breaking high school swimmer and football champion and a Navy SEAL, but he sees himself more as an entertainer than an athlete, and his pre-gubernatorial memoir *I Ain't Got Time to Bleed* is replete with examples of how he used his media savvy and communications skills to win both his mayoral and gubernatorial elections in Minnesota. To Ventura, wrestling was a "performance art" in which he excelled at working the crowds, and a lot of aspects of politics require a performer's skillset. "It's [being an entertainer] all about communicating and being able to see things from a bunch of different perspectives . . . When you're serving in a public office, you have to be able to communicate extremely well."[23]

But as much as campaigning can often benefit from a candidate who is decisive and confident in her skillset, governing, as Kemp learned many times, Congress is often no place for a quarterback calling the shots. As a freshman congressman eager to dictate tax policy, Kemp was quickly cut down to size by his more senior colleagues. "I'd call out a play and expect everyone to carry out his assignment," Kemp said in an interview. "I . . . realized it isn't that way in government. Leadership here means finding where people want to go and figuring out a way to take them there. That's what democracy is all about. A football huddle is not a democracy."[24] Many star athletes also talk about the slow pace of governing taking a lot to get used to. "I think some people thought I would be tremendously frustrated by the slow pace of change in Washington," said Osbourne. "I came to Congress with a coaching background that gave be an ability to get to know a great many members of Congress rather quickly. I was seen as something of an oddity and there was a curiosity factor."[25]

No matter how many comparisons athletes draw between sports and politics, the uncomfortable truth remains: running track is not like politics, playing or coaching in the NFL is not like politics, body building is not like politics. Professional wrestling is not like politics. Basketball is not like politics. Not one of these athletes would suggest that a person with no training can throw on a jersey and start playing in the Super Bowl simply because the fans supported the idea, or because the person relished a challenge, or had watched a ton of games and met a lot of professional athletes. Yet that is pretty much the equivalent of going from zero to United States Congressman, or Senator, or Governor, or President. Politics is one of the only jobs in the world that does not require applicants to have some degree of experience or expertise. The startup costs to inexperience in governing are very high, even if one is not a celebrity novelty, as Kemp and Osbourne described. Congress in particular is a hierarchical and stuffy place in which newcomers from any profession must wait their turn to come up the ranks. The formal obstacles to making change are there for a reason, but the polarized nature of Congress makes change even harder, as do the ideologues who are generally elected. Resentment against freshly elected sports stars on the part of traditional politicians is real. Most members of Congress have been working together for years, if not within the House and Senate, then at lower levels of government, in law practices, and in the private sector, where most of them started. They have a shorthand, a lifetime of experience and the benefit institutional memory, all tools that help to steer them away from the failures and pitfalls of the past. Two-year election cycles in the House also ensure that every member is preoccupied with her reelection; there is no time, or benefit, to mentoring newcomers. As Campbell mentioned in an interview, ". . . the people who get things done around here [Congress] are not necessarily the smartest or the best, but the ones who won't give up. Just keep doing it, keep doing it. Get knocked down, get back up, and redo it again next year."[26] Every athlete describes an experience having to get over the insecurity (and reputation) of being a dumb jock, or as Kemp says, the feeling of "I'm just a P.E. major."[27] Bob Mathias says:

> The truth is . . . I didn't think I was qualified to be a congressman nor did I have any particular desire to be one. Most of the congressmen I had ever been exposed to were just old guys in dark suits. I knew their jobs were important to governing the country, but I was pretty much ignorant of what they did and how they did it.[28]

What becomes clear throughout the process of studying the memoirs of sports stars turned politicians, though, is that the vulnerabilities they report battling once they are elected are the precise strengths that they campaign on and make celebrities of all different backgrounds very difficult for politicians to beat. The 'jock factor' is just one of these. While congressional representatives might avoid working with former athletes out of concern for their own reputation or because of the perceived lack of government experience and knowledge of athletes, poking fun at a star athlete on the campaign trail for being inexperienced often backfires on the perpetrator. Athletes do not try to hide but rather run on their outsider status, their related ability to level with and understand the experiences of their constituents, and by painting their opponents as entrenched, jaded establishment figures.

Sports stars seem to benefit in a campaign setting when their opponents underestimate them. Jim Mathias says, "He [Harlan Hagan] . . . apparently decided I wasn't a serious contender, so he ignored me. Meanwhile, McGee [Mathias's campaign manager] was busy putting together a newspaper ad campaign featuring me as the bright new savior, and for comparison, he found a picture of Harlan that must have been taken after an all-night binge or something."[29] The bitter debate between Jack Kemp and Bob Dole throughout the 1980s on this front is a poignant example. Dole used to call Jack Kemp "the quarterback" (and not as a compliment). He thought Kemp was undeserving of his status and popularity, had skipped steps in his political ascendancy and was ignorant and overly idealistic about the ability of tax cuts to help the American economy. ". . . some of us do all the dirty work," Dole said during one of his many speeches about dealing with the deficit. "They [Kemp and his allies] never made a hard choice in their lives."[30]

But as all skilled performers know, and President Trump frequently exemplifies, if you are good enough at your job, you can turn any personal attack back on your opponents; a strategy akin to the "I'm rubber, you're glue" riposte. Trump successfully re-branded "fake news" during his 2016 campaign. Once seen as a phenomenon that benefitted the GOP candidate, Trump transformed "fake news" into a label that could be attached to any news organization that was critical of his campaign. During Robert Mueller's investigation the president turned the dominant news story about Russians interfering in the U.S. election on its head by propagating a misleading narrative about the FBI and the White House "spying" on his campaign. It is precisely this strategy that Kemp used to retort one of Dole's comments at a GOP event.

Dole sneered that Kemp wanted to include "a deduction for hair spray" in tax reform. Kemp replied, "In a recent fire, Bob Dole's library burned down. Both books were lost. And he hadn't even finished coloring one of them."[31] In the 2003 California gubernatorial debate, Schwarzenegger handled slights about his lack of experience and knowledge in a similar way. He describes Cruz Bustamante's strategy of "prefacing just about every remark he made to me with "I know you may not know this, but . . ." Schwarzenegger continues:

> Being condescending backfired because it made people dislike him . . . that made an impression, and so did my humor. When things got especially intense, with everyone shouting over everyone else, I'd say something outrageous that would make the audience laugh. Arianna [Huffington] and I got into it a couple of times . . . she was blaming the state's budget crisis on tax loopholes . . . I said, "What are you talking about Arianna? You are using tax loopholes so big that I could drive my Hummer through." The next day's polls put me on top. My numbers jumped from 28 to 38, while Bustamante's fell from 32 to 26.[32]

Any responsible political scientist, of course, would caution that it is nearly impossible to causally attribute a jump in polling numbers to one campaign event, let alone one joke during one campaign event, when so many competing forces in the political environment are occurring simultaneously. Broadcast coverage of the speeches candidates make and the events in which they participate is consumed by very few people. The group that *is* usually watching is the least politically persuadable. And considering how difficult political attitudes are to influence in general, getting viewers to actually change their opinions and behavior and vote a certain way, as Schwarzenegger and other celebrities claim to do, is an extremely tall, if not nearly impossible order. But none of this changes the fact that all politicians *do* go public, they *do* campaign, and that as long as campaigns remain media events, celebrities like Schwarzenegger have an upper hand. The below section summarizes the campaign advantages enjoyed by celebrities that came to prominence as sports stars, like Schwarzenegger.

Reps, Reps, Reps

Perhaps because athletes seem to suffer from the insecurity that they do not know as much about political issues as their opponents, or because they are so accustomed to a great deal of practice in their respective sports, celebrity athletes, somewhat surprisingly, do not count on their talents as a 'natural' politicians, even if they feel they possess these talents. Instead, celebrity athletes follow the directions of experienced advisors as closely as they would follow those of an athletic coach, and they rehearse, rehearse, and rehearse. Jim Ryun refers to practice as a series of "small things done well" and attributes his athletic and political success to it.³³ Here, Schwarzenegger's memoir is again illuminating. Describing his speech at the RNC, Schwarzenegger says:

> I was making such a splash that the Republican leaders asked me to help in the push to get President Bush reelected . . . they knew I could attract attention . . . I stood at the podium at Madison Square Garden—my first time in the spotlight there since my victory as Mr. Olympia thirty years before . . . my heart was pounding, but the cheering crowd reminded me of Mr. Olympia, which had a calming effect. As I began to speak and heard them respond, I felt like it was no different than posing. I had them in the palm of my hand. I'd prepped for this appearance more intensively than any in my life. The speech had been revised and revised, and I'd practiced it dozens of times, doing my reps.³⁴

Kemp was not nearly as disciplined a speechmaker as Schwarzenegger. In fact, he had a Trumpian habit of ignoring the guidance of aides and advisors to shorten his speeches and follow the text as written, "so the sound bite of the day did not get lost," as Press Secretary John Buckley said. At one point during his 1988 presidential bid, aides put Kemp on "a word diet" and gave him a timer to put on his podium. "Jack would nod his head obediently and behave for a speech or two. Then it was back to the mumbo-jumbo . . ." wrote Ed Rollins, who chaired Kemp's 1988 campaign.³⁵ But Kemp did read constantly. When he was first elected he was insecure about his lack of knowledge about the economy and worried he would not be able to help his constituents in Buffalo, even going so far as to ask neoconservative thinker Irving Kristol for reading lists.³⁶

Under Pressure

Another theme that comes up constantly in the professional reflections of celebrity athletes is their ability to perform under pressure. Bill Bradley attributes his success in his first congressional campaign to this: "Although I had no experience in government, I had appeared on television in people's living rooms for ten years. They had seen me perform under pressure as a player; they felt they knew me. In my first poll, I had higher name recognition than Clifford Case, the Republican incumbent of twenty-four years."³⁷ No matter how much candidates practice for high-pressure campaign events like debates, they still battle nerves and self-doubt. The best performers can stay relaxed in these environments and give the audience the impression that they are in command of the information and even having fun. Schwarzenegger recalls these feelings bubbling up before his first big press conference and his first gubernatorial debate:

> I reminded myself, don't get caught up on detail. Be likable, be humorous. Let the others hang themselves. Lure them into saying stupid things . . . Sixty

seconds before we started, I did a mental spot check. "Health care: what would you change?" I quizzed myself. But all of a sudden I could remember absolutely nothing about health care . . . Once or twice in movies I'd experienced a brain lock like this, but it was very rare. And in movies, you can always ask for your lines. Luckily, I still had my sense of humor. "This will be interesting," I thought.[38]

An Irresistible Challenge

Most professional athletes turned politicians describe their decision to run for office as another opportunity to prove their detractors wrong, just like they did in sports. They see politics as an elite accomplishment with low odds of success, and they relish the opportunity to beat those odds. They are compulsive about winning, and when their sports careers are over, they look for another way that drive can be satisfied. Running for office for many retired athletes is not a calling or a long-planned career path. It is just a way to quell the drive to make a major push toward "something," as Tom Osborne said, or the designated "next mountain to climb," according to Arnold Schwarzenegger.[39] When Ben Nighthorse Campbell was snubbed by a Democratic Party leader who told him he had "two chances" of winning a state legislature seat, "little . . . and none," Campbell recalls that "my old Olympic competitive drive began to rise up inside of me."[40] Both Jack Kemp and Schwarzenegger describe with detail how they were doubted in their sports careers and how that carried over the success in politics: ". . . and they said I would never make it. I came from the wrong schools. I was too short. I threw too hard. I was too optimistic. I didn't have it. And I'll tell you what. I never gave up. I got traded, hurt, sold, cut, booed, knocked out, but I never gave up."[41] His staffers and children described his spirit in a similar fashion: "Someone has to take the risk, someone has to step up, someone has to cast the vision, someone has to have confidence when others are faltering or worries or fearful. Whether on the field or in the Capitol, Kemp aspired to be that person."[42] Schwarzenegger's description of beating the odds at every stage in his career is remarkably similar: "That was the way people in Austria reacted when I said I wanted to be a bodybuilding champ . . . And it was the way that Hollywood agents had reacted when I said that I wanted to become an actor."[43] Schwarzenegger relays a specific story about how political operative Karl Rove snubbed him when he visited his office to gauge his support. Rove told him that the 2003 recall would never happen and that nobody could unseat Gray Davis, and that the GOP had already picked their candidate for Governor of California in 2006, Condoleezza Rice. "I understood why Condi was getting the nod," Schwarzenegger recalls.

> She's intellectual, she's Stanford, she's the National Security Advisor. I'd heard that story before about 2006 . . . it stung. But I reminded myself right away, "Actually, this is good! This is one of those situations where someone dismisses

you, and you come from behind and surprise the shit out of them." I never argued with people who underestimated me. If the accent and the muscles and the movies made people think I was stupid, it worked to my advantage.[44]

Bill Bradley recalls meeting with local Democratic kingpin Ed Eversole in his hometown of Crystal City, Missouri when he first considered running for political office. "He told me what many others would tell me in the years ahead. If I wanted to get into politics, I had to start at the bottom. Run for City Council, he said, and then try for county office."[45] He continues later in his memoir, "Many said that if you ever wanted to enter elective politics . . . then you had to be a veteran, preferably a decorated veteran."[46] Bradley did none of those things. His interest in politics, his confidence in his abilities, and his status as a public figure were sufficient to convince him he could skip several steps. Athletes tend to see athletic ability as a unique set of talents but political leadership as something anyone can do if they put their mind to it. That someone may as well be them. "Some of us are blessed with unique talents. I had the gift to run, and that is something not everyone is given," says Jim Ryun. "I am convinced, however, that all of us can learn skills and qualities in life, and one of those is leadership."[47] ". . . someone has to do it,"[48] writes Tom Osborne. ". . . if a guy like me can become governor, so could you. That's the way American government is supposed to work," writes Jesse Ventura.[49]

A Different Kind of Candidate

It is somewhat ironic that the most common factor celebrity athletes attribute to their political success is their ability to stand out from the crowd. Again, Jesse Ventura's colorful comparison of himself to his competitors does not disappoint:

> They also voted for me . . . because I'm not easy to ignore. I'm big, I'm loud, and I'm not afraid to say what I think . . . The bottom line is that my opponents were boring. They were the same old brand of career politicians, the kind that comes out of the woodwork every four years, spouts the same old rhetoric about the same issues, and then disappears . . . My campaign was anything but run-of-the-mill. My opponents were in suits. I was wearing jeans and a Minnesota Timberwolves jacket, and my campaign slogan was "Retaliate in '98."[50]

During both his push for the ballot proposition that served as a precursor to his campaign in 2002 and his gubernatorial bid in 2003, Schwarzenegger was sure to craft entertaining and media attention-getting campaign events.

> Instead of a boring press conference, I did a two-day fly-around of cities up and down the state, with rallies and kids and hoopla to get us on TV and pump up support . . . This is when I discovered that raising cash from the set

of a movie was a huge advantage, and Terminator 3 was the greatest set of all. People loved coming to see the special effects, the loading of weapons, the explosions. Sometimes I'd meet them with my makeup still on.[51]

And later:

If I did jump in, my campaign would have to be truly unique, because I was a nonpolitician responding to a populist revolt. We needed to avoid trying to win over the press and instead play to the people. When I went on TV, I'd go on entertaining national shows like Jay Leno, Oprah, David Letterman, Larry King . . . rather than wonky local broadcasts.[52]

Bill Bradley discusses how despite the fact that professional athletes are fundamentally somewhat unrelatable, it is common for people to project their own life experiences onto athletes. Maybe it is easier to understand what a basketball player does for a living—almost every child in America is exposed to the basics of sports at some point—than it is to understand the background of candidates who come from investment banking or law or politics. ". . . when we played basketball in Detroit during my years as a Knick, I would go with my roommate Dave DeBusschere, to his family's bar across from one of the large Chrysler plants . . . the autoworkers knew Dave, the basketball star, who played the game the same way these men approached their jobs: Work hard and get it done. Give a few blows and take a few. No complaints."[53]

Perhaps the best example of a candidate that understood the importance of emphasizing a contrast between his campaign and the campaigns of his competitors was Ben Nighthorse Campbell. Campbell and his staff seized on his unique name and his varied background to attract voters in his first congressional campaign. Even though he had already been elected to the state legislature, he did not campaign on his applied experience there. He campaigned on his identity and life experience. ". . . being part Indian gave Ben an air of novelty, a refreshing breeze in the political landscape, especially compared to his white-bread opponent," said Campbell's campaign treasurer and eventual chief of staff Ken Lane. In fact, the media was already portraying the race as "cowboy versus Indian," but campaign manager Sherrie Wolff was careful to portray Campbell as a "Renaissance man" rather than a native American.

The idea was to get voters to identify with Ben as one of them, and this was easy to do because of his wide experience—semiorphan, high school dropout, Korean war veteran, small businessman, Olympic athlete, artist, truck driver, teacher, rancher . . . each component of Campbell's unique background appealed to a different set of voters and contrasted sharply with Strang's, which seemed largely one-dimensional in comparison. "He simply could not compete with Ben in terms of personality, excitement, and appeal," repeated Lane.[54]

Friends in High Places

Savvy campaign staffers like Campbell's, who told him to keep his long ponytail and the name "Nighthorse" for example, but to ditch his dark sunglasses and tendency to cross his arms in front of him when talking to voters, are not accessible to everyone who aspires to run for political office. But because of their years in the public eye, athletes are often solicited by political parties and convinced to run, or they know exactly who to call when they become interested on their own. Athletes travel extensively, participate in fundraisers and community events, and have sometimes even stumped for other candidates by the time they jump into politics for themselves. As a New York Knick, Bill Bradley developed a habit of compiling "lists of interesting people . . . journalists, government officials, academics, businessmen, social activists" when he traveled abroad. "When I arrived in town, I'd call their offices, usually giving a mutual friend as a reference, and ask if I could meet them. Often they said yes."[55] It is easier for sports stars to meet elites and build support than it is for an unknown politician. Bradley also recalls being surprised that he "raised more money from NBA players than Princeton alumni" and that "California, fertile ground from the Laker-Knick rivalry of my basketball days, yielded an impressive amount."[56] Beloved athletes have no trouble filling seats at a fundraiser, and they are often wealthy enough themselves that they can play up the "I didn't need this job" and "I don't need to get reelected" angles, which Trump did constantly in 2016.[57] Arnold Schwarzenegger benefited greatly not only from his own star power, but from his wife Maria Shriver's deep connections to the Democratic Party and her wealth of political knowledge as a former NBC reporter and a member of the Kennedy family. Because of this, Schwarzenegger not only received endorsements and advice from prominent Californian Republicans, but from Democrats. He describes a meeting his mother-in-law arranged with her brother Ted Kennedy leading up to a big press conference that resulted in invaluable advice: "Arnold, never get into specifics," Kennedy said. "Right away, from the top, all you say is, 'I'm here to fix the problem.' Make that your approach. In California, you need to say, 'I know we have major problems—we have blackouts, we have unemployment, we have companies leaving the state, we have people who need help—and I will fix it.'"[58]

In their memoirs, Jim Ryun and Bob Mathias both describe the experience of being approached by party leaders in their home districts who encouraged them to run for office. "Visibility" and name recognition always crops up in these discussions. "People know you and respect you" was the pitch Bob Mathias was given.[59] While an Olympian turned actor like Bob Mathias might have sufficient fame to succeed in a race in other areas of the country, experienced political operatives that draft professional athletes into political contests often advise them to run where they are known, not where they are from. This proved to be the right move for both Jack Kemp, who was raised in Los Angeles but became famous playing for the Buffalo Bills, and Bill Bradley, who was raised in Missouri but became famous playing for the New York Knicks. Tom Osborne, of course, was born and raised in Nebraska where he launched his political career, and was well aware of the advantages he had there as a household name. "I had 'name recognition'—people already knew who I was, so I could concentrate on communicating what I stood for rather than on introducing myself. Many candidates must spend huge sums of money just so their name will ring a bell with voters when they go to the polls," Osborne wrote.[60]

As I mentioned earlier, there are complications to each of these campaign advantages that spill over into governing. Athletes are used to being coached, but also like to feel that they are in charge. It seems the campaign managers that are most successful in these cases understand the importance of building and maintaining the candidate's self-confidence. Bob Mathias recounts a story in his memoir about how he decided to hire campaign manager Bob McGhee, who someone recommended he call. "When I introduced myself there was a silence, then he said, 'Who is this really?' When I repeated myself he asked: 'Bob Mathias the movie star?' I was already in love with Bob McGhee," writes Mathias.[61] Entire sections of the memoirs of Bob Mathias, Tom Osborne, and Jim Ryun are devoted to quotes from loved ones, former teammates and athletes describing their leadership qualities and how special they are as people. The star athletes studied here are all exceptionally hard workers, but their memoirs also reflect that they do not take well to criticism and they do not like to lose or be overlooked. Kemp in particular stands out here. His son Jeff Kemp described him as selfish and "narcissistic even" and his staff recalls his quick temper which included "screaming profanity" and his determination "to avoid being manipulated." He was chronically late and very difficult to control. And at the end of his career, Kemp reflected on this. "As congress and a political career replaced football, I began to realize how ego and pride were inextricably bound up in what I was doing . . . I had put too much of my ego and pride into football and political accomplishments."[62]

Macho Culture

Finally, it is impossible to overlook how central the comfort and familiarity with a "macho culture," as Bill Bradley calls it, translates from sports to politics.[63] As Tom Osborne writes, "As a culture, we have not always appreciated the contributions of women as equal to those of men. This is particularly true in the world of sports . . . but it reaches into every sector of society."[64] Osborne goes on to describe the important support functions his nearly all female congressional staff served, such as "superb organizational skills," which underlines the stereotype of women as helpers and men as leaders. Some of Osborne's early alliances in Congress were with other former male athletes, and he notes the importance of working out in the congressional gym for forming friendships across party lines. The Congressional gym was not open to women until 1982 and the pool was not open to women until 1970. Former Speaker of the House Dennis Hastert, a former high school wrestling coach who admitted to sexually abusing teenagers in 2015, was one of Osborne's closest colleagues while Osborne was in Congress in the early 2000s. Hastert used sports analogies to describe the importance of party loyalty to Osborne. "Denny . . . [compared] the House of Representatives to an athletic contest in which the two teams are pretty evenly matched. Giving the other team a point could change the game, and the winning side (us) might never regain the advantage."[65] Indeed, in the United States, politics are often described in macho terms. Interactions between parties and candidates are described as "fights" or "battles" or "barroom brawls," campaign conference rooms are "war rooms" and the candidates and themselves are "players" with "weaknesses" and "strengths." Male vitality was a noticeable undercurrent in the 2016 presidential election, with Donald Trump famously defending the size of his hands, branding Jeb Bush "low energy" and remarking that Hillary Clinton did not have "a presidential look."[66]

Male predominance was a theme of Arnold Schwarzenegger's victory in the 2003 recall election, too. Schwarzenegger is no stranger to the prevailing perception that the public desires strong leading men, both in their movies and in politics. He recalls a debate among the producers of *Collateral Damage* "about whether firefighting was a macho enough profession for an action hero."[67] The goal in his campaign was to get voters to see him as "the real terminator."[68] Schwarzenegger's planned one-liners for gubernatorial debate opponent Arianna Huffington revolved around portraying her as an excitable and emotional woman. "If she got overly dramatic," during the debate Schwarzenegger writes, he could say, "I know you're Greek" or "switch to decaf."[69]

But the most overt example by far of attributing electoral success to physical prowess and masculinity is provided by Jesse Ventura, whose memoir is itself called *I Ain't Got Time to Bleed*. He writes of his gubernatorial opponents:

> It didn't hurt that I was in direct contrast to them physically. I'm a six-foot-four monstrosity. I towered over them. These guys were puny by comparison. I deliberately sat between them. I looked strong and powerful. Neither one of them looked powerful at all. I think your physical bearing plays a large role in leadership. People looked at me and saw a leader. As a general, or an admiral, or a governor, you have to carry yourself with dignity and power.[70]

Where does that leave women candidates and non-sports-stars, you may ask? "Being short, four feet eleven," said Senator Patty Murray, as Bill Bradley recounts in his memoir, "people underestimate you."[71] Women face many challenges throughout the election process, but they do win when they run, and actually, according to empirical research on the topic, they make for better government representatives across the board. Women work in a more bipartisan manner, sponsor and co-sponsor more legislation than their male counterparts, and bring more money home to their districts. As political scientists Sarah Anzia and Christopher Berry adeptly summarize in their article "The Jackie (and Jill) Robinson Effect," "If voters are biased against female candidates, only the most talented, hardest working female candidates will succeed in the electoral process. Furthermore, if women perceive there to be sex discrimination in the electoral process, or if they underestimate their qualifications to run for office, then only the most qualified, politically ambitious female will emerge as candidates."[72]

The point here is not that women cannot be perceived as tough or authoritative, or that there have not been successful women athletes who enter politics. Congresswoman Cheri Bustos (D-IL), and Senators Kelly Ayotte (R-NH) and Kirsten Gillibrand (D-NY) were all successful athletes in college. The point is that success on the campaign trail, as many famous (male) athletes have enjoyed, does not necessarily translate to success in governing. And the people who are very good at governing are often not the best campaigners.

Politics as Show Business

In his 1990 memoir, Ronald Reagan writes, ". . . I had always believed a candidate doesn't make the decision whether to run for president, the people make it, the people let you know whether you should run for office."[73] As much as entertainers like to be in control of their own careers (just ask them), they also like to point out that they were recruited into politics, rather than choosing it. Aside from rare moments of candor—Ronald Reagan famously said, "there have been times in this office when I wonder how you could do the job without having been an actor"—entertainers are more likely to report that they were chosen because of their business acumen, or trustworthy character, or simply because there was nobody else who could solve the problems at hand, than because of their fame and popularity.[74] That is P.T. Barnum's and Roy Acuff's story, at least. Barnum, the originator of The American Museum, which later became the renown Ringling Bros. and Barnum & Bailey Circus, has been widely credited as one of the original public relations professionals. "I was a party man, but not a partisan, nor a wire-puller, and I never sought or desired office, although it had often been tendered to me," Barnum writes in his autobiography.[75]

Politics Chose Me

Barnum honed a skillset over a lifetime that made him adept at campaigning. He initially came to fame by way of a variety of hoaxes on the public and the media, including the promotion and exhibition of a slave named Joice Heth, who Barnum claimed was 161 years old and had the papers to "prove" she had been a nurse to George Washington. In addition to writing copy and manipulating the press into covering his traveling attraction, Barnum would send fake angry letters to the editors of newspapers complaining that Heth was a fraud, which only boosted ticket sales. Barnum rented billboard space, draped oversized banners over buildings to advertise his upcoming attractions (a strategy used by national museums to this day), hired advance teams to scout potential event sites (now a bread-and-butter tool of political campaigns), wrote press releases, and arranged "behind the scenes" interviews with journalists who were delighted to gain exclusive access to his facilities when the circus first arrived in town.[76] A fascinating article in the *Brooklyn Daily Eagle* from February 1867 about Barnum's fledgling candidacy for U.S. Congress argues that Barnum's experience as the caretaker of a large menagerie of circus animals would prove useful in Congress. "Mr. Barnum is a candidate for Congress," the reporter writes, "and if Connecticut has any sense of the fitness of things, he will succeed . . . although the connection between a showman and a legislator may not be apparent at first, the most pig-headed will soon perceive that, as things are at present, that the latter office is only the proper complement and higher stage of the former."[77] Yet despite Barnum's apparent instinct for politics and his success in City Council races, he despised the work of campaigning. He did not particularly like interacting with people, even giving hints in his book of what appears to be a lot like Donald Trump's brand of germaphobia. In an almost Trump-like rant about his failed congressional campaign in, Barnum shares:

> I possess naturally too much independence of mind . . . regardless of party expediency, to make a lithe and oily politician . . . to do the dirty too often demanded by political parties; to be "all things to all men" though not in the apostolic sense; to shake hands with those whom I despised, and to kiss the dirty babies of those whose votes were courted, were never political requirements which I felt I could acceptably fulfill. Nevertheless, I had become almost a man of leisure; and some of my warmest personal friends insisted that a nomination to so high and honorable a position as a member of Congress was not to be lightly rejected, and so I consented to run.[78]

Later, when Barnum lost, he gave what we might have imagined to be a Trump-like (and indeed, Sinclair-like) half-admission of defeat. He felt vindicated after the election when he 'learned' of allegations against his opponent—who, bizarrely, was a distant relative of P.T. Barnum's named William H. Barnum—of bribery, fraud and corruption during the election and writes that he "concluded that if I had been defeated by fraud mine was the real victory." Reporting at the time, though, indicated that Barnum's campaign was also using money to buy votes, and that it may have been Barnum himself who stoked rumors that resulted in "trumped up" charges against his opponent. An October 1867 *Brooklyn Daily*

Eagle article scathingly concludes that "The tactics of the show business do not answer in politics."[79] Nonetheless Barnum writes:

> I was neither disappointed nor cast down by my defeat . . . the filth and scandal, the slanders and vindictiveness, the plottings and fawnings, the fidelity, treachery, meanness and manliness . . . my personal efforts in the canvass were mainly confined to the circulation of documents, and I did not spend a dollar to purchase a vote.[80]

In other words, the system is rigged, and I didn't even try that hard.

Roy Acuff, the country music star of the 1930s and 1940s who helped popularize the Grand Ole Opry, describes his entrance into race for Governor of Tennessee in 1948 in a similar manner to P.T. Barnum. "I have been nominated three times friends; two times I refused to accept the nomination . . . this year I told them to leave my name on . . . it isn't easy for a country boy like me to stand up here and try to make a political speech. I intend on staying up here with you, being one of you, and I promise not to bring politics again to the Ole Opry."[81] Bringing politics to the Ole Opry, of course, is exactly what Acuff was doing, and some of his later public statements indicate he was not completely honest about his lack of political ambition. "I imagine that every American boy dreams that someday he might become Governor of his state, and, frankly, I was no exception," said Acuff.[82]

Legendary author, playwright and public intellectual Gore Vidal writes in blunt terms about his decision to run for Congress in the 29th district of New York in his memoir *Palimpsest*. Unlike Upton Sinclair, who drew a clear parallel between his muckraking career, his books, and his drive to become personally invested in politics, Vidal, more like P.T. Barnum and Arnold Schwarzenegger, was bored. "I was now looking forward to the 1960 election," Vidal writes. "I was also getting restless . . . I was through with Hollywood. Live television was sputtering out, and I had just done what was to be my last play for television . . . Time now to go to Washington; or to go away to write."[83] There were plenty of practical reasons for Vidal to run; he, and the Democratic leadership understood the importance of his fame and connections. Vidal was endorsed and closely counseled by Eleanor Roosevelt and Harry Truman, and Paul Newman and Joanne Woodward campaigned for him. Speaking of his entrenched opponent incumbent Ernest Wharton, Vidal says, "Thanks to a decade of television appearances (where I preferred to talk not of my work but of the state of the union), I was far better known than the congressman, whose career had been devoted to enriching the great insurance companies . . ."[84]

It is difficult to provide a clear modern parallel to the televised political debates at the RNC and DNC that made liberal playwright Gore Vidal, and his conservative counterpart, editor of the *National Review* William F. Buckley, so famous in 1968. The best comparison is probably a series of debates between former Fox News anchor Bill O'Reilly, and former *Daily Show* host and comedian Jon Stewart during the Obama presidency, the most hyped of which was called the "Rumble in the Air-Conditioned Auditorium" in 2012. Though neither O'Reilly—who was fired from Fox News for sexual harassment in 2017—nor Stewart, who retired from *The Daily Show* in 2015, had aspirations to run for elective office (both Buckley, who ran for Mayor of New York in 1965, and Vidal, who ran for Congress in 1960, did), both O'Reilly and Stewart understood the entertainment value of hyperbolic political debate. But had they decided to run for office eventually, one can clearly see how the hyper-partisan, attack-laden debates may have helped propel both forward in their parties' respective primary contests. The debates increased public exposure to both men, showcased new aspects of their personalities and intellect, and synonymized their names with the political parties their views represented. Increased exposure, and a public intimacy with Buckley and Vidal, is precisely what the 1968 ABC debates accomplished for both writers. Buckley and Vidal differed from other public intellectuals at the time because they understood the importance of public relations. Being a weekly presence in the living rooms of millions of Americans, even if it required formal thoughts to be boiled down to TV-made soundbites, and eloquent arguments to occasionally give way to personal insults, was a worthwhile exercise for two men who always secretly dreamed of being politicians. But not everyone in the 1960s agreed that the emergence of media-centered politics was a good thing.

Besides being a personal friend and confidante of Vidal, Eleanor Roosevelt clashed with him on issues of political strategy. She did not think the private lives of politicians should play a role in campaigns; Vidal did, and had just written a play to that effect, *The Best Man*. Roosevelt resisted the glamorized style of modern campaigning that emerged in the 1960s, and she strongly dismissed Jack Kennedy as the likely Democratic nominee for president, instead urging the candidacy of Adlai Stevenson in her massively influential column, *My Day*, even publicly chastising delegates at the DNC. Vidal, Mrs. Roosevelt's son Frank Roosevelt Jr., and another close advisor Walter Reuther, were concerned with the issue of Stevenson's electability. He was stubborn, idealistic, and unwilling to be molded into the ideal Democratic candidate. "And that," Reuther asserted as recounted by Vidal in a conversation before the 1960 convention, "is why we don't want him as the candidate."[85]

But for all the advantages Vidal had as a celebrity and his assertion that the public was "comfortable" with him, his celebrity status would also prove to be an obstacle. When Vidal, like most celebrities, pointed out that he did not need the job for he had made plenty of money, journalists suggested that he was bragging about his wealth. When he, like most celebrities, used tales from Hollywood and show business gossip as an enticing opener to his fundraisers and campaign speeches, reports implied he was unserious and his ideas lacked substance. Like Sinclair nearly 30 years before, Vidal was widely portrayed as a hypocritical elitist, a tactic that is still used by the GOP today, despite the fact that many Republican candidates have been celebrities. A *New York Times* column by Ira Freeman in September 1960 that Vidal calls a "smear job" is an almost eerie reflection of the way in which *The San Francisco Chronicle* used Sinclair's wealth and Beverly

Hills home against him; a subheading in the article about Vidal is actually "Lives Alone in a Mansion," directly after which, Vidal's lifestyle is described as one of "lonely splendor."[86] Perhaps in an attempt to convey the careless nature of Vidal's candidacy (and admittedly, he does at times seem indifferent to victory, more passionately commenting on campaigns other than his own), Freeman writes, "Mr. Vidal shrugs and lets his cocker spaniel lick the Chateau Yquem off his fingers" after which Vidal reportedly said, "If I am swamped like that, I'll quit."[87] "The thought that I might be elected was sufficient cause for a Jihad," Vidal writes.[88]

One of Vidal's frequent intellectual sparring partners, Norman Mailer, describes his foray into the New York mayoral race in 1969 in even more haphazard terms than Barnum and Vidal, if possible. But by all accounts other than Mailer's, the contest for Mayor of New York in 1969 was quite an important one in American political history. Much like Sinclair's gubernatorial bid in 1934 and Trump's campaign in 2016, the election proved to be more about personality than policy. Here is an excerpt from a letter Mailer wrote to Lamed G. Bradford, once Chief Editor at Little, Brown & Company:

> It looks as though I'll be running for mayor in the Democratic primary elections on June 17th. At first this gave me some concern at the thought of conflicting with the moon shot but I like it better and better the more I think about it as a take-off pad, because the difficulty in approaching the story this summer is that I didn't know how to locate my self in reference to it. While this may sound terribly egotistical it's actually a most practical manner since one's stance determines one's style. As a defeated candidate in the Democratic primary I'll have all the stance and focus in the world with much to muse over the stations of the cities and planets. If by any disastrous miscalculation of the Gods I should win the primary—but there Ned, why should I add another grey hair to that fine crop you have already?[89]

One difference between Mailer's tone in this letter and the way in which Sinclair and Trump speak about themselves is Mailer's obvious talent for self-deprecation. By acting as if he merely stumbled onto the campaign trail and could not care less if he wins or loses, Mailer opened an opportunity for his opponents to point out his apathy. But the strategy of not letting on quite as strongly as traditional politicians that he was desperate for the job and ambitious may have allowed him to extract some favor, if not votes, from New Yorkers. Mailer's campaign manager, Joe Flaherty, evoking Trump campaign managers Cory Lewandowski and Paul Manafort's strategies in 2016, was conscious not to manage Mailer, and to let him be himself. When other campaign staff members suggested that Mailer's running mate, columnist Jimmy Breslin, instead run for Mayor, while Mailer switched to run for City Council president, Flaherty said, "You can't just shuffle National Book Award Winners around like subservient aldermen."[90]

Mailer, like Trump, was such an outrageous campaigner that at the height of his candidacy, he attacked his own supporters, calling them "spoiled pigs" at a rally at a nightclub, and prompting Breslin to draw a comparison between his behavior and Ezra Pound's.[91] It is worth noting here how similar Donald Trump's 2015 rant on the campaign trail in Iowa was. Attacking opponent Ben Carson, Trump exclaimed, "How stupid are the people of Iowa? How stupid are the people of the country to believe this crap?"[92] Mailer's vulgar campaign slogan, "No More Bullshit," could not even be printed in papers. But Mailer and Breslin's ticket did not fail to entertain. Neither did Trump's. Like Trump, Mailer was so famous for his former career that it took a while for the public, and even party leaders, to realize he was a serious candidate. ". . . in a sad city with a grimace of despair carved into its face . . . Mailer and Breslin, for a short season, [turned] that grimace into a grin."[93]

Celebrities often also seem surprised, after stumbling in to politics, about how difficult it is. Ronald Reagan provides a poignant example of his steep learning curve in office in his 1990 memoir *An American Life*.

> Yes, I was learning that it is one thing to preach a sermon about reducing the size of government, another to put it into action when you're fighting a hostile legislature determined to expand it. In Hollywood, Nancy and I had become used to having critics take shots at us and reading things about ourselves in the papers that weren't true. But what we found in Sacramento made our Hollywood experience seem mild by comparison . . . I came home one day and told Nancy: "I spent thirteen years at Warner Brothers and they couldn't give me an ulcer, but I think I'm getting one now."[94]

Reagan also learned during his time as Governor of California that his showmanship and communication skills, which at times, he admitted "worked better than I ever dreamed it would" were not sufficient to enact change in government.[95] He also needed to bargain. ". . . I thought the professional politicians in Sacramento and I were natural enemies . . ." Reagan writes. "Although that sentiment never changed . . . I'd have to do some negotiating with them . . . and that meant meet with them socially, invite them over for a drink, get to know them."[96]

Always the Ringmaster

Roy Acuff traveled throughout Tennessee in 1948 with a circus-like campaign of which P.T. Barnum might have approved. Not only did Acuff refuse to put his music career on hold while he sought the governorship, he brought his whole band with him, even coaxing one member out of retirement to hit the campaign trail. Acuff held two campaign events a day on average, one "performance" at 2:30 and one at 7:30, in which he would play music for the crowd before making a political speech. Saturdays were largely off limits for campaign activity because the band had to get back to the Opry, where they were still performing. Acuff's campaign staff also included politicos, including a 24-year veteran of Congress and former chairman of the Republican National Committee B. Carroll Reece, who supported Acuff's campaign strategy of drawing the largest crowds possible, but wanted him to spend more money on traditional campaign tools. A journalist covering the Acuff campaign wrote, "I've never seen anything like it, they're really coming out to hear Roy . . . he still sings and fiddles, but they meet a new man, a plain, sincere man . . . It's evident that they are sold on Roy Acuff, as an honest . . . politician, just as much as they were sold on Roy Acuff the troubadour."[97] When Acuff was heckled at one campaign event by a man who yelled out, "You're nothing by a sideshow performer!" Acuff barked back ". . . you've got me mixed up with someone else . . . I've always been the main event!" "I'm the main attraction" became one of Acuff's signature campaign lines.[98]

Few people understand the relationship between politics and entertainment more than Jerry Springer, once the Mayor of Cincinnati, and eventually the host of a controversial talk show that became known for the brawls that erupted on stage between guests. Springer's path is the opposite of the other entertainers in this chapter—he became a local news anchor and television personality *after* he left political office—but Springer's experience in radio, both as a student at Tulane, and from the two-minute segment he hosted on WEBN in 1976 when he was a City Council member, preceded the peak of his political career. Springer credits that radio spot, called the "Springer Memorandum" with building his name recognition and popularity in Ohio. ". . . I guess it was a combination of the success of the radio stint—and my following as the mayor—that led the television stations to believe that I could be a successful news anchor . . . I . . . knew the community and the community knew me," Springer writes in *Ringmaster!* his autobiography.[99] Springer's propensity toward all things dramatic was previewed during his time as Mayor when the Russian circus visited Cincinnati and Springer volunteered to wrestle a bear for charity, which ended up pinning him down and giving him a welt on the side of his face, to the delight of his constituents. "So there I am, the reigning political figure of Cincinnati, and I'm wrestling a bear," Springer shares.[100]

Singer and songwriter Sonny Bono, who eventually became Mayor of Palm Springs, writes in his memoir of running for political office, "Phil Spector had taught me the value of shocking the public."[101] And shock the public he did. Bono describes a dramatic outburst he had in public on one night of his campaign, which simultaneously reveals his desire to be in control, his desire to be the center of attention, and the deep insecurities that underlie both of those desires. Bono skipped a campaign forum with the other candidates to tend to his pregnant wife at the hospital and the media did not report the details, instead sharing that he had to tend to other affairs. Furious, Bono drove to the venue where the candidate forum was taking place and tore into the moderator Ed Kibby, who told Bono repeatedly, "Mr. Bono, you are out of order." Bono replied, "You know Ed . . . you are not my mother. Don't tell me what the hell I can do and what I can't do."[102] While it is possible that this kind of exclamation would have made the average political candidate appear unhinged, Bono seems to have gotten away with it, recalling that the public appreciated his passion and honesty. The singer was indeed very worried about losing out on an opportunity to win.

Bono describes deep feelings of inadequacy the night before he won the election. His ex-wife Cher was in the running for an Academy Award the same night. He writes, "He [God] was going to have Cher win the Academy Award, and all the old aguish and feelings of inadequacy were going to tumble down like a landslide—especially if I lost the election the next day."[103]

Not in My Backyard—or State—or Country

Sonny Bono stumbled into politics in a remarkably similar fashion to Jesse Ventura, who claims that he did not get into politics, rather, "politics came to me." Ventura was living in Brooklyn Park, a suburb of Minneapolis, which he felt was run by "one of the greediest packs of good old boys" who, in order to please developers who wanted to reap maximum profit from the remaining spare land in the area, required residents to pay for new curbs, sewers and gutters.[104] Sonny Bono, a restaurant owner in Palm Springs who began to build a new home in the community, ran up against zoning and permitting issues and inefficiencies in local government. ". . . in the course of remodeling my disheveled property, I began to see City Hall as a tired complex of unfair contradictions," Bono says. "The town's leaders . . . were entrenched in an abuse of power, like the pudgy bullies one encountered in grammar school. They were elitist. They had an attitude that Palm Springs was their town."[105] P.T. Barnum, too, was suspicious of the railroad executives in New York he feared were becoming monopolies. Though he acknowledged the advantages and blessings brought to the public by the railroad enterprises, he said, "the vaster the enterprise and its power for good, the greater its opportunity for mischief if its power is perverted."[106] What a profound statement about the power of celebrity might the founders have found this?

'If it has to be someone, why not me?' is the question that jolts many celebrity candidates who (admittedly) depend on public attention and approval for happiness into action. That, or pure revenge, as former *Saturday Night Live* cast member and former U.S. Senator Al Franken's memoir describes. But rather than get back at the bullies running City Hall or imposing unfair regulations on one's neighborhood, Franken's precipitous rise to political power started with sitting Minnesota Senator Norm Coleman insulting his political mentor and close friend Senator Paul Wellstone. After Wellstone died, Coleman insensitively touted his political prowess, stating "I am a 99 percent improvement over Paul

Wellstone." "When I read that quote on the Roll Call website, my immediate thought was this: "Somebody's got to beat this guy . . ." writes Franken in his memoir *Al Franken: Giant of the Senate*. He continues, "Now, that's a really bad reason to run for office. And over time it would become less about beating Norm Coleman, and more and more about the people of Minnesota."[107] Later Franken writes:

> . . . no one debating whether or not to run for office is worried about the upside. The problem is the downside. Sure, as an empty nester who had already had a successful career, I was playing with house money . . . I was confident I could do a lot of good, it would feel great to beat Norm Coleman, and also, like a lot of people, I kind of really wanted to be a senator . . .[108]

The point here is not necessarily that Franken was called to action by the intrusion of government into his own life, like Ventura and Bono, but that similarly, a lot of Al Franken's decision to run was about Al Franken. Running for Senate in Minnesota filled a void in Franken's life that had previously been filled by comedy. The word Franken uses to describe this is "validation," and he describes his political supporters as a built-in following, something to which I will devote more attention in the next chapter. Writing about his direct mail campaign, Franken says, "And because I had something of a following from my books and radio show, instead of just tossing my envelopes in their trash cans . . . people tended to open them." Franken's celebrity was not only a benefit to him, but a benefit to all progressive candidates supported by the Midwest Values PAC in 2008.[109]

Loveable Roles

Franken first received accolades for his contributions to American politics when he published *Rush Limbaugh is a Big Fat Idiot and Other Observations* to the delight of liberals. It seems doubtful that anyone other than a famous comedian—or a famous reality television star—could get away with such a brash entrance into national politics. Franken explains, "I'd always thought there was nothing better than hearing people laugh. But hearing people tell me they were not only entertained, but also energized to go out and take these guys on themselves, was thrilling."[110] By publicizing his books, Franken had a ready-made opportunity to promote himself, share his sense of humor, and demonstrate that he could hold his own in a political debate. The most infamous example of this is perhaps the shouting match that ensued between Franken and Bill O'Reilly at BookExpo American in Los Angeles over Franken's lengthy account—while O'Reilly was sitting right next to him—that O'Reilly had lied when he said on more than one occasion that a "tabloid" show he had anchored, Inside Edition, won two Peabody awards. After Franken needled O'Reilly for quite some time, O'Reilly appeared to lose his temper, calling Franken an "idiot" and telling him to "shut up" while Franken remained relatively calm.[111]

Franken understood, as many entertainers do, that winning over voters often has "nothing to do with politics." ". . . being an extrovert," for example, was a skill Franken benefitted from, in addition to being able to present himself in a "friendly and approachable" manner.[112] As Franken said, Minnesotans loved Paul Wellstone because of his warmth, his humility, and his wit.[113] Franken was a likeable public figure, a comedic actor, to be exact, who had spent his entire career learning how to endear himself to people and make them laugh, but he did not see himself that way. Celebrities manage to convince the public that they are outsiders and concerned citizens, even as they are using the specific tools of celebrity to accomplish this. For example, in Franken's memoir, he explains the format of his radio show, *The Al Franken Show*, on Air America as progressive radio, different from other formats such as "Hot Adult Contemporary," which he jokes in a footnote, "I think it's Rihanna and Justin Bieber and stuff like that?" One of the show's ground rules was even "No actors talking about politics."[114]

For famous actors in particular, it seems, becoming a politician and running for office is akin to adopting another role. Speeches are scripts. Stumps are stages. Voters are fans. And the specific role that celebrities feel they are playing is one of the relatable but heroic protagonist, or the underdog. Sonny Bono provides great examples here. "The more I thought about the problems facing Palm Springs, the more I began thinking of ways to inject new life into Palm Springs. I likened the situation to show biz. The city was a good concept in need of a rewrite," Bono writes. "I was like the protagonist in . . . a TV movie. I wanted to take action . . . to fight back."[115] Bono continues, "I did not play by the established rules. I was a rabble-rouser, a troublemaker. I was also Joe Q. Citizen—an honest, ordinary, but frustrated businessman, and I was not afraid to say what I thought." Not everyone was impressed with Bono's 'act,' however. Indeed, some actors are better than others. Sitting Palm Springs Mayor Frank Bogart, for example, said comparing Sonny Bono to Ronald Reagan and Clint Eastwood is like "comparing chicken shit to chicken salad."[116]

Ronald Reagan conceived of the presidency as "The Role of a Lifetime." As journalist Lou Cannon, whose book bears that exact title, reveals, Reagan "was not really a politician at all . . . but simply an actor on loan from Hollywood who had entered politics."[117] Indeed, it is impossible to talk about Reagan's gubernatorial or presidential legacy with talking about his abilities as an actor and entertainer. Reagan benefitted both from the roles he played and the opportunities being an actor presented him.

Reagan identified so closely with some of the characters in his movies that sprinklings of their lines and the "fantasy world" that Reagan "had . . . created in Hollywood . . . out of material he brought with him from the Midwest" often seemed to be mapped on to his real life and real political career. Reagan, for example, would forever be synonymized with "The Gipper," a nickname given to an all-American football player Reagan played in *Knute Rockne, All American* named George Gipp, who died tragically of pneumonia in 1920 while he was a student at Notre Dame. Like the real Gipper, who excelled at football despite having no experience with the sport when he entered college, Reagan was portrayed on and off the campaign trail as an unlikely political success. "Let's make it one more for the Gipper," Nancy Reagan said at the end of her 1984 speech to the Republican National Convention.[118] The other character that became closely associated with Reagan was Drake McHugh in *Kings Row*, a young man whose legs were unnecessarily amputated in a vindictive surgery but refused to wallow in his misfortune, instead appearing liberated and optimistic at the end of the movie. When Reagan's character wakes up from surgery, he says, "Where's the rest of me?" a line that would grace the cover of Reagan's 1965 memoir. Reagan also played numerous cowboys in Western films during his career. Whether a starring, supporting, or cameo figure, Reagan's characters represented bravery, toughness, rebelliousness, pride, and chivalry. Reagan writes about another one of these characters, Johnny Hammond, an allied air force pilot in World War II, in his memoir. "I received a telephone call from my brother on a Sunday morning telling me that the Japanese bombed Pearl Harbor. Very shortly I started another picture costarring with Errol Flynn. It was called Desperate Journey and we played RAF pilots shot down behind the German lines."[119] Another heroic role.

Reagan projected the image of a cowboy in his real life too, as author Gene Kopelson indicates. Images of Reagan riding horses and working with his hands on his ranch in California did not hurt his electoral prospects. Reagan's time in the media spotlight, like Al Franken's, also endowed him with valuable skills and chances to show them off. As the host of General Electric Theatre on CBS, Reagan became a household name and polished his camera skills. Knowing where to stand, where to look, how to look, and how to speak is no small feat for a politician, and one that many take for granted. These skills were on full display in a town hall style debate between newly elected California Governor Reagan, and New York Senator Bobby Kennedy in 1967 about Vietnam. While a lack of knowledge about foreign policy was and continued to be Reagan's Achilles heel throughout his political career, Reagan prepared for the debate as he would have for a big scene in a movie. He had an answer planned for every question, and he knew those answers cold, allowing him to appear completely relaxed when he delivered them. He also knew to look into the cameras when he answered a question. If Reagan had to choose between addressing a "flesh-and-blood" audience in front of him or a broadcast crew, he tended to choose "the larger electronic audience that he saw as America," as Francis Clines wrote.[120] Also in Reagan's back pocket was his ability to act quickly on his feet if necessary, which also contributed to the former actor's confidence. Reagan experts often point to Reagan's early career as a sportscaster as the genesis of this particular skill. One time, during a Chicago Cubs baseball game Reagan was announcing, Kopelson explained, the telegraph wire from which Reagan dictated his comments was cut off, and the 23 year old Reagan was forced to ad lib his announcement.

How is it that Reagan managed to hone a likeable image, even when he made mistakes? Reagan smiled, told jokes and anecdotes, and made an effort to get to know the reporters that traveled with him. Because Reagan was likeable, Kopelson theorizes, attacks on him on the basis of his acting career were not well received, as the Democratic candidate for Governor of California in 1966 learned when he aired an attack ad to this effect. In 1968, the public had become even more open to an actor running for political office, as Kopelson illustrates by citing a *Seattle Times* poll from the same year.[121] Of Reagan's ability to deliver a broadcast, the White House television and radio director Elizabeth Board said, "He has absolute perfect timing, better than any news correspondent I've ever worked with . . ."[122] The result of the 1967 debate with Kennedy appeared to be a heap of news coverage in Reagan's favor. Joseph Lewis said Reagan "talked easily and precisely without a hint of uncertainty or hostility" (despite the well-known fact that Reagan despised Bobby Kennedy) and *Newsweek* printed that Reagan, a "political rookie" left "old campaigner Kennedy blinking when the session ended."[123]

Just as Reagan gained experience as the host of GE theatre, Al Franken mastered the stage early in his career. In comedy, as in political debates, there are no re-dos. Yet as is the case with every celebrity-turned politician (and traditional politician) who succeeds, raw or cultivated talent is not enough to win an election. Someone on the campaign needs to know what they are doing. Arnold Schwarzenegger, Bill Bradley, and Ben Nighthorse discussed the importance of surrounding themselves with seasoned campaign professionals at length. Al Franken hired several operatives who used to work for Paul Wellstone, a luxury he had as a result of coming to know Paul Wellstone while stumping for him on the campaign trail. Franken speaks of two kinds of candidates who run for office for the first time: "Category 1: I've been successful because I'm incredibly smart, I've always followed my own instincts even when people said I was wrong, and I know what the hell I'm doing . . . Category 2: I've been successful in my field, and one reason I've been successful is that I know what I don't know and when I should rely on expert advice."[124] Franken, by his own admission, was the second kind of candidate.

Franken also had political opportunities most candidates do not as a result of his fame, above and beyond establishing his reputation as a good stump speaker for other candidates. Franken had the chance during several Christmases to travel with the sergeant major of the Army's USO tour to Kuwait, Iraq, and Afghanistan to perform for the troops. Ironically, it was a picture of Franken appearing to fondle a woman while she slept on one of these tours that ultimately forced him to resign as a Senator. But other pictures from these events concurrently emphasize Franken's talents as an entertainer and his patriotism. Even an unknown political candidate who cares deeply about the military does not necessarily have an opportunity to visit troops abroad.[125] One of Reagan's most important political advantages was the mentorship of Dwight Eisenhower, a president who despised the enterprise of celebrity, but was arguably the first American president to master it, and was won over by Ronald Reagan. Reagan, in return, was completely loyal to Eisenhower and hung on to his every word and suggestion. Reagan wrote in a letter to Eisenhower in 1966, "Freeman called and read your letter to me with the very sound advice and suggestions—some of which are already being put into action."[126] In another 1966 letter, he writes to Eisenhower, ". . . you hit home with some sound philosophy I'll long remember . . . As I told you I'm working on a speech designed to make plain what are my fundamental beliefs. If you wouldn't think it presumptuous I'd like to submit it to you once it takes shape and have the benefit of your judgement."[127]

Different Rules for Women

Male actors who run for political office often benefit from playing macho heroes on screen—legendary athletes, risk-taking cowboys, firefighters, policemen, decorated military veterans—the kinds of strong responsible people we imagine we would want to be our elected representatives, even when they are not real. Women do not often get to play roles like these, which has been a longstanding and long-fought battle in Hollywood. Instead, women entertainers play the girl next door, the damsel in distress, the seductress, the glamorous assistant, or the sweet and agreeable helpmate. None of which probably first comes to mind when picking a leader. This is the issue that child star Shirley Temple Black and actress Helen Gahagan Douglas both faced in their congressional elections despite their different electoral fates.

Temple Black campaigned as many women did in the 1960s and have continued to do to this day. Women actors cannot brag about their accomplishments or chastise their male competitors with the same freedom that men are afforded. If they do this, they risk being stereotyped even further than they already are. So they choose a noncontroversial message, not too strong but not too weak, and one that touts the value of a woman's perspective. "Our country is in great trouble," said Temple Black on the congressional campaign trail in California in 1967. She was running in the GOP primary for the 11th district against Pete McCloskey. "I think men are fine and here to stay but I have a hunch it wouldn't hurt to have a women's viewpoint expressed in that delegation of 38 men." But the newspaper did her no favors. The first line of the AP story about Temple Black's candidacy was about her hair color and facial expression. "Brunette Shirley Temple Black, dimpling her cheeks the way she did when millions knew her as a blonde, curly-haired child star, announced today she will go out on the sidewalks and campaign to become the only woman in California's 38-member congressional delegation." The article continues later to describe Temple Black displaying "a petulant pursing of her lips, remindful of the *Good Ship Lollipop* days."[128] In her defense, Shirley Temple even felt the need to say, "Little Shirley Temple is not running."

Her campaign coordinator Forden Athearn was not convinced her name recognition was enough to carry her to victory, since the public had to first realize "she has grown up."[129]

Gahagan Douglas faced a similar gender-related fate in her 1950 Senate campaign against Richard Nixon, a race made famous by Nixon's excoriating comment that Douglas was "pink right down to her underwear." It may have taken a certain amount of star power for Douglas to get where she was in the first place. In addition to enjoying notable success on Broadway, Douglas starred in the classic 1935 film *She*, a portrayal of a female villain so effective that it inspired the evil queen in Disney's *Snow White and the Seven Dwarfs*. She was one of only nine women in Congress when she decided to run for the Senate, and if she won the Senate race against Nixon, she would have become only the fourth woman ever elected to the Senate, and the first woman to get there without a husband who preceded her and died in office. Author and journalist George Mitchell says she was the first actor ever to run for higher office in New York. Nixon's branding of Douglas as "The Pink Lady," a strategy aimed to frame Douglas a communist sympathizer, was far from the worst thing said about her during the campaign. She was called "gushy," "emotional," a "scolding woman," "excitable," and Nixon joked that she and President Truman were in bed together in more than a political sense.[130] Congressman John F. Kennedy, who supported Nixon in the 1950 race, told a group of students at Harvard that Douglas "was not the sort of person I like working on committees with," a thinly veiled reference to her gender.[131]

Celebrities run for political office because they can. The talents sports stars and other entertainers possess are perceived to be valuable campaign tools by experienced party elites and operatives. The exercise of campaigning satisfies the same hunger for public attention, validation, adulation, awards, and influence that drives celebrities to enter the entertainment industry in the first place. Fundraising, for celebrities, is not nearly as challenging as it is for the average politician. Many times, celebrities have become experienced campaigners and fundraisers on behalf of other politicians, businesses, and charities. They have wealthy and powerful friends. And they know who to ask about getting into politics in the first place, if they are not approached outright. They have time on their hands, a built-in base of fans and followers, and perhaps most of all, a deep desire to prove themselves to be more than just a "dumb jock" or a shallow entertainer.

To be clear, not all of the themes enumerated in this chapter are strictly specific to celebrities. Traditional politicians, too, are ego-driven, selfish, hounds for the spotlight, and often have terrible reasons, or no reasons, to run for office. But they do not generally own up to any of that. Traditional politicians cannot risk saying something like "Man, it would just be cool to be a Senator" or "I have no idea what I'm doing, but I have good instincts, trust me," or ". . . sometimes a little naiveté is exactly what is needed"—Cynthia Nixon, former *Sex and the City* actress and candidate for Governor of New York, actually said that last one.[132]

There appear to be substantial differences in the ways that celebrity candidates and traditional politicians discuss American politics and negotiate their positions within it. Take the following presidential campaign announcements from our last four presidents, for example.

> Today, as we stand on the threshold of a new era, a new millennium, I believe we need a new kind of leadership, leadership committed to change. Leadership not mired in the politics of the past, not limited by old ideologies . . . Proven leadership that knows how to reinvent government to help solve the real problem of real people.
>
> That is why today I am declaring my candidacy for President of the United States. Together I believe we can provide leadership that will restore the American dream—that will fight for the forgotten middle class—that will provide more opportunity, insist on more responsibility and create a greater sense of community for this great country.
>
> —*Bill Clinton, Little Rock, Arkansas, October 3, 1991*

> I have come here today to tell you this: I am running for President of the United States. There's no turning back, and I intend to be the next President of the United States.
>
> I'm running because our country must be prosperous. But prosperity must have a purpose. The purpose of prosperity is to make sure the American dream touches every willing heart. The purpose of prosperity is to leave no one out—to leave no one behind. I'm running because my party must match a conservative mind with a compassionate heart. And I'm running to win.
>
> —*George W. Bush, Cedar Rapids, Iowa, June 12, 1999*

> It was here, in Springfield, where North, South, East and West come together that I was reminded of the essential decency of the American people—where I came to believe that through this decency, we can build a more hopeful America.
>
> And that is why, in the shadow of the Old State Capitol, where Lincoln once called on a divided house to stand together, where common hopes and common dreams still, I stand before you today to announce my candidacy for President of the United States.
>
> —*Barack Obama, Springfield, Illinois, February 10, 2007*

> You know, all of my life, I've heard that a truly successful person, a really, really successful person and even modestly successful cannot run for public office. Just can't happen. And yet that's the kind of mindset that you need to make this country great again.
>
> So ladies and gentlemen . . . I am officially running . . . for President of the United States, and we are going to make our country great again.
>
> —*Donald Trump, New York, New York, June 16, 2015*

Trump's announcement is reminiscent of the rhetoric of many of the celebrity candidates we examined earlier in the chapter. The self-centered nature of the announcement, the way Trump frames himself as the underdog, and the familiar reasoning that underlies it—that the candidate is running because someone told him he could not and he relishes the impossible—do not appear in the campaign remarks of traditional candidates. Since celebrities are atypical political candidates, they are not expected to follow the typical rules. In the next chapter, we will explore each factor that I hypothesize differentiates traditional candidates and celebrity candidates and makes celebrity candidates particularly electorally deadly. Outsider status and looser standards for personal and professional conduct are merely a couple of these attributes. Crafting a theory that operationalizes and measures the star power of celebrities across a variety of characteristics is a critical step to understanding whether American voters prefer celebrities to traditional politicians when given the choice.

Notes

1. Sinclair, Upton. 1934. *I, Candidate for Governor: And How I Got Licked*. Berkeley, CA: University of California Press. Page 31.
2. Ibid. Pages xviii, 36, 214
3. Ibid. Page 36
4. For "Criminal conspiracy" see Ibid. Page 186; "Fascism" and "would-be Fascists" Pages 185 and 187; "sham proceedings" Pages 188 and 189.
5. Ibid, Page 99.
6. Ibid, Page 191.
7. Ibid, Page 144.
8. Ibid, Page 135.
9. Ibid, Page 166.
10. November 1, 2007. World News with Charles Gibson. ABC News.
11. Bradley, Bill. 1996. *Time Present, Time Past*. New York, NY: Vintage Books. Page 200.
12. Mathias, Bob and Robert Mendes. 2001. *The Bob Mathias Story*. New York, NY: Sports Publishing LLC. Page 46.
13. Ryun, Jim. 1979. *The Courage to Run*. Ventura, CA: Regal Publishing. Page 104.
14. Latimer, Clay. August 5, 2004. "Injury Diminished Proud Moment for Senator Campbell." *Rocky Mountain News*.
15. Ryun 1979, Page 108.
16. Bradley, Bill. 1996. *Time Present, Time Past*. New York, NY: Vintage Books. Page xi.
17. Schwarzenegger, Arnold. 2012. *Total Recall*. New York, NY: Simon & Schuster. Pages 476–477.
18. Osbourne, Tom. 2009. *Beyond the Final Score*. Ventura, CA: Regal Publishing. Page 113.
19. Ibid. Page 109.
20. Kondracke, Morton and Fred Barnes. 2015. *Jack Kemp: The Bleeding-Heart Conservative Who Changed America*. New York, NY: Sentinel. Page 4.
21. Bradley 1996, Page 158.
22. Ryun 1979, Page 109.
23. Ventura, Jesse. 1999. *I Ain't Got Time To Bleed*. New York, NY: Villard.

24. Kondracke and Barnes 2015, Page 33.
25. Osbourne 2009, Page 70.
26. Viola, Herman. 2002. *Ben Nighthorse Campbell: An American Warrior*. Boulder, CO: Johnson Books.
27. Kondracke and Barnes 2015, 112.
28. Mathias 2001, Page 115.
29. Mathias 2001, Page 122.
30. Kolbert, Elizabeth. September 29, 1996. "Dole, Choosing Kemp, Buried a Bitter Past Rooted in Doctrine." *The New York Times*.
31. Kolbert 1996 and Kondracke and Barnes 2015, Page 149.
32. Schwarzenegger 2012, Pages 509–510.
33. Ryun 1979, Page 24.
34. Ibid. Pages 520–521.
35. As quoted from Ed Rollins's book *Bare Knuckles and Back Rooms* in Kondracke and Barnes 2015, Page 209. Also for "undisciplined and impatient" see Page 10.
36. Kondracke and Barnes 2015, Page 30.
37. Bradley, Bill. 1996. *Time Present, Time Past*. New York, NY: Vintage Books. Page 31.
38. Schwarzenegger 2012, Page 509.
39. Osborne 2009, Page 65 and Ibid, Page 466.
40. Viola, Herman. 2002. *Ben Nighthorse Campbell: An American Warrior*. Boulder, CO: Johnson Books. Page 196.
41. Kondracke and Barnes 2015, Page 6.
42. Ibid, Page 14.
43. Schwarzenegger 2012, Page 469.
44. Ibid, Page 485.
45. Bradley 1996, Page 9.
46. Ibid, Page 125.
47. Ryun 1979, Page 100.
48. Osborne 2009, Page 64.
49. Ventura 1999, Page 4–5.
50. Ibid, Pages 4, 6, 9.
51. Schwarzenegger 2012, Page 477.
52. Ibid, Page 487.
53. Bradley 1996, Page 251.
54. Viola 2002, Page 227.
55. Bradley 1996, Page 128.
56. Ibid, Page 172–173.
57. Ventura 1999, Pages 3 and 8.
58. Schwarzenegger 2012, Page 500–501.
59. Mathias 2001, Page 114.
60. Osborne 2009, Page 68.
61. Mathias 2001, Page 121.
62. Kondracke and Barnes 2015, Page 111.
63. Bradley 1996, Page 253.
64. Osborne 2009, Page 71.
65. Ibid, Page 95.
66. Parker, Ashley. September 6, 2016. "Donald Trump Says Hillary Clinton Doesn't Have 'a Presidential Look.'" *The New York Times*.
67. Schwarzenegger 2012, Page 474.
68. Ibid, Page 508.
69. Ibid, Page 509.

70. Ventura 1999, Page 165.
71. Bradley 1996, Page 187.
72. Anzia, Sarah and Christopher Berry. 2011. "The Jackie (and Jill) Robinson Effect: Why Do Congresswomen Outperform Congressmen?" *American Journal of Political Science* 55 (3): 478–493. Page 478.
73. Reagan, Ronald. 1990. *Ronald Reagan: An American Life*. New York, NY: Pocket Books. First page of Chapter 31.
74. Wilkinson, Alyssa. June 29, 2017. "The Reagan Show Is a Terrifically Entertaining and Unnerving—Take on a Presidency." *Vox*.
75. Barnum, P.T. 2017. *Barnum's Own Story*. Mineola, NY: Dover Books. Page 357. (Note: *Barnum's Own Story* is a condensed volume of two autobiographical books by P.T. Barnum published in 1855 and 1869 respectively, *The Life of P.T. Barnum*, and *Struggles and Triumphs*).
76. Burgeson, John. July 4, 2010. "P.T. Barnum: Master of Advertising and Promotion." *CT Post*.
77. Unknown author. February 21, 1867. "Barnum for Congress." *The Daily Brooklyn Eagle*. Page 2.
78. Barnum 2017, Page 361.
79. Unknown author. October 12, 1867. "The Two Barnums." *The Daily Brooklyn Eagle*. Page 2.
80. Ibid, Page 362.
81. Schlappi, Elizabeth. 1997. *Roy Acuff: The Smokey Mountain Boy*. Gretna, LA: Pelican Publishing Company. Page 189.
82. Ibid, Page 190.
83. Vidal, Gore. 1995. *Palimpsest*. New York, NY: Penguin Books. Page 338.
84. Ibid, Page 338.
85. Ibid, Page 343.
86. Freedman, Ira Henry. September 15, 1960. "Gore Vidal Conducts Campaign of Quips and Liberal Views." *The New York Times*.
87. Ibid.
88. Ibid, Page 348.
89. Lennon, Michael, ed. 2014. *Selected Letters of Norman Mailer*. New York, NY: Random House. Page 397.
90. Roberts, Sam. November 18, 2007. "Mailer's Nonfiction Legacy: His 1969 Race for Mayor." *The New York Times*.
91. Ibid.
92. Schlesinger, Robert. November 13, 2015. "The Epic Trump Rant." *U.S. News & World Report*.
93. Ibid.
94. Reagan 1990, Pages 166–167.
95. Ibid, Page 169.
96. Ibid, Page 170.
97. Ibid, Page 192.
98. Ibid, Pages 192–193.
99. Springer, Jerry and Laura Morton. 1996. *Ringmaster!*. New York, NY: St. Martin's Press. Page 70.
100. Ibid, Page 63.
101. Bono, Sonny. 1991. *And The Beat Goes On*. New York, NY: Pocket Books. Page 263.
102. Ibid, Page 269.
103. Ibid, Page 271.
104. Ventura 1999, Page 137.

105. Bono, Page 261.
106. Barnum 2017, Page 357.
107. Franken, Al. 2017. *Al Franken: Giant of the Senate*. New York, NY: Twelve. Pages 51–52.
108. Ibid, Page 63.
109. Ibid, Page 66.
110. Ibid, Page 44.
111. C-SPAN2. 2003. "Book TV." Video of Al Franken and Bill O'Reilly's presentations to booksellers at BookExpo at the Los Angeles Convention Center.
112. Ibid, Pages 68–69.
113. Franken 2017, Page 48.
114. Ibid, Pages 56–57.
115. Bono 1991, Page 263.
116. Bono 1991, Page 266.
117. Parmet, Herbert. May 5, 1991. "Eight Years of Living Languorously." *The New York Times*.
118. C-SPAN. 1984. "Republican National Convention, Day 3." Video of Nancy Reagan speaking at the RNC in Texas.
119. Reagan 1990, Page 96.
120. Clines, Francis. March 31, 1985. "The Reagan Play-By-Play Still Plays." *The New York Times*.
121. Gene Kopelson is the author of *Reagan's 1968 Dress Rehearsal* (Figueroa Press, 2016). I conducting an interview with him in May 2018 about the findings in his book.
122. Ibid.
123. Kengor, Paul. May 22, 2007. "The Great Forgotten Debate." *The National Review*.
124. Franken 2017, Page 75.
125. Ibid, Page 72.
126. Skinner, Kiron and Annelise Anderson and Martin Anderson, eds. 2003. *Reagan: A Life in Letters*. New York, NY: Free Press. Page 700.
127. Skinner et al. 2003, Page 701.
128. Associated Press. August 30, 1967. "Shirley Temple Running for Congress in Calif." *The Pittsburgh Post-Gazette*. Page 1.
129. Marinucci, Carly. February 12, 2014. "Shirley Temple Black excelled in 2nd Career in Diplomacy." *The San Francisco Gate*.
130. Mitchell, Greg. February 4, 1988. "Tricky Dick and the Pink Lady." CSPAN 2 "About Books" talk. Video.
131. Mitchell, Greg. August 23, 2016. "When JFK Backed Nixon Against a Famous (Female) Democrat." Blog Article.
132. Wright, Lauren. March 27, 2018. "Cynthia Nixon Is No Donald Trump." *The Hill*.

Chapter 3

Celebrities, They're Not Like Us

Bucking the Status Quo

"I said, 'Hey Donald, you got a script?' and he pulled it out of his pocket," recounted Senate Majority Leader Mitch McConnell on Bloomberg's "Masters In Politics" podcast in June 2016. McConnell was telling a story about his encounter with Donald Trump at the National Rifle Association rally in Louisville, Kentucky. McConnell continues:

> He said, "You know I hate scripts, they're so boring." And I said, "Put me down in favor of boring. You've demonstrated that you have a lot of Twitter followers and you're good at turning on a big audience. Now you need to demonstrate you have the seriousness of purpose that is required to be President of the United States, and most candidates on frequent occasions use a script."[1]

Donald Trump, unlike many of the other celebrities discussed in this book, has never liked following a script. He is a reality television star—not a trained actor like Ronald Reagan or Arnold Schwarzenegger or Al Franken. Trump's skill set involves unpredictability and shock and awe and attention-grabbing, no matter how controversial. Not unlike a drunken brawl on MTV's *Jersey Shore* in which one person is pulling another person's hair and someone else is getting a drink thrown in his face, it is impossible not to be captivated by Trump, even if the basis of the captivation is sheer horror. Yet Trump, not Mitch McConnell, turned out to have the last laugh in 2016.

Celebrities are not like average politicians, and they do not behave like them. They do not campaign like them. And because of this, it is not unreasonable to suppose that they might not perform like them in elections. That is the basis of this chapter—to begin to explore the possibility that *celebrity candidates* (famous entertainers seeking elective office who have not held office before), due to a host of attributes that differentiate them from *traditional political candidates* (politicians running for office who have held elective office before and may or may not be well-known by the public), are preferable to voters and better positioned to win elections at a variety of levels. Simply put, I theorize that when celebrities run for public office, they are well-poised to win. I hypothesize that this is not only true because celebrities have higher name recognition on average than traditional politicians. Rather, because of a variety of skills and advantages gained from their entertainment careers, voters might prefer celebrities to traditional political candidates who are equally famous.

The mere idea of celebrity politics makes the establishment upset, whether celebrities are advocating for other candidates, or celebrities are the candidates themselves. It has been this way in the United States since at least the 1920s, when Broadway stars and performers started to become central fixtures of the presidential campaign trail. *Liking Ike* author David Haven Blake traces the star-studded spectacles we often see on the campaign trail today, as well as the appearances of presidential candidates on *Saturday Night Live*, the use of Twitter to communicate with voters, and modern campaign machinery as a whole to Dwight Eisenhower's campaign for president in 1952. "The path to these contemporary activities runs directly through him,"[2] writes Blake of Eisenhower. He describes a particular scene that one cannot help comparing to the Democratic and Republican national conventions we have become accustomed to in recent years. When Irving Berlin's hit play "Call Me Madam" opened in The Imperial Theatre on Broadway in October of 1950, it served two purposes. One, surmises Blake, was to make as much money and draw as large of an audience as possible. But the other was to try to recruit Dwight Eisenhower to run for President of the United States. Actors from the play walked to Eisenhower rallies after they were finished performing for the night and played a part there too. At one particular rally in Madison Square Garden, Ethel Merman sang her famous song "There's No Business Like Show Business" and Clark Gable spoke. "As if politics were a combination of pugilism and show business," Blake writes, "all the performances took place within the confines of the Madison Square Garden boxing ring."[3]

Elite criticism of Eisenhower's celebrity-centered political strategy—the sort Mitch McConnell and other Republican standard-bearers could be seen dishing out to Trump at the early stages of the 2016 Republican primary—was swift and intense from both sides of the political aisle. Arthur Schlesinger said of the spectacle, "If the Eisenhower campaign were going to succeed, then someone must take it out of the hands of the advertising man and jack it up to the level of a ten-year-old intelligence."[4] On the more conservative end of the spectrum, George Sokolsky called the Eisenhower-Broadway alliance "cheap" and "vulgar." The

New Bedford Standard Times wrote "Horseplay and lavish star-studded spectacles are no substitute for a candidate or a program."[5]

Eisenhower himself did not relish any of this. In fact, he found celebrities and show business mostly abhorrent. But he understood their value. Asked one time to wear makeup for a television appearance in Abilene, Kansas, Eisenhower remarked, "To think that an old soldier has come to this."[6] Eisenhower's ambivalence and distaste for the campaign process only seemed to work to his advantage. It made him seem more statesmanlike, enhancing his political desirability. Blake puts it well when he says, "The irony of this resistance was that Ike could afford to be such a detached politician because he had entered the campaign with fame ... celebrity gave him license to bypass the partisan maneuvering that occupied his opponents."[7]

Why did someone like Dwight Eisenhower, a celebrated war hero with a big smile and a charming family, need celebrities and media consultants to glamorize his 1952 and 1956 campaigns? Television is a medium that requires expertise. The personal lives of candidates and trivial details have become interesting to the press. Celebrity was becoming more important than political parties. Television turned politicians into actors, and a growing political alliance between television, advertising, and celebrity became evident. Being a beloved military general was, historians and communications scholars argue, not enough for Eisenhower. To succeed on the campaign trail and in the White House, Eisenhower needed to learn how to become a television star.

More than ever today, the intense focus of television on personality and the personal lives of politicians gives everyone a chance to participate. Policy is complicated. Sex scandals are not. Family feuds are not. Fashion choices are not. In many ways television and celebrity involvement in campaigns is one of the most democratic features of American politics. Celebrities can be everything to everyone, which creates an "illusory intimacy."[8] Ronald Reagan, for example, was a down to earth working rancher, a glamorous movie star, a star football player, a brave and heroic protagonist, and a sports announcer. There was something in Ronald Reagan for everyone.

Is the connection between celebrity and political parties strictly a Republican phenomenon, as the stories of Eisenhower and Reagan (and Ventura, Schwarzenegger, Kemp, Thompson, and Trump) might lead us to believe? It really is not. As Table A.1. in the Appendix demonstrates, the list of celebrities who have run for prominent offices since the 19th century is almost evenly split between Republicans and Democrats.[9] While there is nothing about the Republican Party platform that fundamentally links celebrities to the GOP, the histories of political activism and Hollywood are deeply intertwined. The heads of the large Hollywood movie studios in the era of Eisenhower and Reagan were prominent Republicans. MGM was headed by Louis Mayer, who Steve Ross writes "brought Hollywood to the Republican party and the Republican party to Hollywood."[10] In fact, Ross goes so far as to say that Hollywood has always been privately conservative and publicly liberal. In the 1920s, it was Mayer's idea to have Broadway and movie stars appear with "tired-looking" politicians in need of some glamour and stardust. "What united all these stars was that they saw their fame as an invitation to become leading voices in the ongoing conversation about the future of the United States."[11] Stars were becoming more comfortable with political advocacy and politicians were learning the benefits of opening up their personal lives to the public, an activity that was, until Eisenhower, mostly done in the Hollywood sphere. Harriet Van Horne, a *New York Times* critic, wrote of the coverage of one of Eisenhower's birthday celebrations, that it "may have been, as Republicans were at pins to state, entirely not political . . . But it is hard to imagine a more effective piece of campaign strategy than a picture of the Eisenhower family, gathered in the White House library, happily watching the TV screen."[12]

Then again, it is worth noting that what successful politicians like Eisenhower have had to painstakingly and often begrudgingly learn on the campaign trail, celebrities already know. Traditional politicians fantasize about skipping the tedious campaign tasks of handshaking, picture-taking, smiling and energizing a crowd. Hillary Clinton actually did skip them, many times, in 2016, particularly in the last two weeks of the presidential campaign, when political science research consistently shows voters are paying the most attention. Trump, in contrast, happily crisscrossed the United States, making a total of 133 visits to Florida, Pennsylvania, Ohio, North Carolina, Michigan, and Wisconsin in the final 100 days of the campaign. Hillary Clinton made just 87 visits to the first five states—she did not visit Wisconsin once after the convention.[13] For the most wonky candidates, repetitive travel and glad-handing are the irritating responsibilities to which one must tend on the campaign trail to have the opportunity to do the work of governing. For celebrity candidates, the work of governing is drudgery. The work of campaigning is what they live to do. Even politicians who have been described as possessing many of the qualities celebrities have—relatability, popularity, and sharp communications skills—candidates like Barack Obama and John F. Kennedy—have expressed Eisenhower-like dismay of life on the campaign trail. Robert Draper reported a story in the *Independent* about Barack Obama's final days on the South Carolina Democratic primary campaign trail in 2008, excerpted below.

> On 25 January 2008, the day before the South Carolina Democratic primary, Barack Obama endured a gruelling succession of campaign events across the state. When his staff informed him the evening would conclude with a brief show-up at the Pink Ice Ball, a gala for the African-American sorority Alpha Kappa Alpha, Obama flatly refused to attend. "We're not gonna change anybody's mind," he said. Rick Wade, a senior adviser, Stacey Brayboy, the state campaign manager, and Anton Gunn, the state political director, took turns to beseech their boss . . . "Man, it's late, I'm tired," he snapped . . . At the day's penultimate event, a rally in Columbia, Gunn, Brayboy and Wade pleaded their case to Jarrett, the Obamas' long-time friend and consigliere. Jarrett informed

Michelle [Obama] of the situation and when the candidate stepped offstage from the rally, Obama's wife told him he had one last stop to make before they called it a night. "I told Anton I'm not going to any Pink Ice Ball!" Obama barked. Then Jarrett glided over to the fuming candidate. Her voice was very quiet and very direct. "Barack," she insisted, "you want to win, don't you?" Scowling, Obama affirmed that he did. "Well then. You need to go to Pink Ice." "And he shuts up," Gunn recalls, "and gets on the bus."[14]

The point of this story, for the purposes of this book, is not to emphasize the persuasive power of Valerie Jarrett and Michelle Obama, but to demonstrate that even for the most talented politicians, campaigning is difficult, taxing, and unnatural. For lifetime self-promoters like Donald Trump, Arnold Schwarzenegger, and Jesse Ventura, there is much less distance between the work to which they became accustomed over a lifetime in the entertainment industry, and what is required of candidates on the campaign trail, particularly at the presidential level. The next section of this chapter describes each of the valuable qualities and attributes celebrities possess in detail.

The Seven Deadly Ins

1. Name Recognition

Name recognition—the extent to which a voter is aware of a politician—is by far the most potent tool that celebrities have on the campaign trail. The mere absence of it is enough to kill a candidate's electoral prospects, especially in a primary election when voters must choose among candidates from the same political party. In this situation, it is highly unlikely voters will choose a candidate whose name they do not recognize over one who they do. Despite its power, name recognition is only one heuristic that voters use to make choices at the ballot box. Others, such as a candidate's party, or incumbency status, can be even more critical, even though they are closely linked with the concept of name recognition. For example, a party may choose to devote more resources to a candidate with high name recognition in a primary, or may even recruit a political amateur with high name recognition to run for office. Incumbent candidates often gain high name recognition from holding office, and voters may assume a candidate is politically experienced if they are familiar with her name.

While it may seem an obvious point that being familiar to the public is an asset on the campaign trail, political scientists have debated whether and how name recognition factors into elections for decades. Because political candidates spend so much time and money on establishing their names to voters through tools like direct mail, television, print and radio advertising, and yard signs, it is important to know whether these efforts actually bear fruit, or if candidates are wasting time engaging in these activities when they could be doing something else. Would they have done just as well in the election in the first place?

Some scholars such as Larry Bartels have asserted that name recognition is a necessary, although not sufficient ingredient to win elections.[15] Others such as Warren Miller and Donald Stokes have made much stronger statements, asserting that the reason name recognition is so important is because it carries a positive valence, that is, that "to be perceived at all is to be perceived favorably."[16] Miller and Stokes's perspective is consistent with research in marketing and cognitive psychology which asserts that consumers consistently prefer product brands they recognize over products they do not.[17] This conclusion is in line with common cultural references to name recognition, such as the line famously attributed to P.T. Barnum: "There is no such thing as bad publicity" or another to Oscar Wilde: "There is only one thing in life worse than being talked about, and that is not being talked about." In a recent episode of *Comedians in Cars Getting Coffee*, comedian Jerry Seinfeld debated this point with President Barack Obama. "With all due respect," says Seinfeld, "I remember very well not being famous. It wasn't that great." "Yeah. You think being famous is better?" asked Obama. "Yeah," responds Seinfeld, laughing.[18]

Alan Abramowitz, on the other end of the spectrum, has asserted that name recognition breeds neither contempt nor affection.[19] In 1975 Abramowitz tested name familiarity as the driving force behind the incumbency advantage and found it an unsatisfactory explanation. Instead, he finds support for the reputation hypothesis, that is, that the incumbency advantage is a function of one's reputation among voters in her constituency, not her name recognition. More recent empirical research in both the United States and other countries, however, has found conclusively that name recognition affects candidate support.

Through a series of laboratory experiments, including those that subliminally prime participants to become familiar with certain candidates' names, Cindy Kam and Elizabeth Zechmeister confirm that name recognition has a powerful effect on candidate preference, but that the mechanism behind it—that is, the inferences participants are drawing based on recognizing a candidate's name—rather than certain traits or experience, is the perception of viability.[20] That is, when voters recognize a candidate's name, assuming there are no competing cues about other predictors of vote choice such as partisan affiliation or incumbency status, they assume the candidate has a good shot at winning the election. Research shows that voters consistently prefer candidates they perceive to be viable over those they do not.[21]

Kentaro Fukumoto and Hirofumi Miwa expand on Kam and Zechmeister's study with their investigation of the role of name recognition in elections to the upper house of the Japanese legislature. Through natural experiments, they find that all else held equal, national candidates in high-name recognition districts obtain a 69% larger vote share than those in low-name recognition districts. More to the point, the authors assert based on collected evidence that voters do engage in the "unprincipled behavior" of casting a ballot just because they recognize a candidate's name. Even more interestingly, their findings hold regardless of a candidate's past performance, policy record, personal traits, or even party affiliation.[22]

Also leveraging data from Japan, Justin Reeves finds that when celebrity candidates run for seats in the upper house in national Japanese legislature, they win more than half the time. The phenomenon of celebrity candidates running for elective office in is even more common in countries like Japan, Finland, Brazil, and Greece than the United States, because electoral systems and rules allow slates of up to 200 candidates to enter the race. Similarly to Fokumoto and Miwa, Reeves finds that even when accounting for gender, age, education, income, political knowledge, and willingness to support a celebrity candidate in the hypothetical long-ballot races he designs, celebrities outperform the control group candidates (who have the exact same professional backgrounds), receiving triple the support.

Indeed, one of Reeves's most interesting findings is that the respondents in his surveys often support celebrity candidates even though they claim to reject the very idea of them.[23] Reeves asserts that in contrast to literature claiming that name recognition is only important in low-information races in which voters are not concerned with candidates' political or policy experience or ideology, research on decision-making often shows that voters use the most simple, least intellectually demanding heuristics to make decisions rather than more complicated ones. In addition, voters may associate celebrities with certain positive attributes and traditional politicians with more negative ones. Support for celebrities, he finds, is linked to levels of trust in government, and the presence of political scandal can also increase support for celebrities. Moreover, as I will discuss later in the book, Reeves weighs in on the debate over whether celebrities are in fact less effective legislators than their non-celebrity counterparts. At least in Japan, he finds no discernable differences between the legislative productivity of celebrities and non-celebrities once in office. Celebrities may be even *more* effective, he finds, when it comes to bill sponsorship and parliamentary questioning.[24]

Even more difficult for non-celebrity candidates is the fact that advertisements geared toward increasing a candidate's name recognition are often ineffective. This is to say that politicians, in addition to expending considerable resources and time trying to introduce themselves to voters, probably still will not be able to match the deep level of name recognition that celebrities have achieved over time. A short stint of exposure to a certain candidate's name is no match for a lifetime of positively associated exposure to a celebrity's name. This is what a recent study by David Broockman and Donald Green demonstrates. The authors randomly assigned voters to be exposed to ads for little-known congressional candidates on Facebook an average of 38 times over the course of a week. Broockman and Green found that voters were no more likely to positively evaluate or even recognize the candidates who were the subject of advertisements over the candidates who were not. In their own words, "evidence remains sparse that impersonal mass communications are able to affect large, enduring changes in individuals' attitudes or behaviors, online or not."[25]

Celebrities Have Higher Name Recognition Than Prominent Politicians

To review, name recognition is a potent factor in voter decision-making. There is a direct relationship between name recognition and vote choice. And the debate that exists in this regard seems to be over what information voters infer from a name with which they are familiar. Experience, popularity, and viability are several of these ideas. Figure 3.1 clearly demonstrates the point that celebrities, on average, have higher rates of name recognition than politicians.[26] The first set of differences (in open-ended name recognition questions) between celebrities and politicians in Figure 3.1 are statistically significant. In order to gauge name recognition of celebrities and politicians, I conducted a survey of 1,083 respondents using Amazon's Mechanical Turk

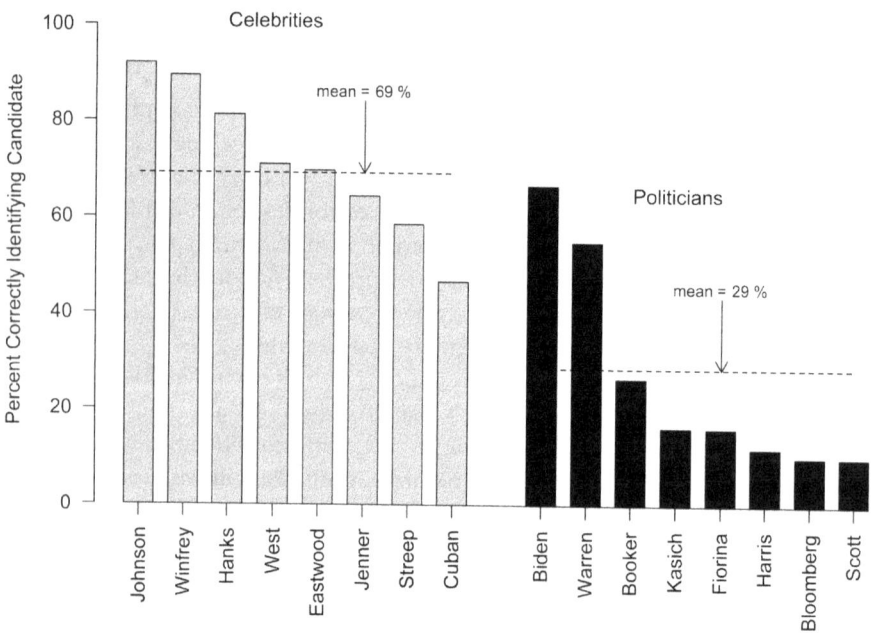

Figure 3.1 Name Recognition, Open-Ended Responses

Candidates as they appear from left to right on the graph include: Dwayne "The Rock" Johnson, Oprah Winfrey, Tom Hanks, Kanye West, Clint Eastwood, Caitlyn Jenner, Meryl Streep, Mark Cuban, Joe Biden, Elizabeth Warren, Cory Booker, John Kasich, Carly Fiorina, Kamala Harris, Michael Bloomberg, and Tim Scott.

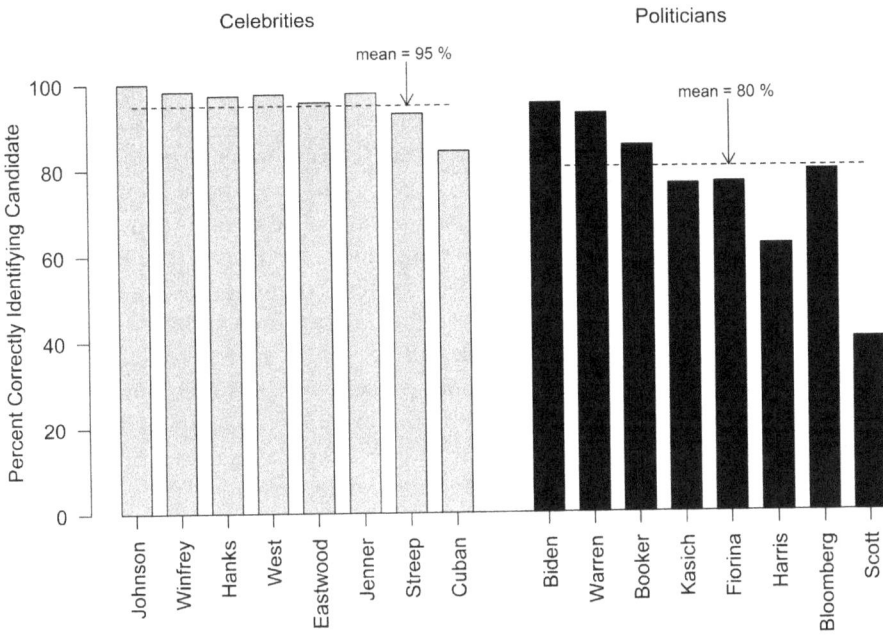

Figure 3.2 Name Recognition, Multiple Choice

Candidates as they appear from left to right on the graph include: Dwayne "The Rock" Johnson, Oprah Winfrey, Tom Hanks, Kanye West, Clint Eastwood, Caitlyn Jenner, Meryl Streep, Mark Cuban, Joe Biden, Elizabeth Warren, Cory Booker, John Kasich, Carly Fiorina, Kamala Harris, Michael Bloomberg, and Tim Scott.

service. I chose prominent celebrities who have either floated running for elective office or who have shared strong opinions about politics in public. An equal number of Republican and Democratic celebrities were presented, as were politicians. I chose politicians who have a national presence and appear frequently in the media. I also presented an equal number of white and non-white celebrities in each group, and an equal number of men and women in each group. In the first name recognition question, respondents were shown pictures of celebrities and politicians and asked to identify them by name. This is a much tougher test of name recognition than a multiple choice question, the results of which are summarized in Figure 3.2. After they were asked to identify politicians and celebrities in an open-ended format, respondents were asked to identify the person shown on the previous screen among a set of three names. For celebrities, the choices included another prominent celebrity, the correct celebrity, and a randomly generated name. With three choices, respondents had a 33.33% chance of getting the answer right, even if they did not truly know the celebrity's name. This is one explanation for the much smaller difference in name recognition rates between celebrities and politicians in Figures 3.1 and 3.2.

It should also be noted that if these results are unrepresentative in any way, they are likely biased upwards, meaning that the name recognition of politicians could be even lower than these results suggest. Survey sampling research has shown that Mechanical Turk respondents consume more political news and are more educated than other survey respondents such as those in the American National Election Series surveys and the general public.[27,28] The results in Figure 3.1 deserve additional attention here. A former vice president (Joe Biden) has only 67% name recognition among a relatively politically knowledgeable sample. Two 2016 presidential candidates (John Kasich and Carly Fiorina) who continue to make plans to run for national office in the future, have just over 16% name recognition in this survey.[29,30] Three popular U.S. senators who are also weighing presidential bids (Elizabeth Warren, Cory Booker and Kamala Harris) weigh in at 55%, 26%, and 12%, respectively. Tim Scott, the only African American Republican in the U.S. Senate, has only 10% name recognition when respondents are asked to identify him in a fill-in-the-blank question, and only 46% when asked to identify his name out if three multiple choice options. If name recognition is as important a factor in vote choice as the research suggests, one may conclude that Joe Biden and Elizabeth Warren are by far the best candidates to face Donald Trump in 2020. These results are only partially consistent with recent surveys conducted by firms such as Vox Populi Polling that ask respondents outright which candidates they would support in the 2020 election, which analysts have admitted are "wildly speculative."[31]

Despite their very low name recognition, Kamala Harris and Cory Booker are usually featured at the top of these lists. Celebrities, by contrast, are usually featured at the bottom. As previous celebrity research has suggested, many people will not admit to supporting a celebrity candidate, especially in phone interviews where they may be concerned with the interviewer's opinion of them, but when faced with a choice of names in a ballot box, their choices often do not reflect their stated preferences. Still, recent polling suggests that there is a strong positive correlation between candidate awareness and candidate consideration.[32] As the authors of *The American Voter Revisited* so aptly put, ". . . electoral choice is guided by a simple premise: Whatever does not register in the voter's mind cannot make a difference in the voter's behavior."[33]

Moving to the celebrity side of Figure 3.1, Dwayne "The Rock" Johnson's name recognition is extremely high. When shown a picture of Johnson and asked to fill in the blank below it, 92% of respondents get the answer right (a good amount more than Oprah Winfrey at 90% and Tom Hanks at 81%, to be clear). When asked the same question in a multiple-choice format, more than 99% of respondents correctly identify Johnson.

As we take a deep dive into the research behind each of the attributes that culminate in a theory of celebrity preference, it is important to note that successful politicians have many of these attributes too. Traditional politicians, to succeed, must have a certain degree of name recognition. They must have a certain degree of likability, at least among a core group of supporters. They must have supporters and followers, cultivate that following, and must continue to grow public awareness of themselves through media appearances. They must be good fundraisers. They must have a compelling personal story or qualities, or they must play on their individuality as politicians, even if they are not political outsiders. They must try to appear relatable, and some do achieve that.

Instead of asserting that politicians do not have any of these qualities, I am hypothesizing that celebrities have more of them. They are wealthy in these areas and politicians are often not. A good example of this wealth is political advertising, which we touched on briefly in our discussion of research on how to build name recognition. Politicians must promote themselves, and they do. But the way in which they do this—television and internet and mail ads—seems disingenuous at its core. The way politicians advertise themselves is opportunistic. Paid ads and sanctioned interviews are not the same as the TV shows, movies, and interviews that celebrities have earned over a lifetime. Voters can tune out ads. But they tune in to celebrity content by choice. Perhaps the preeminent study in this area is that of Gerber, Gimple, Green, and Shaw which was the first large-scale field experiment measuring the effectiveness of paid political advertising within a gubernatorial campaign. The authors deployed television and radio ads on behalf of Rick Perry's 2006 campaign for Governor of Texas, randomly varying the media market, launch dates and volume of ads. When the authors reviewed the results from their tracking poll, they discovered that the ads did significantly improve perceptions of the candidates, however these changes were very short-lived, only about one week long on average. Political ads do not influence political opinion in the long term.[34] One particular finding, however, is very useful for my study here. Gerber et al. also finds that the maximum dose of advertising produces the biggest effects. In some ways, the public appearances of celebrities, including their television shows, movies, performances, and interviews, can be considered a large dose of advertising that is deployed long-term. That advertising dose is mostly positive, nonpartisan, and it is not countered by negative attack ads. It is also not as opportunistic—or some might say—desperate—as political advertising. When celebrities appear on television they are merely doing their jobs, not trying to persuade public opinion in a controversial direction at a high cost.

2. Favorability

Another important consideration in the process of differentiating celebrity political candidates from traditional political candidates is favorability. Favorability is a common measure in political science of how well-liked a candidate or politician is. Favorability is closely related to approval—that is, how well a politician is doing her job—but it is substantively different. While approval may be a more germane measure of a sitting politician's electoral prospects, favorability is a measure most often found on the campaign trail. We want to know whether voters *like* a presidential candidate, while we want to know whether voters *approve* of the job a sitting president is doing. Favorability is typically assessed by asking survey respondents to rate a politician on a feeling thermometer that ranges from 0 to 100. The thermometer is described as a scale that ranges from cold to warm feelings toward a person, designed to assess the gut-level, emotional reaction a person has toward a political candidate. This measure has become increasingly important as theories of voter behavior have moved away from rational choice theory, which assumes an economic model of voting wherein voters cast ballots strictly according to their best interest, and toward social-psychological models of voting, which are focused on voter attitudes. According to the latter models of voter behavior, voters form subjective evaluations of candidates. Positively-toned perceptions are likely to motivate voters to support candidates they feel positive about. Negative perceptions, by contrast are likely to help the other candidate.[35]

Although the relationship between favorability and vote choice seems self-explanatory, it is actually quite complicated. First, because the way you vote for someone affects how you feel about them and how you feel about them affects how you vote for them (i.e., favorability and vote choice are endogenous) it is difficult to prove that a candidate's favorability has a causal effect on vote choice. The media also acts as a filter for favorability, meaning that voters do not form positive or negative views about a candidate in a vacuum; they consume information about the candidates and see coverage of campaign events that often also has a discernably positive or negative tone. Research has shown, for instance, that favorable *media coverage* of a candidate accounts for a significant amount of change in voter attitudes over the course of a campaign, and plays a significant role in voter preferences.[36] Another valid question is *whose* favorability are we talking about? The favorability of candidates' opponents, running mates, co-partisans and predecessors, in addition to their own favorability, also has a powerful effect on vote choice. For example, researchers studying the 2008 election found that voters who had a "somewhat unfavorable" view of John McCain in June were 15 points more likely to transition from undecided to support for Barack Obama in September than voters who had a "somewhat favorable" view of John McCain. The same study found that contrary to a classic theory of voting behavior which alleges that the reason elections are predictable is because people vote retrospectively—that is, they are not casting their ballots based on how they feel about the current candidates, they are casting ballots based on how they feel about the previous administration—George W. Bush's legacy did not play a significant role in voters' decision-making process come election day.[37] As the campaign progresses, however, voters tend to more heavily weigh prospective evaluations of candidates than retrospective evaluations of their predecessors. Celebrities might benefit from these tendencies of voters in a couple of ways.

First, celebrities (who I define as athletes and entertainers who have not previously run for elective office) may not be as closely tied to either political party in the minds of voters as politicians who have spent their entire careers saddled with a party label. Of course, traditional politicians also have their own legacy to worry about, in addition to the sins and mistakes of the political party to which they belong. For instance, if Senator Elizabeth Warren runs for president in 2020, she would have a closer association with the Democratic party and the legacies of her predecessors such as Obama and Clinton, than someone like Dwayne "The Rock" Johnson, who happens to be a Republican, but is known mostly as an apolitical actor. In fact, in the open-ended name recognition surveys I conducted, it was much more likely for respondents to include a politician's partisan affiliation in their responses than a celebrity's, even though all of the celebrities and politicians included in the survey have publically indicated an allegiance to one political party over the other. For example, a few respondents who could not name Carly Fiorina and Elizabeth Warren in the survey were still able to link them to a political party. One person typed in "Democrat" under Warren's picture, and one person typed in "GOP hopeful" below Fiorina's. I did not observe the same phenomenon for celebrities. Because of their utter political inexperience, celebrities cannot be as easily burdened with the mistakes of co-partisans. Politicians have experience, but as Donald Trump put it on the 2016 campaign trail, if it is "bad experience"[38] (or can be easily framed as bad experience) the extent to which voters evaluate a politician favorably could be overshadowed by an outsider's ability to paint her opponent's past as unfavorable. A celebrity is more likely to be viewed prospectively than retrospectively by voters.

While it may not be surprising to those who recall the historically low favorability ratings of both Hillary Clinton and Donald Trump surrounding their primary victories—a period when candidates generally enjoy high favorable ratings and a post-convention polling bump—just because favorability is highly correlated with and indeed predictive of vote choice under certain circumstances does not mean that it is impossible for an unpopular candidate to clinch a victory. Not since George H.W. Bush in 1992 had there been a majority unfavorable candidate in June of an election year. In June 2016, after Donald Trump swept the Republican primary contest, 70 percent of Americans viewed Trump unfavorably according to an ABC News/Washington Post poll. Virtually every other major national poll also had Trump "upside down" with regard to favorability—his unfavorability was much higher than his favorability—(66 percent according to a Bloomberg poll, 64 percent according to a Marquette poll, 63 percent according to Gallup, all significantly higher figures than Clinton).[39] Writing in *Politico* in June 2016, Steven Shepard said, "In 2016's race to the bottom, Donald Trump is going to find out if you can

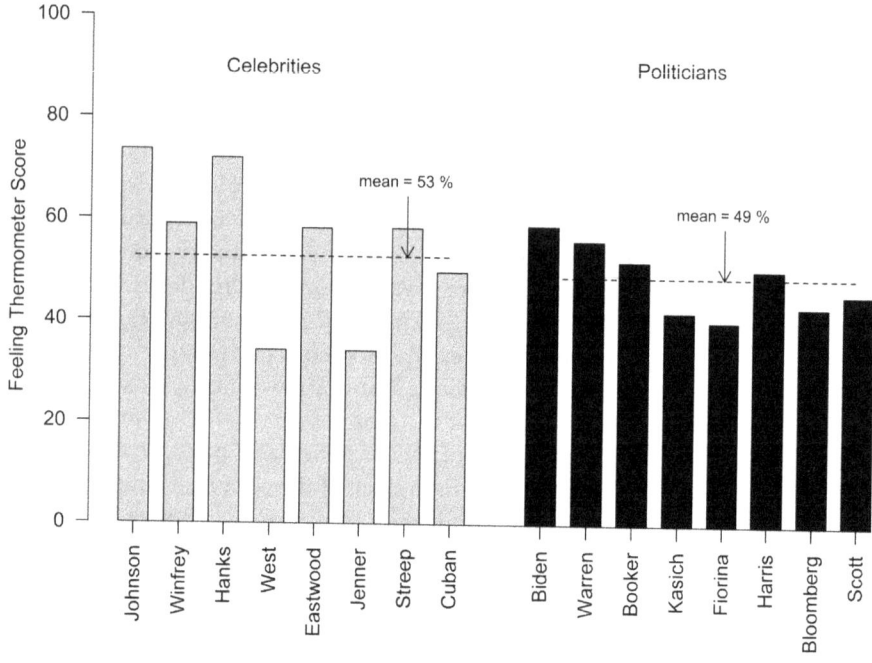

Figure 3.3 Favorability

For ease of comparison, the order in which candidates' names appear is the same in Figures 3.1, 3.2, 3.3, and 3.4 although their scores on each measure fluctuate. Candidates as they appear from left to right on the graph include: Dwayne "The Rock" Johnson, Oprah Winfrey, Tom Hanks, Kanye West, Clint Eastwood, Caitlyn Jenner, Meryl Streep, Mark Cuban, Joe Biden, Elizabeth Warren, Cory Booker, John Kasich, Carly Fiorina, Kamala Harris, Michael Bloomberg, and Tim Scott.

become president when two-thirds of Americans don't like you—and a majority can't stand you."[40] Apparently you can. While it is possible that Donald Trump's high marks on a host of other celebrity attributes discussed here helped pull him over the general election finish line in key areas of the country, average favorability among Americans was clearly not one of them. In fact, as Figure 3.3 shows, celebrities only have slightly higher favorability ratings on average than traditional politicians.

When asked to rate the celebrities and politicians on this list on a sliding scale ranging from 0 to 100 in the same survey I conducted to assess name recognition in 2018, respondents gave celebrities a mean feeling thermometer score of 52.6 out of 100, and politicians a mean feeling thermometer score of 48.7 out of 100. Though the difference between these two figures appears meaningful, since celebrities are popular on average (their mean feeling thermometer score is above 50) and politicians are unpopular on average (their mean feeling thermometer score is below 50), it is not statistically distinguishable from zero.

3. Relatability

How do you win a national election if you are unpopular? Setting the important institutional and idiosyncratic factors aside that helped propel Donald Trump to a general election victory in 2016 (Trump benefitted heavily from the electoral college system, the fact that a Democrat had been in office for eight years, and the scandals and negative associations surrounding Hillary Clinton) there are several other individual attributes of celebrities that are important to explore. Relatability is perhaps the most fascinating example of these. Whether a candidate is relatable to voters captures the extent to which voters can understand and sympathize with a candidate and in turn whether than candidate makes voters feel that they and their own experiences are understood. A relatable candidate is a candidate that reminds voters of themselves. Candidates that appear relatable appear to be genuine, down-to-earth, and normal. They are the opposite of elitist, cold, out-of-touch, unapproachable, and insensitive. While there is a lack of literature in political science that directly addresses the quality of relatability, the concept has long been discussed by journalists and social psychologists. One measure that is constantly used in elections to assess relatability is the "who would you rather have a beer with" test. Trump, like Bush over "up-tight Al Gore" in 2000 and "pinot-sipping Kerry" in 2004, and Obama over "likeable enough" Clinton in 2008 and "pompous" Romney in 2012, won this contest handily in 2016 over his primary opponents and Hillary Clinton.[41,42] Describing the measure in 2016, Seth Stevenson writes in *Slate*:

> Of course, Trump doesn't drink. Neither did W. The want-to-have-a-beer-with measure is metaphorical in nature. It's more a measure of the voter's own id and imagination than of the candidate's likely behavior . . . For the people who want to drink with Trump . . . he is their champion. He assures them that, as long as they're hanging with him, they are champions too. Nothing tastes better than an ice-cold bottle of winning.[43]

Writing on the same topic in Town Hall, Joseph Bilello writes:

> Ever since Nixon's sweaty, uncomfortable, seemingly disgruntled face appeared side-by-side with the more youthful, charming and charismatic John F. Kennedy on the TV sets of millions of Americans in 1960, there has only been one tried-and-true . . . factor in choosing the President of the United States . . . personal politics and outside influences often cloud one's judgement and distort one's honesty. But if an individual was able to put all politics aside, the choice is usually quite clear.[44]

Indeed, in June 2016, Rasmussen discovered that among likely voters not affiliated with either major party (who also happen to be the most likely to be undecided and the most important swing group in an electorate) 50% preferred to have a beer with Trump (compared to 25% for Clinton) and 46% (compared to 27%) would rather have dinner with him. 53% of all men in the same survey said they would rather have a beer with Trump.[45]

NYU psychologist Jonathan Haidt asserts that Republican candidates are more skilled than Democrats at tapping into the tendency of voters to gravitate towards values-based messages that make them feel like they live in a safe, strong and fair country.[46] Of course, this is a book that is focused more on individual candidates within parties rather than party-based messages, but Haidt's point is reminiscent of a young literature in political science referred to as expressive voting that is useful to my inquiry. Alexander Schuessler's definition of expressive voting is based on the following interpretation of Anthony Downs's seminal work on rational vote choice: "It is often overlooked that Anthony Downs noted how voters' choices of political candidates could be motivated by factors other than the desire to determine the outcome of an election . . . at least for some voters, voting is a means to express political beliefs and preferences, and, in doing so, to establish and reaffirm their own political identity."[47] In other words, voters may not choose a candidate because they are best qualified or best equipped to govern, but because they are expressing something about themselves or their own beliefs. For example, a voter who is angry at the state of society, her own success or lack thereof, or at government in general might vote for an unqualified outsider to 'send a message' to Washington, in other words, an *expression* of political frustration, rather than a vote for a candidate who is most viable or most likely to succeed or most likely to help the most people. In their study of 'angry' voters, Dwight Lee and Ryan Murphy provide an additional helpful definition of expressive voting:

> the literature on . . . expressive voting . . . begins with the observation that, except in a small-numbers setting, the probability of an individual's vote being decisive—i.e. determining the election's outcome—is vanishingly small. The immediate implication of this observation is that in a high-turnout election, the probability of a voter casting a decisive vote is miniscule, and therefore he is far less interested in how his vote affects the election's outcome than in how it affects him emotionally.[48]

Because celebrities are political outsiders, they are less experienced and less qualified to hold public office, on average, when compared to traditional politicians. It is easier to make the argument that a vote for a celebrity is an expressive vote, rather than a vote for a traditional politician, who represents the political establishment.

Another area of political science research that helps explain the concept of relatability is a more established area of literature having to do with representation. Candidates who are relatable are candidates that voters perceive are better representatives of their own lives and experiences. Voters often believe they are better represented by people who look like them, share their occupation or social status, live where they live, or are more like them in other ways. There are several types of representation. One of the original political representation scholars, Hanna Pitkin, describes representation as the activity of making citizens' "voices, opinions and perspectives" "present" in the policymaking process.[49] Jane Mansbridge expanded on the work of Pitkin and other representation scholars in her study of the ways in which disadvantaged groups benefit from having "descriptive" political representatives, that is, people who in their own backgrounds mirror "some of the more frequent experiences and outward manifestations" of group belonging.[50] To relay a few of Mansbridge's examples, the idea is that African-American voters benefit from electing African-Americans to represent them, that women benefit from electing women, and that farmers benefit from electing people with experience in farming. One of the only requirements to become President of the United States, in fact, is to have been born in the United States. The logic behind this? A United States citizen will be more loyal and more responsive to U.S. interests than a non-U.S. citizen. In the same way, one wonders, voters might believe that a non-politician, with whom they can better relate, might better represent their interests than a politician who is professionally invested in political outcomes. The argument against descriptive representation? "Nobody would argue that morons should be represented by morons," wrote Roland Pennock in 1979.[51]

In order to assess whether celebrities are in fact more relatable on average than traditional politicians, I included a question about relatability in the previously discussed Mechanical Turk survey I conducted in 2018. After respondents were shown a picture of the hypothetical candidates listed in the figure, asked to name them, asked to rate them on a feeling thermometer, respondents were also asked the following question: "Think about [Candidate's Name]. Do you agree, disagree, or neither agree nor disagree with the following statement: [Candidate's Name] can relate to people like me." As Figure 3.4 shows, respondents in my survey did not find the celebrity candidates to be very much more relatable on average than the traditional political candidates (about 29% of respondents found celebrities to be relatable and about 28% of respondents found politicians to be relatable). Dwayne "The Rock" Johnson, Tom Hanks, and Oprah led the pack of celebrities and Joe Biden and Elizabeth Warren performed best on this question among politicians, although no candidate achieved 60% relatability. What does seem clear from these results, however, is that the best-known and best-liked candidates are also the most relatable. This makes sense, since voters have more of a chance of getting to know a candidate the more media exposure they receive.

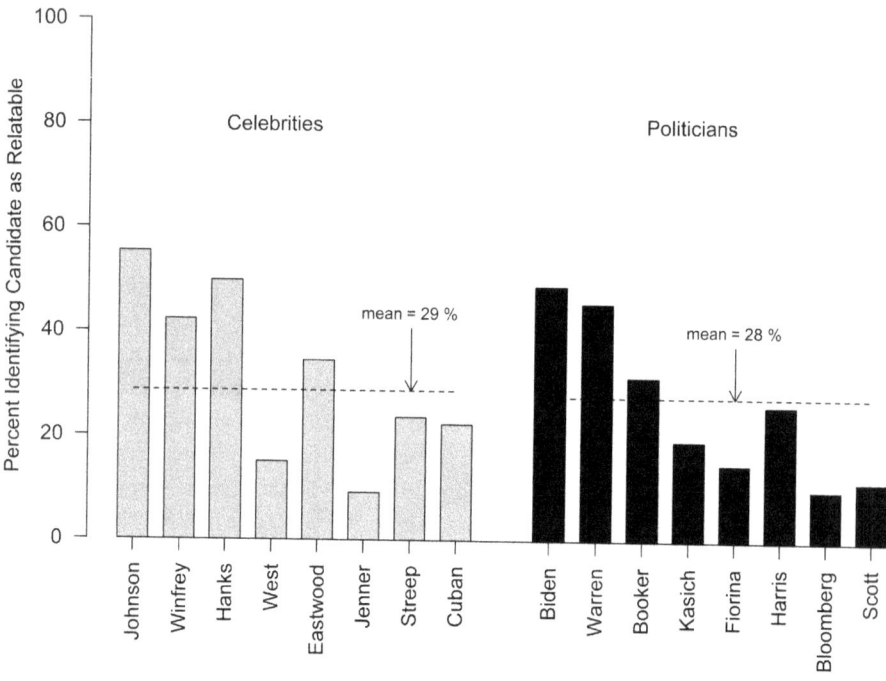

Figure 3.4 Relatability

For ease of comparison, the order in which candidates' names appear is the same in Figures 3.1, 3.2, 3.3, and 3.4 although their scores on each measure fluctuate. Candidates as they appear from left to right on the graph include: Dwayne "The Rock" Johnson, Oprah Winfrey, Tom Hanks, Kanye West, Clint Eastwood, Caitlyn Jenner, Meryl Streep, Mark Cuban, Joe Biden, Elizabeth Warren, Cory Booker, John Kasich, Carly Fiorina, Kamala Harris, Michael Bloomberg, and Tim Scott.

4. Outsider Status

Outsider status is a binary variable. Either a political candidate has held elective office before, or she has not. This information is highly accessible to voters, since politicians spend a lot of time on the campaign trail touting their political experience, while celebrities proudly trumpet their lack of experience and their fresh outlook on politics. Outsider status is also a big part of the way in which media outlets frame elections. Journalists delight in discussions of campaigns as "battles" and "wars" and face-offs between a political newcomer or underdog and an experienced politician defending his or her title or throne. Outsider status is closely linked to relatability because a lack of political experience is a key attribute celebrities have on the campaign trail that politicians do not. Voters can imagine themselves figuring out the ropes on the campaign trail, even stumbling, or living a normal life with a career prior to politics like most outsider candidates describe. It is much more difficult to imagine yourself walking the halls of the Capitol or cutting deals with politicians or engaging in the aspects politics that often appear phony and ingratiating.

According to presidential scholars there are several reasons candidates might want to leverage outsider status. The first is that not all candidates can claim outsider status, so merely being able to do is a political asset. Political candidates are not typically in the habit of ignoring low-hanging political fruit. For example, governors running for president often adopt an anti-Washington outsider stance, as do businesspeople and entertainers, but congressional representatives running for president have a much harder time mobilizing this tactic and do so less often. Congressional representatives are Washington insiders, and thus they are considered part of the problem.

Another reason candidates are concerned with outsider status is that it may allow them to tap into political forces larger than themselves, such as the populist wave that accompanied the Tea Party in 2010, or rising distrust in government institutions, or a bad economy.[52] There is also some political science research that suggest it is valuable to be considered an outsider in a presidential election, but that most politicians fail to succeed at doing so. In their study of the 2008 presidential election, Melvin Hinich and coauthors discovered through survey research that 68% of people agreed "the federal government is mostly incompetent" and 82% agreed that "the federal government is mostly corrupt," conditions the authors argue are ripe for non-establishment politicians to succeed and establishment politicians to suffer.[53] However, despite the frequent appeals to voters by both Barack Obama and John McCain for reform and against 'the old way of doing things'—and especially by McCain's running mate Sarah Palin, who often described herself and McCain as "mavericks"—the majority of voters did not see any of presidential or vice presidential candidates as outsiders.[54]

Voters do, however, fascinatingly consider *themselves* outsiders, which bolsters the argument that to be a political outsider is to be relatable.[55] To be an insider in American politics is to be part of the political or Washington elite. Voters of both parties have trouble identifying with the elite. Washington elites are perceived to be stiff and uncompassionate snobs who eat at expensive restaurants and belong to expensive clubs and take off work for the entire month of August. And no matter how wealthy or politically experienced they are, politicians are constantly trying to distance themselves from these images on the campaign trail by engaging in activities normal Americans do, like using public transportation, eating at diners and fast food stands and having coffee in peoples' living rooms and doing yardwork.

Yet it is a common theme in political science research that voters consistently inaccurately portray themselves and their lifestyles in surveys. For example, Americans consistently over-report the amount of political news they consume and the amount of political knowledge they have, and under-report their incomes. Most Americans, in fact, no matter how poor or wealthy they are, claim to be in the middle class.[56] There is a bias towards wanting to be sophisticated in certain regards, and average in others. Donald Trump seized on these preferences during the 2016 election by fashioning himself as a "blue-collar billionaire."⁵⁷ Although he attended elite schools, he does not speak like an elitist, or even how elitists might imagine a normal person speaks. Although he can afford expensive food, he prefers diet soda, McDonald's and Kentucky Fried Chicken. It is important to him to differentiate himself from the political establishment. Susan Hunston at the University of Birmingham provides a great description of the way in which Trump uses language to define himself as an outsider.

> It is tempting to agree with commentators, themselves professional writers, who are 'simply appalled by Trump's savage mauling of English.' To do so may, however, be to miss the point. All language use contributes to a persona—we continually reinvent ourselves as we write and speak—and Trump's persona is, arguably, carefully crafted as the antithesis of the conventional politician.⁵⁸

As Hunston indicates above, Trump's ability to redefine and vilify the political elite even from within it has been a key part of cultivating his persona as a blue-collar billionaire. Here is Trump at a 2018 rally in North Dakota engaging in precisely this exercise while speaking directly to a crowd of supporters.

> I hate it. I mean these people, they call it the elite . . . We got more money, we got more brains, we got better houses and apartments, we got nicer boats, we're smarter than they are and they say they're the elite. You're the elite, we're the elite . . . Let's call ourselves, from now on, the super elite.⁵⁹

Speaking to supporters in South Carolina on the presidential campaign trail, Trump remarked, in a similar fashion, "I'm telling you, I used to use the word incompetent. Now I just call them [the Obama administration] stupid. I went to an Ivy League school. I'm very highly educated. I know words, I have the best words . . . but there is no better word than stupid."⁶⁰ Once again, it is much easier to dismiss Trump as unknowledgeable or unintelligent than it is to acknowledge that the rhetorical strategy he is using, whether it comes naturally or not, is a multilayered one most politicians would be at pains to master. Not unlike a mob member who has to perform a brutal act against the out-group to prove his loyalty to the in-group, Trump's all-out assault on the elite class of which he has been part his entire life can be conceived as a love letter to his working-class supporters. When Trump attacks elites, he is saying "I'm not one of them anymore, I'm one of you." Yet Trump still leans on his elite life experience to give him credibility. Because he has brushed shoulders with the Washington "swamp" his whole life, Trump purports to know first-hand how depraved it is. Recall Trump's 2016 RNC acceptance speech in which he declared, "Nobody knows the system better than me, which is why I alone can fix it."⁶¹ There is something in Trump's rhetoric everyone can relate to. Unabashed wealth and success for the coastal capitalists, a clear distinction between friends and enemies—and good people and

Figure 3.5 Donald Trump at Trump Steaks Event

Donald Trump eats a piece of steak in 2007 at a Sharper Image launch event for Trump Steaks. Trump's preference for well-done steak was the subject of elite criticism on the 2016 campaign trail, although research has demonstrated that many Americans, like Trump, do tend to order their steak this way in restaurants. Diet and lifestyle are examples of the kind of personal information that has become interesting to voters in the era of candidate-centered campaigns.

bad people, aliens and citizens, and takers and makers—and what sociologists Michele Lamont and coauthors call "moral absolution" for white working class men without college degrees.[62]

Even something as trivial as Trump's preference for well-done steak (see Figure 3.5) can be seen as a small part of his credibility with working people. Even though a majority of Americans report that they prefer to eat steak medium-rare (the "better" and socially desirable way to order, according to elites in the food community)[63] when they are asked in surveys, real data from Longhorn steakhouse suggests that when it comes to actually ordering the food they want, Americans ask for their steak more well-done, just like Donald Trump.[64]

5. Large and Passionate Following

The size of a political candidate's social media following matters because in addition to becoming a vehicle for interacting with voters and shaping one's public image, social media channels like Instagram, YouTube, Facebook, and especially

Twitter have themselves become mass media channels. In 2016, 44% of people reported to Pew Research that they learned about the election from social media, as opposed to the 24% that learned from television and print outlets.[65] In the last three major presidential election cycles (2016, 2012, and 2008) the most successful candidates have been the most savvy users of social media to both promote their campaign messages and to engage and energize voters. Perhaps no year was a clearer example of this than 2008, what scholars have deemed the "first social media election."[66] Barack Obama used his large social media following as a data collection and mobilization tool, in addition to keeping his followers engaged and informed about the status of his campaign. In 2012, the Obama campaign was using four more social media channels than the Romney campaign, and by 2016, the way presidential candidates were using social media, particularly Twitter, had changed completely.

Donald Trump de-professionalized the use of social media by sharing his thoughts extemporaneously, many times with grammatical errors, imperfect syntax, and messages that had not been vetted by a communications staff. Trump's Twitter account gave his supporters the impression that they were hearing directly from him, for better, or for worse. According to Enli et al., 78% of Trump's total retweets during the 2016 election came from ordinary users rather than campaign staffers, media outlets, or other public figures, a risk Hillary Clinton's mistake-averse campaign was too careful to take.[67] Ordinary users and voters were the people Clinton, like Trump, wanted to empower, but they were also unpredictable. Trump, more than Clinton, understood that Twitter is an attention-getting tool, not just an additional channel the campaign could use to disseminate information. The main purpose was to make Trump's supporters feel close to him, and to build the impression that he was accessible and authentic. Not only did Trump's number of social media followers dwarf Clinton's (he had 54.1 million followers as of August 2018, compared to Hillary Clinton's 23.3 million followers) but even when Trump, Clinton, and Bernie Sanders tweeted at the same rate, Americans were more responsive to Trump's tweets. They received more attention.[68]

Most celebrities, like Trump, excel at using social media, because they understand that it is a unique public relations tool, a useful way to allow fans and supporters a glimpse into their world without the filter of print and television. Speaking about model Chrissy Teigen, *US Weekly* writes, "One look at Chrissy Teigen's social media accounts and it's clear that the model doesn't hold back—and that's what makes her so relatable. That candor has helped her gain more than eight million followers on Twitter, as well as earning her a block from the President of the United States Donald Trump in 2017."[69] Some celebrities, such as Justin Bieber and Kim Kardashian, even achieved fame through social media, and have perfected ways to engage fans using various platforms. And that world is probably more interesting than the world of politicians. At 107 million followers, singer Katy Perry leads the pack in terms of her Twitter presence, and professional soccer player Christiano Ronaldo has the most followed Facebook and Instagram pages, with 122 million and 169 million followers, respectively. (Keep in mind only 139 million people voted in the 2016 election). Of these channels, Twitter features more political content and is the most impersonal. 48% of Twitter users predominantly follow people on Twitter they do not know personally, while only 3% of Facebook users mostly follow people they do not know.[70]

Figure 3.6 illustrates a significant statistical difference in the number of Twitter followers that celebrities have—an average of 18.1 million—versus the number of followers politicians have—an average of 1.9 million. Meryl Streep and Clint Eastwood do not have Twitter accounts, which suggests this difference could be even larger had they been included. As we have discussed here, social media is not only a measure of fame, like name recognition, but it is a measure of interest and a possible willingness to support someone. These are critical tools for politics. Celebrities who have used social media their entire lives either

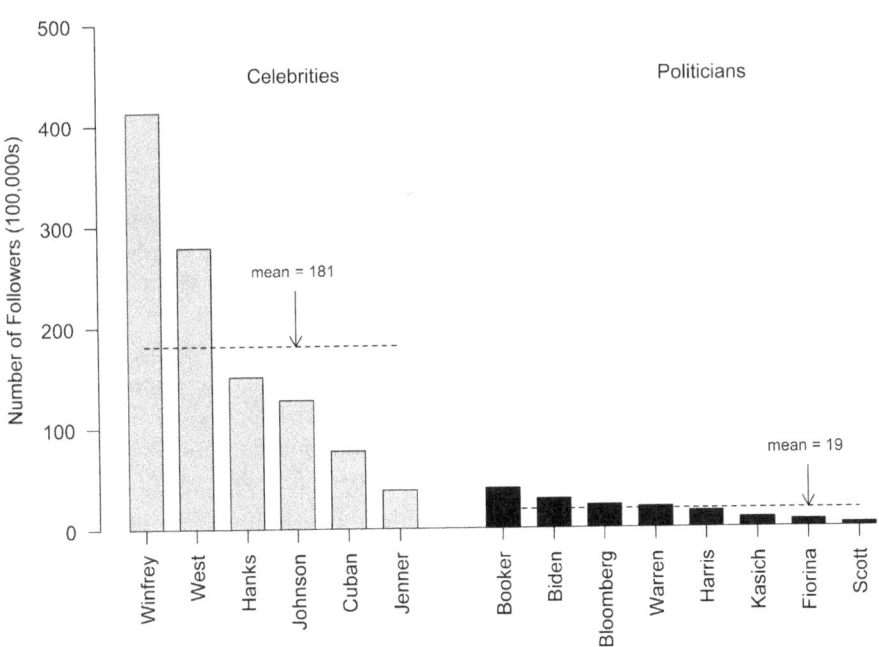

Figure 3.6 Twitter Followers

For ease of comparison, the order in which candidates' names appear is the same in Figures 3.6 and 3.7 although their scores on each measure fluctuate. Candidates as they appear from left to right on the graph include: Oprah Winfrey, Kanye West, Tom Hanks, Dwayne "The Rock" Johnson, Mark Cuban, Caitlyn Jenner Cory Booker, Joe Biden, Michael Bloomberg, Elizabeth Warren, Kamala Harris, John Kasich, Carly Fiorina, and Tim Scott. Clint Eastwood and Meryl Streep did not have Twitter accounts at the time of the study and are thus not included.

to gain notoriety or make themselves seem more accessible and transparent for fans also have a leg-up in this regard. While politicians must do the tedious work of humanizing themselves and making themselves appear relatable, celebrities have already done this for many years, in part through the use of social media. Finally, there is a direct relationship between social media and political action. Social media platforms may inspire Americans to visit their polling place, send a candidate money, or attend a political rally.

6. Fundraising

Among the most consistent and enduring findings in political science research is that in order for a political candidate to be viable at any level of elective office she needs to have adequate funds to run a competitive campaign. Fundraising ability, like name recognition and favorability, is a classic component of what election scholars most often refer to as "challenger quality" or candidate quality. The idea is simply that certain people make better political candidates than other people, and the better candidates possess a common core of attributes and resources, the most obvious of which is having previously held elective office (since winning a previous campaign is evidence that voters responded positively to the candidate in the past). Fundraising, in fact, is such an integral part of challenger quality that some scholars have even used money raised in a campaign as a proxy for candidate quality as a whole.[71] Despite a variety of disagreements in the congressional research about how to code candidate quality, every major study on the topic since 1980 has consistently shown that higher quality House and Senate candidates are the candidates that raise more money and get more votes.[72] Moreover, congressional scholars have found that the stage at which candidates collect funds matters, whereas early money raised significantly predicts fundraising success later on in a campaign, and is therefore more important that late money raised no matter the source it comes from.[73] Yet other scholars have argued that fundraising is not the only factor that determines how well outsiders and challengers fare in elections, because self-funded candidates more often lose elections than win them.[74] Moreover, the candidate with the most funds is not always the winner, as we have seen many times at all levels of the electoral process.

The interplay between celebrity status and fundraising challenges the scholarship on candidate quality and money spent in elections in several other ways. First, the congressional elections literature assumes that incumbents have an easier time raising funds than challengers on average. This makes sense, since incumbents have built-in donor networks. Yet celebrities who are running for office for the first time also have access to donor networks that they have called on for other purposes, such as charity, or perhaps they have been avid fundraisers for other candidates. Donald Trump again proves to be a valuable example of the celebrity fundraising advantage. Trump, in previous election years, such as 2012, had been a powerful part of the Republican fundraising machine. Trump was called on extensively to bring glamour and excitement to the Romney campaign. Despite Romney's concern with Trump's controversial birther conspiracy against Barack Obama in 2012, it was not enough to prevent him from courting the candidate's endorsement at a high-profile Las Vegas event with Trump in February 2012. Romney took the stage with Trump and reluctantly declared, "There are some things that you just can't quite imagine in your life; this is one of them."[75] Donors were so enthusiastic about attending a Trump-hosted Romney fundraiser in the reality star's Manhattan penthouse in April 2012, in fact, that the event had to be split up into two shifts of 400 people total, each paying $50,000 to attend. The Romney campaign asked the Trumps to host a similar event again after Romney clinched the nomination. John Dickerson, who compared Romney's Las Vegas event with Trump to a movie in which "the straight-laced square goes to Vegas with his outrageous friend" hit the mark exactly right in his description of the strategy involving Trump:

> For Romney, Trump is a useful tool. As the Donald himself put it, "Part of the beauty of me is that I'm very rich." He says he's noodling a super PAC, and he can raise money for Romney and gather together other people who can raise money. Romney certainly could never distance himself from Trump (let alone denounce him) for fear of alienating those donors the campaign is trying to reach by offering a dinner with the host of *The Apprentice*. Trump is probably popular with some of the working-class voters who cheer for a pugnacious loudmouth and whom Romney wants to attract.[76]

Interestingly enough, Romney also deployed Trump to make hard-hitting robocalls in Michigan attacking Rick Santorum. "I'm tired of Rick Santorum pretending he's some kind of D.C. outsider," Trump said in the call. "Rick Santorum is a career politician that's never had a job in the private sector—he doesn't know about producing jobs."[77] Now imagine if a celebrity candidate were to open her rolodex and wield those assets on her own behalf, as Trump did in 2016. It brings us to another aspect of celebrity fundraising that does not match up with the congressional fundraising literature.

Congressional studies argue that the reason fundraising success is so closely associated with electoral outcomes is because of what it buys a candidate—namely the ability to increase her name recognition through media buys and to buy more opportunities to convince voters why she is the better candidate. Celebrities, as I have already established, do not need tools to build their name recognition, so money spent on media can be used exclusively for getting their message out and attacking their opponents. There is also some evidence that celebrities, like other political outsiders, may have different media strategies than incumbents. For example, one study by Christine Williams and Jeff Gulati suggests that "outsider" candidates

Barack Obama in 2008 and Donald Trump in 2016 spent a higher proportion of their funds on digital marketing strategies than "traditional" media buys (such as television advertising) giving them an advantage over their establishment opponents who were less willing to adopt new technologies.[78] To make a long story short, celebrities rival incumbents and traditional candidates with their access to high-quality donor networks, but require fewer funds to accomplish the goals politicians must fulfill. Celebrities are already known and beloved, and they have better and more innovative channels for sharing their messages. This might be one reason why Donald Trump got away with spending so much less than Hillary Clinton throughout the course of his campaign. Trump's total expenditures of $340 million, including more than $66 million of his own money, were dwarfed by Hillary Clinton's $581 million. It is also important to note that by spending his own money, Trump was able to benefit from another message—he did not need donors and he did not need the party to fund the campaign—he was able to send a message that he was not asking anything of the public.

"First of all, I don't know why I need so much money," Trump said in an early campaign appearance in New Hampshire. "You know, I go around, I make speeches. I talk to reporters. I don't even need commercials, if you want to know the truth."[79] Trump also spent his money differently, with a smaller, more flexible staff, less allotted to travel, and more investment in digital get-out-the-vote efforts in his final days in Michigan, Florida, Pennsylvania and Wisconsin, although Hillary still out-spent him in the end.[80]

Donald Trump, was of course, not the only person to rely on celebrity status to fundraise during the 2016 election. Even with her deep donor networks stretching back to her husband's 1992 presidential bid, Hillary Clinton still saw the value of enlisting the support of Hollywood elites to excite other donors and justify huge price tags for fundraising dinners. At a San Francisco Bay Area fundraiser in April 2016, Clinton charged couples $353,400 to sit with George and Amal Clooney at the head table at the event.[81] Over the course of her campaign, she enlisted the support of Anna Wintour, Eva Longoria, Busy Phillips, Seth MacFarlane, Diane Von Furstenberg, Steven Spielberg, Justin Timberlake, and Jessica Biel, to name a few. Even if the events were hosted by celebrities, many times, donors were also promised a surprise appearance by "a mystery guest or two" to make the event even more glittery.[82]

Even if it is unclear whether celebrity candidates do, on average, raise more campaign funds than traditional politicians, it is evident that many causes, both political and apolitical, have relied on the support of celebrities to survive for many years. Of the efforts of celebrities like Bono to raise funds on behalf of organizations like Save the Children, CEO Justin Forsyth writes, "In my experience, the benefits of celebrity are not fables but real—and can produce very concrete results."[83] Public relations experts claim that aside from actual funds raised or donated by celebrities and their friends, celebrities bring credibility and attention to the fundraisers they attend, which then encourages other donors to support the same cause. In a complex and fast-moving media environment, public attention, whether garnered on behalf of a candidate, a charitable organization, or one's own campaign, is the most valuable ingredient to success.[84]

7. Media Attention

Even when celebrities run traditional political campaigns, their campaigns differ substantially from those of traditional politicians. When celebrities raise money, they tend not to use as much on television ads. They are already well-known, many times well-liked, and have invested an entire career molding their persona into something Americans find appealing. When celebrities appear in the media, they seem to be a breath of fresh air for television producers, who detest the wrote lines of traditional politicians, the way the evade questions, and the stiffness that comes with constantly having to protect yourself from making a mistake on a news broadcast. Not only do celebrities wiggle their way out of uncomfortable questions with ease from decades of practice, they are often not asked difficult questions to begin with. News anchors often lower the bar for celebrities. They understand first, that hard-hitting interviews are not requisite for ratings when it comes to popular athletes, musicians, and actors—audiences tune in to be entertained—and second, that their own popularity might be at risk if they are perceived to be bullying a person with millions of devoted fans.

Most of the time, celebrities do not have controversial political track records to defend, and they do not have to swat away accusations of being obstructionist or a hyper-partisan or of trying to amass political power for their own professional stake. Instead, when celebrities give interviews on political shows, they are often asked about themselves, why they are running, or really, anything else they want to talk about. This often happened with Donald Trump on the 2016 campaign trail. He was not taken seriously as a Republican primary candidate early in the race, so news shows invited him on for fun, and he delivered on fun every time. Trump was also given the advantage of telephone interviews on TV shows such as *Morning Joe* (MSNBC) and *Fox & Friends* (Fox News), where his presence was so desired that the traditional rules of face-to-face journalism were thrown out. Trump was given a platform where he could talk at length, perhaps with notes in front of him, and could dominate interviews by making it difficult for anchors to interrupt him. His rallies were so entertaining and bombastic that television stations aired them without interruption, sometimes even before he was on stage, cut into the rallies of other candidates, and in effect, gifted Trump hours of unfiltered coverage that amounted to billions in free advertising dollars. By February 2016, when Donald Trump was racking up primary wins despite his comparatively tiny campaign budget, this discrepancy became quickly apparent. Donald Trump had only spent $10 million on television advertising, less than John Kasich, Chris Christie, Ted Cruz, Hillary Clinton, Bernie Sanders, Marco Rubio, and especially Jeb Bush, who led the pack at $82 million.[85] By the end of the campaign in November 2016, Donald Trump had benefitted from $6 billion of free media. Hillary Clinton received less than half that figure at $2.8 billion.[86]

To understand the extent of Trump's complete saturation of the airwaves in 2016, it is important to first distinguish between earned and paid media. Earned media, of the kind we just mentioned—television interviews, Twitter and Facebook mentions, print articles—is far more valuable than paid media in a campaign. Candidates do not get more airtime because they bought it, they get more airtime because they deserve it. And the way they demonstrate to producers that they deserve it is because they provide raw ingredients that make for good television. Andrew Tyndall enumerates these ingredients as follows.[87] Trump's candidacy, and the candidacy of all celebrities for that matter, was newsworthy in and of itself. Never before had a candidate with no political or military experience made it so far in an election, and neither had someone who had so confidently tossed decades of accumulated campaign knowledge in the trash can. Trump is also a master of sound bites. He makes nicknames for his opponents (who can ever forget the phrases "Crooked Hillary" "Lyin' Ted Cruz" or "Low Energy Jeb Bush"), says politically incorrect things—breaking the rules is news after all—and unapologetically inundates the public with his political messages. Even now that he is in the White House, Trump continues his "Make American Great Again" slogans, along with describing Washington as a rigged system and a swamp. By speaking in simple and memorable phrases, Trump makes it easier for the media to get his points across for him. He provides unfettered access to himself and his campaign, rarely turning down interviews, even as he wages war on the news media itself. His television appearances *are* his 2020 re-election campaign, rather than coverage of his campaign.

As Figure 3.7 shows, Donald Trump is not the only celebrity who excels at garnering media attention. In order to assess the amount of media interest in each candidate, I tabulated total Google search results associated with each celebrity and politician's name. Although Google search results are blunt approximations of media interest and fluctuate depending on the amount a particular person is in the news, they are valuable indications of cumulative multimedia attention. Results were collected in August 2018 using a Google "Incognito" search to ensure than no previous search results and learned browser preferences played a role in the search results that appeared. On average, a search for a celebrity's first and last name yielded 53.2 million results, while a search for a politician's name yielded an average of 34.1 million results, a significantly lower number. Search

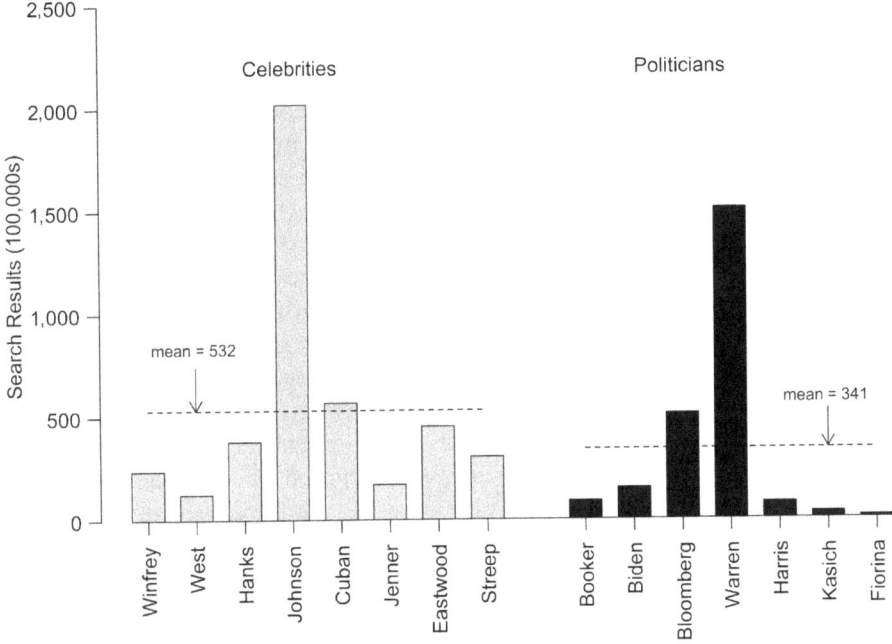

Figure 3.7 Google Search Results

For ease of comparison, the order in which candidates' names appear is the same in Figures 3.6 and 3.7 although their scores on each measure fluctuate. Candidates as they appear from left to right on the graph include: Oprah Winfrey, Kanye West, Tom Hanks, Dwayne "The Rock" Johnson, Mark Cuban, Caitlyn Jenner, Clint Eastwood, Meryl Streep, Cory Booker, Joe Biden, Michael Bloomberg, Elizabeth Warren, Kamala Harris, John Kasich, and Carly Fiorina. Tim Scott was not included in the graphic because his name is too common to yield accurate results. Google "Incognito" mode was used in order to ensure that information from past searches did not skew the results.

engine results are a good proxy for media attention because the results are an accumulation of news stories, video clips, and social media conversations about the person. Again, we see that Dwayne Johnson and Elizabeth Warren are each pulling the mean upwards in their respective categories. This makes sense, since Elizabeth Warren is frequently at the center of discussions about possible 2020 contenders to challenge Donald Trump, and Dwayne Johnson was the most highly-paid, well-liked actor in 2018.

It is also important to consider structural factors that have played a role in the ability of celebrities to garner more media attention and recognition than their traditional political counterparts. The expansion of media choice that has occurred in the 21st century—more outlets, more channels, the proliferation of news on the internet—rather than increase political knowledge among the public, has actually contributed to its decline. Instead of giving the public more opportunities to consume news and learn new information, the diversification and expansion of the media has allowed people to choose entertainment instead of news, and when people choose news, they now have an opportunity to choose news outlets that reinforce their preexisting political views, a phenomenon political scientists call partisan selective exposure. To make matters worse, the same set of forces has given rise to infotainment—a combination of hard and soft news, politics and Hollywood gossip, or news packaged as entertainment (think panels of politically polarized cable contributors screaming at each other during primetime, or President Donald Trump calling former *Apprentice* contestant and White House senior staffer Omarosa Manigault Newman a "dog" via Twitter).

There is an active debate among scholars about whether infotainment is good for democracy. On the one hand, scholars argue that if people are tuning into news channels that look more like dramatic television, they are getting information they may not be exposed to otherwise, no matter how unserious the packaging. On the other hand, these types of forums have made it even easier for candidates like Donald Trump to succeed. If political campaigns look increasingly like reality shows, maybe we should not be so surprised when an actual seasoned reality television star wins. Low political knowledge in the electorate also plays a role, because voters cannot hold certain parties and politicians accountable if they do not know who they are. They also cannot adequately fact-check what political candidates are saying. As we saw from the name recognition survey earlier, just over 60% of respondents in the Mechanical Turk sample could identify former Vice President Joe Biden. In an Annenberg Public Policy Survey released in 2014, only 36% of Americans could name all three branches of government, only 38% knew who controlled the House and Senate, and only 27% knew it takes a two-third majority in the House and Senate to override a presidential veto.[88] Further evidence from psychology suggests that the politically ignorant do not even know they are politically ignorant. In fact, they are more confident in their political knowledge than respondents who have high political knowledge, a phenomenon known as the Dunning-Kruger effect. This over-confidence in knowledge is even further exacerbated when partisanship becomes salient, such as when one is arguing with someone she knows belongs to the opposite political party.[89]

Moreover, celebrity candidates do not shy away from appearing on nonpolitical shows to advocate for themselves. They understand that shows with no political content often have more viewers and a different demographic of viewers than political news shows. For example, when Donald Trump visited *The Dr. Oz Show* to perform a "big reveal" of his medical records on the 2016 campaign trail, Hillary Clinton declined to do the same. While she released a clean bill of health from her physician to the public, politicians like Hillary Clinton, especially after being elected, often shy away from media outlets that present opportunities to make gaffes or are not very structured. The same theme can be seen in how both candidates used Twitter throughout the campaign. While Donald Trump's tweets were, like many of his interviews, an unedited stream-of-consciousness, Hillary Clinton's are packaged and professionalized and seem much less transparent than the rantings of her opponent.

There is also, of course, a gender-related difference in the way in which male and female candidates garner media attention, which cannot be excluded from comparisons of media coverage of Hillary Clinton and Donald Trump in 2016. Even though recent studies on gender and congressional elections have shown that only negative attention with regard to a candidate's appearance can affect electoral outcomes, and that these negative impacts are identical for male and female candidates, Donald Trump, as a performer, explicitly used Hillary Clinton's appearance against her often on the campaign trail. He floated stories about her lack of stamina, her mental and physical wellness and whether she was up to the job of being president, and as a result, these stories were reported and recirculated in the media. Perhaps nobody will forget when Donald Trump, in a veiled reference to gender, suggested that Hillary Clinton could not be president because she did not have "a presidential look." Trump later echoed the statement in front of a mostly male audience, saying, "And she looks presidential, fellows?"[90] The advantage for Trump, in making attacks like these, is that it is part of his act as an entertainer. As long as Trump has been in show business, he has fixated on the physical appearance of women, and he has assailed women on the basis of personal character.

When Trump is confronted over comments like these about Hillary Clinton, he can say, and the White House often does, that Trump is a counter-puncher, and that voters knew his personality when he was elected. But it does not change the fact that for male and female celebrities, there are also gender dynamics at play. We might expect, for this reason, for female celebrities to be less preferable candidates than male celebrities, for example. Gender and race are two critical forces in candidate perception, and it is important to remember that all celebrity candidates are not created equal. Variables like race and gender affect how candidates are represented in the media. Because there is inherent bias in the way Hollywood, for instance, portrays women, voters may not remember women celebrities as macho sports or war heroes or quirky scientists, but as sex symbols, mothers, caretakers, or neurotic friends, "damsels in distress" or "manic pixie dream girls," not exactly roles that directly map onto political leadership.[91] In political campaigns, too, across years of study, scholars have concluded that "gender stereotypes affect the manner in which the media assess women candidates."[92]

Theory and Expectations

In the next chapter, I will share results from survey experiments aimed to determine whether voters prefer celebrity candidates to well-known traditional politicians. We know from the literature reviewed as part of this chapter that voters claim to prefer politicians to celebrities when they are asked straightforward questions in surveys, but when they vote, they often demonstrate that they do prefer celebrities. We also know, from each of the "deadly ins" presented in this chapter, that celebrities do in fact differ from politicians on several variables that are closely linked to electability. It should not be ignored that even though some differences are much larger than others, on every single variable we measured here—name recognition, favorability, relatability, followers, and media attention—celebrities scored higher on average than well-known politicians. Even when compared to politicians that are frequently in the news, celebrities get more media attention. Even when compared to politicians who are the most famous among their peers, celebrities are more famous. Even compared to politicians who are the most popular, celebrities are more popular. Even when compared to politicians who are considered to be down to earth, who interact with supporters often, and who work hard to cultivate an ordinary image, celebrities are more relatable. And even when compared to politicians with the largest social media following on the most used platform by politicians, Twitter, celebrities have more followers.

The three key variables that drive differences in evaluations between celebrities and politicians include name recognition, where we saw vast and statistically meaningful differences, a large and passionate social media following, where we saw celebrities trounced politicians in the number of people who pay attention to them, and media attention as a whole, where celebrities generated a significantly larger number of search results than their politician peers. Those findings help motivate the following hypotheses that are tested in the next chapter.

Hypothesis 1: Respondents prefer celebrity candidates to politicians when both candidates belong to the same party. Based on what we know about the power of partisan identification, it is not a reasonable expectation that celebrity status is a more overwhelming predictor of vote choice than party ID. However, within party, in a primary contest for example, I predict that celebrity candidates will outperform traditional politicians. I predict the results will be the same in the Democratic and Republican mock primaries described in the next chapter.

Hypothesis 2: Respondents are more likely to choose celebrity candidates when celebrities are running for lower offices, such as Congress, rather than higher office, such as the presidency. We know from previous research that a concentration of celebrities can be found in lower levels of office, such as Congress, where political scientist David Canon finds, for example, that the House has been comprised of roughly 30% political amateurs, including celebrities, since the 1960s. Because celebrities are less politically experienced, I expect that voters will be more willing to take a chance on an outsider running for a congressional seat than an outsider running for president. Celebrities also carry a substantial name recognition advantage in lower level races. Whereas the politicians presented in this chapter are all presidential contenders, most congressional and state-level office seekers are relatively unknown.

Hypothesis 3: Because of well-documented gender biases in media coverage of political candidates as well as the roles women play in Hollywood, I expect that the celebrity advantage for hypothetical female candidates is not as strong as it is for male candidates, within both parties. For the reasons discussed in Chapters 2 and 3, many of the advantages male celebrities enjoy on the campaign trail are not available to women. Women's roles in Hollywood, in sports, and in music do not translate as effectively to the political arena as do men's.

Notes

1. Sargent, Greg. June 10, 2016. "Mitch McConnell Just Made a Devastating Admission about Trump—and the GOP." *The Washington Post.*
2. Blake, David Haven. 2016. *Liking Ike: Eisenhower, Advertising, and the Rise of Celebrity Politics.* New York, NY: Oxford University Press. Page 15.
3. Ibid, Page 61.
4. Ibid.
5. Ibid.
6. Ibid, Page 57.
7. Ibid.
8. Blake 2012, Blake 2016, and Lawrence, Cooper. 2009. *Cult of Celebrity: What Our Fascination with the Stars Reveals About Us.* Guilford, CT: Globe Pequot Press. Page 36.
9. While the advent of the Internet has made it much easier to catalogue celebrities who have run for public office in recent years, there is no encyclopedia of celebrity politics that allows us to ensure we have not left any off of this list. A comprehensive list of entertainers and athletes who have run for office throughout United States history would be a valuable tool for future research.
10. Ross, Steven. 2011. *Hollywood Left and Right: How Movie Stars Shaped American Politics.* New York, NY: Ozford University Press.
11. Blake 2016, Page 53.
12. Blake 2016, Page 23.
13. Terrell, Anthony. November 13, 2016. "Trump Out-Campaigned Clinton by 50 Percent in Key Battleground States in Final Stretch." *NBC News.*
14. Draper, Robert. August 10, 2009. "Obama's Keeper: Valerie Jarrett." *The Independent.*
15. Bartels, Larry M. 1988. *Presidential Primaries and the Dynamics of Public Choice.* Princeton, NJ: Princeton University Press. Page 57. As quoted in Kam and Zechmeister 2013.
16. Stokes, Donald E., and Warren E. Miller. 1962. "Party Government and the Saliency of Congress." *Public Opinion Quarterly* 26(4): 531–46. Page 541. As quoted in Kam and Zechmeister 2013.
17. Coates, Sarah et al. 2006. "Implicit Memory and Consumer Choice: The Mediating Role of Brand Familiarity." *Applied Cognitive Psychology* 20(8): 1101–1116.
18. "Just Tell Him You're the President." Comedians in Cars Getting Coffee. Season 7, Episode 1.
19. Abramowitz, Alan I. 1975. "Name Familiarity, Reputation, and the Incumbency Effect in a Congressional Election." Western Political Quarterly 28(4): 668–84. Page 674. As quoted in Kam and Zechmeister 2013.
20. Kam, Cindy and Elizabeth Zechmeister. 2013. "Name Recognition and Candidate Support." *American Journal of Political Science* 57(4): 971–986.
21. Utych, Stephen and Cindy Kam. 2013. "Viability, Information-Seeking, and Vote Choice." *Journal of Politics* 76 (1): 152–166.
22. Fukumoto, Kentaro and Hirofumi Miwa. 2018. "Share the Name, Share the Vote: A Natural Experiment of Name Recognition." *Journal of Politics* 80(2): 726–730.
23. Shaw, Jonathan. July-August 2017. "Star Power in Politics." *Harvard Magazine.*

24. Reeves, Justin. (2015). "Famous Amateurs in a Professional's Race: The Causes and Consequences of Celebrity Politics." Dissertation accessed via the eScholarship database at the University of California San Diego.

25. Broockman, David and Donald Green. 2013. "Do Online Advertisements Increase Political Candidates' Name Recognition or Favorability? Evidence From Randomized Field Experiments." *Political Behavior* 36(2): 263–289.

26. Concerning Figures 3.1, 3.2, 3.3, 3.4, 3.6 and 3.7, Michael Bloomberg was associated with the Republican Party at the time the survey was conducted. This is a sample of prominent Republican and Democratic celebrities and politicians who were frequently in the news at the time the survey was conducted. It is not intended to represent the population of all politically active celebrities. Some increasingly active Republican celebrities, such as Ted Nugent, Roseanne Barr and Stacey Dash, were not included, and some increasingly active Democratic celebrities, such as LeBron James, Taylor Swift, and Will Ferrell were not included.

27. Levay, Kevin and Jeremy Freese and James Druckman. Accessed 2018. "The Demographic and Political Composition of Mechanical Turk Samples." Working Paper.

28. Berinsky, Adam and Gregory Huber and Gabriel Lenz. 2012. "Evaluating Online Labor Markets for Political Research." *Political Analysis* 20(1): 351–368.

29. Green, Miranda. April 18, 2017. "Adviser: Carly Fiorina 'Strongly Considering' Virginia Senate run." *CNN*.

30. Debenedetti, Gabriel. February 23, 2018. "Kasich's Team Gears up for Possible 2020 Bid." *Politico*.

31. Blake, Aaron. September 8, 2017. "The Top 15 Possible 2020 Democratic Nominees, Ranked." *The Washington Post*.

32. Vox Populi Polling. Results collected from June 13, 2016 to June 16, 2018. "2020 Democrat Nomination Consideration." Presentation uploaded by PopPolling on Scribd.com.

33. Lewis-Beck, Michael et al. 2008. *The American Voter Revisited*. Ann Arbor, MI: University of Michigan Press. Page 31.

34. Gerber, Alan, et al. 2011. "How Large and Long-Lasting Are the Persuasive Effects of Televised Campaign Ads? Results From a Randomized Field Experiment. *American Political Science Review* 105 (1): 135–150.

35. Lewis-Beck et al. 2008.

36. Shaw, Daron. 2001. "The Impact of News Media Favorability and Candidate Events in Presidential Campaign." *Political Communication* 16(2): 183–202.

37. Elis, Roy and Sunshine Hillygus and Norman Nie. 2010. "The Dynamics of Candidate Evaluations and Vote Choice in 2008: Looking to the Past or Future?" *Electoral Studies* 29(4): 582–593.

38. Zurcher, Anthony. October 20, 2016. "Presidential Debate: Who Won—Trump or Clinton?" *BBC News*.

39. Shepard, Steven. June 17, 2016. "Trump's Poll Ratings in a Historic Hole." *Politico*.

40. Ibid.

41. Weisberg, Jacob. February 1, 2012. "Romney Is Kerry. Or Maybe Gore." *Slate*.

42. Stevenson, Seth. February 11, 2016. "A Cold One with Donald." *Slate*.

43. Ibid.

44. Bilello, Joseph. May 10, 2017. "Sorry Hillary, 'Who Would You Rather Have a Beer With' Is Still an Exact Science in Choosing the President." *Townhall*.

45. Rasmussen Reports. June 15, 2016. "Would You Rather Have a Beer with Clinton or Trump?" RasmussenReports.com.

46. Haidt, Jonathan. June 5, 2012. "Why Working Class People Vote Conservative." *The Guardian*.

47. Schuessler, Alexander. 2000. "Expressive Voting." *Rationality and Society* 12(1): 87–119. Page 87–88.

48. Lee, Dwight and Ryan Murphy. 2017. "An Expressive Voting Model of Anger, Hatred, Harm and Shame." *Public Choice* 173(3): 307–323. Page 307.
49. Dovi, Suzanne and ed. Edward N. Zalta. 2017. "Political Representation." *The Stanford Encyclopedia of Philosophy* (Winter Edition). Available at https://plato.stanford.edu/entries/political-representation/
50. Mansbridge, Jane. 1999. "Should Blacks Represent Blacks and Women Represent Women? A Contingent "Yes"." *Journal of Politics* 61(3): 628–657. Page 628.
51. Pennock, Roland. 1979. *Democratic Political Theory*. Princeton, NJ: Princeton University Press. Page 314. As quoted in Mansbridge 1999, Page 629.
52. Stewart, Jared Alan. 2018. "In Through the Out Door: Examining the Use of Outsider Appeals in Presidential Debates." *Presidential Studies Quarterly* 48(1): 93–109.
53. Melvin Hinich and Daron Shaw and Taofang Huang. 2010. "Insiders, Outsiders and Voters in the U.S. 2008 Presidential Election." *Presidential Studies Quarterly* 40(2): 264–285. Page 278.
54. Ibid.
55. Ibid.
56. Shenker-Osario, Anat. August 1, 2013. "Why Americans All Believe They Are 'Middle Class'." *The Atlantic*.
57. Cooper, Matthew. November 9, 2016. "How Donald Trump Courted White Americans to Victory." *Newsweek*.
58. Hunston, Susan. 2017. "Donald Trump and the Language of Populism." University of Birmingham "Perspectives" blog post.
59. Sinclair, Harriet. June 28, 2018. "Donald Trump: My Supporters Should Be Called Super Elites Because 'We Got Nicer Boats' and More Money." *Newsweek*.
60. Guest, Steve. December 30, 2015. "Trump: 'I Know Words, I Have The Best Words'—Obama Is 'Stupid'." *The Daily Caller*.
61. Sherman, Amy. July 8, 2016. "Hillary Clinton Says Donald Trump Said 'I Alone Can Fix It.'" *Politifact*.
62. Lamont, Michele, Bo Yun Park, and Elena Ayala-Hurtado. November 8, 2017. "What Trump's Campaign Speeches Show About His Lasting Appeal to the White Working Class." *Harvard Business Review*.
63. Rosner, Helen. February 28, 2017. "Actually, How Donald Trump Orders His Steak Matters." *Eater*.
64. Hickey, Walt and Rachael Dottle. July 3, 2017. "How Americans Order Their Steak." *Five Thirty Eight*.
65. Pew Research Center. July 18, 2016. "Election 2016: Campaigns as a Direct Source of News." Journalism.org.
66. Enli, Gunn. 2017. "Twitter as Arena for the Authentic Outsider: Exploring the Social Media Campaigns of Trump and Clinton in the 2016 US Presidential Election." *European Journal of Communication* 32(1): 50–61. Page 51.
67. Ibid, Page 54.
68. Pew Research 2016.
69. Rodriguez, Karla. October 20, 2017. "The Most Influential Celebrities on Social Media." *US Weekly*.
70. Duggan, Maeve and Aaron Smith. October 25, 2016. "The Political Environment on Social Media." *Pew Research Center*.
71. Squire, Peverill. 1995. "Candidates, Money, and Voters: Assessing the State of Congressional Elections Research." *Political Research Quarterly* 48(4): 891–917. Page 894.
72. See reference to Jacobson 1980 and 1989, Jacobson and Kernell 1981, Squire 1989 and 1992 in Ibid, Page 896.

73. Wilcox et al. 1993. "Seeds for Success: Early Money in Congressional Elections." *Legislative Studies Quarterly* 18(4): 535–551.

74. Steen, Jennifer. 2006. *Self-Financed Candidates in Congressional Elections*. Ann-Arbor, MI: University of Michigan Press.

75. Boxer, Sarah B. April 17, 2012. "Trump-hosted Fundraiser with Ann Romney Set to Raise $600K." *CBS News*.

76. Dickerson, John. May 29, 2012. "Romney Gambles With the Donald." *Slate*.

77. Schultheis, Emily. February 22, 2012. "Trump Robocalls for Romney in Michigan." *Politico*.

78. Williams, Christine and Jeff Gulati. 2018. "Digital Advertising Expenditures in the 2016 Presidential Election." *Social Science Computer Review* 36(4): 406–421.

79. Rogers, Ed. July 1, 2016. "Trump Says His Campaign Doesn't Need Money or Ads. Is He Serious?" *The Washington Post*.

80. Associated Press, Washington. December 9, 2016. "Donald Trump and Hillary Clinton's Final Campaign Spending Revealed." *The Guardian*.

81. Karni, Annie and Kenneth Vogel. March 24, 2016. "Hillary Clinton Asks for $353K to Sit With the Clooneys." *Politico*.

82. Heil, Emily. September 6, 2016. "Hillary Clinton's Celebrity Fundraising Drive Is Getting Bigger." *The Washington Post*.

83. Stanford, Peter and Justin Forsyth. June 25, 2011. "Are celebrities a help or a hindrance to charities?" *The Guardian*.

84. Antunes, Anderson. January 11, 2012. "The 30 Most Generous Celebrities." *Forbes*.

85. Confessore, Nick and Karen Yourish. March 15, 2016. "$2 Billion Worth of Free Media for Donald Trump." *The New York Times*.

86. Sultan, Niv. April 13, 2017. "Election 2016: Trump's Free Media Helped Keep Cost Down, But Fewer Donors Provided More of the Cash." *HuffPost*.

87. Tyndall, Andrew. March 16, 2016. "Why Donald Trump Is King of All Earned Media." *The Hollywood Reporter*.

88. Somin, Ilya. September 18, 2014. "Annenberg Public Policy Center Survey Provides New Evidence of Widespread Political Ignorance." *The Washington Post*.

89. Anson, Ian. 2018. "Partisanship, Political Knowledge, and the Dunning-Kruger Effect." *Political Pscyhology*. Published online April 2. Pages 1–20.

90. Parker, Ashley. September 6, 2016. "Donald Trump Says Hillary Clinton Doesn't Have 'a Presidential Look'." *The New York Times*.

91. Davidson, Renee. February 4, 2016. "The High Cost of Hollywood's Gender Bias." AAUW.

92. Lawless, Jennifer. 2009. "Sexism and Gender Bias in Election 2008: A More Complex Path for Women in Politics." *Politics & Gender* 5(1): 70–80. Page 78.

CHAPTER 4

DO VOTERS PREFER CELEBRITY CANDIDATES TO POLITICIANS?

Evidence From a Paired Comparison Experiment

While the majority of Americans consistently claim in polls not to be interested in or influenced by the political opinions of celebrities, their voting behavior has often suggested otherwise.[1] Research examining this phenomenon in other parts of the world, such as Japan, has even pointed to the tendency of voters to avow to public opinion pollsters that they would never vote for a celebrity, yet in the privacy of the ballot box, celebrities outperform their traditional political counterparts, especially when there is a large field of candidates from which to choose.[2] The evidence collected in Chapter 3 suggests a related pattern may exist in the United States in which survey respondents are reluctant to admit just how warmly they feel toward celebrity candidates. On measures of whether respondents like or feel comradery with celebrities (e.g., favorability and relatability), celebrities are practically statistically indistinguishable from traditional politicians. That is, celebrities are not particularly popular or particularly relatable. On a feeling thermometer, celebrities achieve slightly warmer ratings than politicians, an average of 52.6 out of 100 compared to an average of 48.7 out of 100, respectively. When asked whether celebrities are relatable, respondents barely give celebrities the edge on politicians (28.7% say celebrities are relatable and 27.6% say politicians are relatable). Perhaps the more important finding is that less than a third of respondents felt they could relate to either group.

Yet on the measures intended to gauge interest in and familiarity with celebrities compared to politicians (e.g., name recognition, social media followers, and internet search results), celebrities have politicians soundly beat in every category. An average of 69% of respondents correctly identified celebrities in an open-ended name recognition question that asked respondents to identify a pictured celebrity. Less than 29% of respondents correctly identified politicians in the same exercise. Google searches for celebrities yielded an average of 53 million results. Google searches for politicians yielded an average of 34 million results. Celebrities in the same survey have an average of 18.1 million Twitter followers. Politicians average 1.9 million. What should we gather from this disconnect between the lack of amity toward celebrities, on the one hand, and overwhelming fascination, on the other? Are survey respondents simply lying about their preferences? Are they embarrassed to admit they like celebrities? How could the entertainment industry survive if celebrities were truly so unlikable? How do politicians garner any votes at all?

Political scientists have increasingly turned to survey experiments to gauge the true attitudes and preferences of survey respondents when there is reason to suspect they may not be revealed by simply asking people their views outright. Throughout the 2016 election cycle, political analysts were worried about 'shy Trump voters,' voters who secretly supported Trump but due to his negative public image—which became associated with white supremacy, misogyny, and other socially objectionable attitudes based on his own comments and media coverage of them—would not admit their support for Trump in a survey.[3] In their study of social desirability bias in the 2016 election, for example, Samara Klar, Christopher Weber, and Yanna Krupnikov conclude that respondents were indeed likely to mask the socially undesirable preference of Trump for president, which they attribute to high levels of "self-monitoring" among certain people—in other words, respondents who were most influenced by social norms and social pressure in general.[4] To ascertain this, the authors employed logistic regression models, a statistical model that mimics an experimental setting by holding certain conditions constant, but is not experimental. In almost perfect contrast, a study by Alexander Coppock in 2016 found that respondents who were asked whether they supported Trump outright in a survey were just as likely to admit supporting Trump as respondents who were in the treatment group of a unobtrusive list-experiment (a type of experiment that gives respondents the ability to hide their preferences by asking them to count items on a list rather than name support for specific items).[5] In other words, this second study found no social desirability bias. Until now, different empirical methods have left behind a mixed portrait of evidence. Most importantly, the results are specific to Donald Trump, leaving the public's general preference for celebrity candidates an open question.

In an effort to glean more truthful responses from survey respondents, and to avoid basing conclusions on particular experimental designs that may be idiosyncratic, political scientists have increasingly turned to various forms of paired choice experiments in which respondents register support for two competing options across repeated tasks.[6] Such designs not only allow for more general conclusions, since results can be averaged over many plausible candidate face-offs, but also afford the analyst enhanced statistical power, making it easy to detect differential responses.

At this juncture, it is perhaps useful to recall the three hypotheses outlined at the end of Chapter 3. First, I expect celebrities to garner more support among survey respondents than traditional politicians, within party. Second, I expect survey respondents to be more willing to choose celebrity candidates in races for lower offices, such as a congressional race, than in a presidential race. Third, I expect the celebrity advantage mentioned in Hypothesis 1 to be weaker for female candidates than for male candidates.

The idea of providing voters various head-to-head matchups of political candidates in order to assess who would win under various rules and circumstances has been around since 18th century mathematicians Nicolas de Condorcet and Jean-Charles de Borda identified famous voting paradoxes that still have applicability today. Some scholars maintain the existence of a Borda paradox in the Republican primary in 2016. While Donald Trump consistently beat John Kasich, Ted Cruz, and Marco Rubio in polls in which all the candidates were offered as choices at once, he lost to at least two of them in repeated pairwise contests.[7] A similar dynamic was present in the 1998 Minnesota gubernatorial contest in which Jesse Ventura, running as a Reform Party member, beat the Republican candidate Norm Coleman and the Democratic candidate Skip Humphrey with a plurality of 37% of the votes. Ventura, like Trump, speaks of his victory in terms of his ability to distinguish himself from the other traditional political candidates, but it is also important to remember how numbers and rules can help celebrity candidates distinguish themselves from the rest of the field.

I leverage the pairwise comparison method in this chapter to assess whether voters are more likely to choose celebrities than politicians in a ballot-like setting by offering them many different hypothetical candidate matchups. The matchups include many different celebrities and many different politicians, who vary in race, gender, professional background, and partisan identification. The data come from a March 2018 survey of 6,091 partisans. After a battery of demographic questions, respondents were shown a series of hypothetical candidates for president. Respondents saw two choices at a time, one celebrity and one politician, and were asked for which candidate they would be more likely to vote. Because partisanship is such a powerful determining factor in vote choice, Democrats were only shown Democratic candidates (well-known Democratic politicians, as well as celebrities who have been publicly active in the Democratic party or have expressed an interest in running for elective office), and Republicans were only shown Republican candidates (well-known Republican politicians, as well as celebrities who have been publicly active in the Republican party or have expressed an interest in running for elective office). True Independents—respondents who do not lean toward either party—were not part of this study.

Combinations were drawn at random from the following groups, and each respondent received five pairs of candidates in total. *Democratic Celebrities*: Meryl Streep, Oprah Winfrey, Kanye West, George Clooney, Tom Hanks; *Democratic Politicians*: Elizabeth Warren, Cory Booker, Joe Biden, Kamala Harris, Kirsten

Gillibrand; *Republican Celebrities*: Dwayne "The Rock" Johnson, Clint Eastwood, Caitlyn Jenner, Peyton Manning, Jon Voight; *Republican Politicians*: Donald Trump, Carly Fiorina, John Kasich, Michael Bloomberg, Condoleezza Rice. Recall that randomly drawing candidates from a large pool of celebrities and politicians minimizes the extent to which survey results can be pulled by one particular celebrity or politician about whom a respondent feels strongly. In other words, if there are systematic differences in how respondents in each group evaluate celebrities as a group versus how they evaluate politicians as a group, then we can be more confident that those effects are due to celebrity status as a whole, not to one particular celebrity such as Meryl Streep or Oprah Winfrey. Figures 4.1.A and 4.1.B illustrate how the choices were presented. The question displayed directly above each pair of boxes was "If the election for U.S. President were held today, for which of the following hypothetical candidates would you be most likely to vote?"

For readers who are not familiar with the benefits and drawbacks of survey experiments, it is worth noting why these results are striking. First, by assigning each Republican and Democratic respondent randomly generated pairs from the list of candidates I mentioned before, internal validity is maximized, which means that any variation in outcomes (meaningful differences in how people who received the "treatment" behaved and how people who received the "control" behaved) can be attributed to the treatment itself—in this case, being asked to consider a celebrity candidate—and a valid causal inference can be made. In this experiment, for example, since the pairs of candidates were randomly assigned, we can assume that the Republicans who received certain combinations of candidates rather than other combinations of candidates did not differ in any other way other than the candidates they received. So if we see differential responses depending on whether a celebrity candidate appeared in

Candidate 1	Candidate 2
Meryl Streep	Elizabeth Warren

Figure 4.1.A Example of Democrat Paired Comparison

Candidate 1	Candidate 2
Mike Pence	Jon Voight

Figure 4.1.B Example of Republican Paired Comparison

the matchup, we can be much more confident that differences are due to seeing a celebrity.[8]

As Figure 4.2 shows, the results from this experiment are quite striking and consistent. Democrats appear to be statistically significantly more likely to support celebrity candidates for president than traditional politicians for president, a difference of 21 percentage points ($p < .01$). Republicans are statistically significantly less likely to support celebrities for president than traditional politicians for president, a difference of 26 percentage points ($p < .01$).[9] A few caveats are in order here. While the survey was specifically designed to avoid any particular candidate pulling the results in a certain direction, Donald Trump's popularity among Republicans at the time the survey was launched (87% in June 2018—the highest for any president since opinion of George W. Bush among Republicans in the wake of 9/11) cannot be ignored.[10] It is possible that the strong negative reaction Republicans demonstrated toward celebrity candidates (and the strong positive reaction they had to traditional politicians) could have been pulled by Republican support for Donald Trump. In order to test for this, I re-estimated the results excluding Donald Trump from the analysis. Even after excluding President Trump from the analysis, Republicans still preferred traditional political candidates, as Figure 4.2 shows.

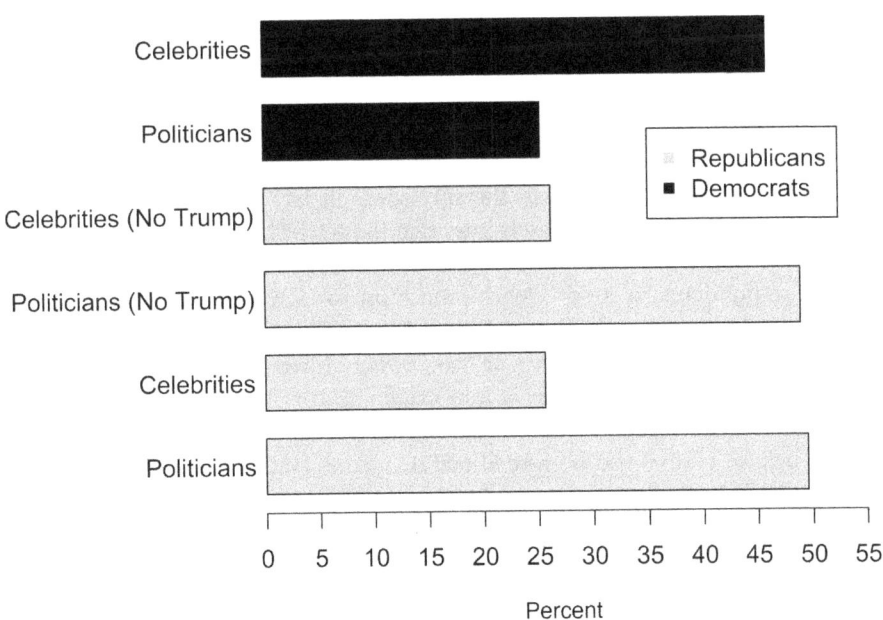

Figure 4.2 Candidate Selection Rates

However, this particular design, in which respondents were assigned random pairs of candidates from which to choose, also has flaws. While random assignment is useful here, the possibility remains that it is not celebrity status, but some other attribute of the individual candidates, that is driving differential support. For example, we may see strong support for Meryl Streep not because she is a celebrity, but because of some unmeasured attribute she possesses that is not considered part of celebrity status. This is the tradeoff of using real-world candidates in experiments: while more realistic (and thus more externally valid) than hypothetical or unnamed candidates, we run the risk that respondents are inferring an unintended treatment from seeing the real-world person's name. However, the paired comparison design helps mitigate this concern. Because we present so many different celebrity candidates and average responses across them, we can relax concerns that an idiosyncratic feature of any one person, rather than celebrity status, is driving results.

Another feature of this experiment that could have played a role in how respondents evaluated candidates is that they were told they were making a choice between two candidates for President of the United States, the highest possible stakes choice a voter must make. For that reason, we cannot rule out the possibility that voters might have chosen differently if they were selecting a candidate for a lower office, such as United States Congress, or Governor of their state. So, while we might expect that Democrats would be even more enthusiastic about a celebrity candidate in a congressional race (if they would vote for a celebrity for the highest office in the land, they would probably vote for them for lower office), for Republicans, perhaps the stakes were too high to select an unqualified celebrity, a person which they may have considered in a lower stakes election.

Finally, it is possible that the Republican narrative surrounding "Hollywood liberals" and strong perceived links between celebrities and Democrats in general could have affected these results. Even though all of the celebrity candidates that were Republican options in the survey are in fact outspoken Republicans, Republican voters might still falsely infer that the celebrities they saw were Democrats (or simply viewed them as Hollywood liberals rather than true Republicans), causing respondents to shun celebrities in most cases. Consistent with this concern, a recent Morning Consult poll found that 61% of respondents viewed the entertainment industry as "very" or "somewhat" liberal, and only 3% viewed it as "very conservative."[11] There is also evidence that Republicans perceive the entertainment industry to be more liberal than Democrats do, although both groups believe Hollywood is more liberal than conservative. In another Morning Consult poll that asked Trump and Clinton voters to place the entertainment industry on an ideological scale ranging from 1 (most conservative) to 10 (most liberal), Trump voters rated the entertainment industry at 7.7, and Clinton voters rated the entertainment industry at 6.8.[12] For example, one can imagine that Jon Voight, while an outspoken Republican who vouched for President Trump before and after his inauguration, might still be associated more powerfully with the Hollywood elite in general, than with the Republican party.[13] If it is the case that fame is a proxy for liberalism, it may mean it is difficult for Republicans to vote for a celebrity candidate no matter what other information is provided. I address some of these potential design flaws in a follow-up experiment in the next section of this chapter.

Despite the low support for celebrities observed among Republicans in these data, the fact remains that Donald Trump managed to make a successful case in 2016 that he was not a celebrity, or not part of the Hollywood elite, despite being at the center of it. Although a reality television star, Trump drove home an anti-Hollywood message throughout his campaign and emphasized his credentials as a businessman (although he also often touted his success as an author and as the star of the Apprentice). During a rally in Hershey, Pennsylvania only days before the 2016 election, for instance, Trump ripped Hillary Clinton for the star-studded get-out-the-vote concert she held. Speaking about packing the building in which he spoke and breaking records for crowd size, Trump said, "And by the way, I didn't have to bring J-Lo or Jay-Z—the only way she [Hillary Clinton] gets anybody . . . I am here all by myself . . . Just me, no guitar, no piano, no nothing."[14] Ironically, successfully convincing the public that one is not a "celebrity candidate" or merely an "entertainer" may be a feat only the most accomplished entertainers and actors can achieve.

Evidence From a Priming Experiment

I address several of the aforementioned concerns with the initial paired-choice experiment in a follow-up survey in September 2018. I also introduce a new experimental treatment: the degree to which the context in which a candidate appears primes their celebrity status in the minds of voters. Rather than choosing one candidate over another, respondents instead were asked whether or not they would support one particular candidate for United States Senate, a scenario more robust to previous concerns that Donald Trump's incumbency status as president would confound results. Respondents were randomly assigned to see either a picture of that candidate interacting with large crowds or signing autographs (the "celebrity" condition—a depiction of what celebrities normally do, how beloved they are, and how many fans they have, per the name recognition literature), that candidate giving a political speech (the "politician" condition—a depiction of what politicians normally do: give speeches in front of lecterns, usually while professionally dressed), and a plain headshot of the candidate, which served as a control condition in each case. Each respondent evaluated eight candidates in total. Respondents were first shown pictures of a single candidate with a prompt that said, "This is a picture of [brief description of candidate's occupation, such as "Senator" "Governor" or "actress" or "musician"] [candidate's name]." They were asked the following after viewing the picture: "Imagine [candidate's name] was running for the [Democratic/Republican] nomination for United States Senate in your state. How likely would you be to vote for [her/him]?" Choices included "very likely," "somewhat likely," "somewhat unlikely," and "very unlikely." By stipulating that the individual was running as a Democrat or a Republican, I eliminate the concern in the previous experiment that Republicans may have failed to infer the partisan leanings of conservative celebrity candidates.

I used the same set of candidates that were used in the previous experiment plus several more who had entered the political fray recently. The list of candidates from which options were drawn for Democrats included: Elizabeth Warren, Meryl Streep, Elizabeth Banks, Tom Hanks, George Clooney, Alec Baldwin, Bruce Springsteen, Lebron James, Kanye West,[15] Eva Longoria, Oprah Winfrey, Jerry Brown, Kamala Harris, Cory Booker, Julian Castro, Kirsten Gillibrand, Andrew Cuomo, Tim Kaine, Joe Biden, Bernie Sanders, and Deval Patrick. The list of candidates from which eight options were drawn for Republicans included: Caitlyn Jenner, Mark Cuban, Kellie Pickler, Trace Adkins, Dwayne Johnson, Jon Voight, Chuck Norris, Ben Stein, Peyton Manning, Clint Eastwood, Condoleezza Rice, Mike Pence, Marco Rubio, John Kasich, Mitt Romney, Nikki Haley, Paul Ryan, Carly Fiorina, and Michael Bloomberg. True Independents (voters who lean neither toward the Democratic nor Republican party) were randomly assigned to either the Republican or Democratic block of candidates. Each respondent was asked to consider eight total candidates, which included a random mix of celebrities and politicians within their party.

Interestingly for this study, it was not difficult to find pictures of either traditional political candidates or the celebrities engaged in any of these activities, prima facie evidence for both the degree to which celebrities are seeking to get involved in politics, and the degree to which political campaigning has actually become more like show business. For example, it is no more difficult to find a photograph online of Elizabeth Warren taking a selfie and stopping to shake hands and sign autographs for a large crowd than it is to find Tom Hanks doing these things. On the other hand, one can just as easily find pictures of George Clooney or Lebron James giving a political speech as one can find pictures of them interacting with fans in stands or along a rope line. These two worlds are merging.

In this experiment, I hypothesized that candidates in general—whether celebrities or politicians—who were pictured interacting with fans would garner more support than candidates represented merely by a headshot or candidates pictured giving a political speech. This is because the pictures of candidates with crowds prime audiences to think of the candidate as well-liked, down-to-earth, and thus electorally viable.

I also expected that celebrities pictured engaging in these activities (signing autographs, taking pictures with fans, or shaking hands with fans) would fare better than politicians engaging in these activities, and that celebrities pictured engaging in political activities (the lectern condition) would also fare better than politicians seen in this traditional setting. Recall that again, Republican respondents were only shown Republican candidates, and Democratic respondents were only shown Democratic respondents. Yet it is important to consider that while the condition in which celebrities are doing "celebrity things" prime the best and most politically relevant attributes of celebrities, the condition in which politicians are doing "politician things" also prime important politically relevant attributes of politicians, such as experience, incumbency, and a professional image. Neither the literature nor the descriptive findings in Chapter 3 provide a clear picture of which contexts will be most beneficial for each type of candidate. With that in mind I turn to the results.

Results of Priming Experiment

Before discussing baseline support for celebrity candidates and traditional politicians within party, I want to mention the effects of the experimental manipulations. For the most part there were no discernable differences in how respondents evaluated candidates after being primed to see candidates behaving like "stars" or "politicians" relative to seeing a simple headshot of the candidate. However, that does not mean there were no priming effects at all. Democratic politicians appear to benefit slightly from being seen as "stars" (with adoring fans or signing autographs) and suffer slightly from being seen as "politicians" (speaking behind a lectern). Democratic politicians shown in a political context do 3.3 points worse on a likelihood to vote scale that ranges from 0 to 100 than Democratic politicians that appear in a plain headshot. When Democratic politicians appear as stars, they do 2.4 points better on a likelihood to vote scale that ranges from 0 to 100 than Democratic politicians that are shown in a political context. While these effects are small in magnitude and specific to one subset of candidates (Democratic politicians) they do reinforce prior research and popular theories of political campaigns that encourage candidates to humanize themselves and appear as accessible to the public as possible.

While the context in which candidates appear does not seem to matter much, respondents support celebrities and politicians to largely similar degrees at the baseline. Figure 4.3 displays the results among Democratic respondents in the survey, and Figure 4.4 displays the results among Republican respondents in the survey. Both figures present results for the "headshot" condition, which merely provided respondents a basic picture of the candidate's face, as opposed to the treatment conditions in which candidates were shown with fans or speaking in front of a podium. Similarly to the paired comparison experiment, the results were measured on a four-point scale, where a four means the respondent is "very likely" to vote for the candidate and a one means the respondent is "very unlikely" to vote for the candidate. To ease interpretation, I rescaled these responses to range from 0 to 100. Like a favorability scale, scores above 50 can

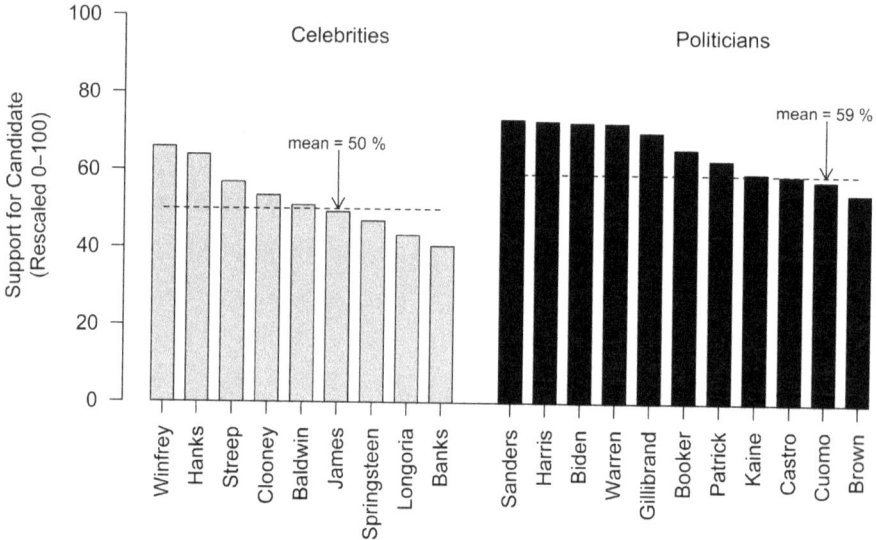

Figure 4.3 Candidate Support by Celebrity Status, Democrats

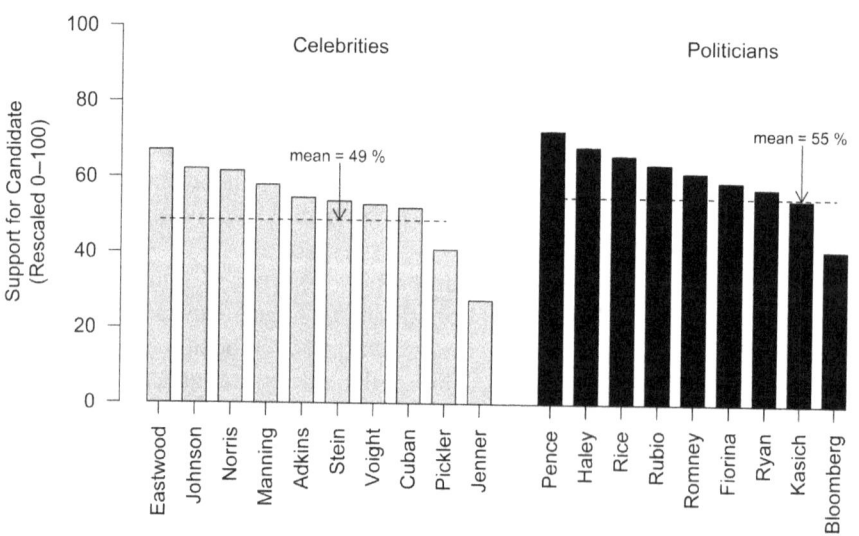

Figure 4.4 Candidate Support by Celebrity Status, Republicans

be thought of as an indication respondents are more likely to vote for someone and scores below 50 can be thought of as an indication that respondents are less likely to vote for someone.

The first and most important conclusion one should draw from these results is that celebrity candidates, both within the Democratic and Republican parties, garner almost as much support as traditional political candidates, and in many cases garner more support. Recall in the first candidate experiment explained earlier in this chapter that Democrats were more supportive of celebrity candidates running for President of the United States than they were of traditional politicians running for President of the United States. That result is not replicated in this experiment, in which politicians running for United States Senate do marginally better (mean level of support is 59 out of 100) than celebrities running for United States Senate (mean level of support is 50 out of 100).

While celebrities do not beat out politicians in this case, the two groups are essentially neck-in-neck, a strong indication of the public's openness to considering these non-traditional candidates. Democratic respondents in my survey asked to consider candidates in a hypothetical U.S. Senate race would be very likely to vote for Oprah Winfrey (she scores a 66 out of 100), Tom Hanks (64 out of 100), Meryl Streep (57 out of 100), George Clooney (53 out of 100), and Alec Baldwin (51 out of 100). This is particularly remarkable when compared to the results of sitting United States Senators and other powerful and experienced politicians who have been rumored to be weighing runs for the presidency in 2020 or 2024. For example, New Jersey Senator and rumored presidential hopeful Cory Booker scores 66 out of 100 among Democrats, very much in line with the scores of leading celebrity candidates within the Democratic Party. Booker is an experienced United States Senator, and yet Democrats are no more likely to vote for him for a job he already has than they are Oprah Winfrey, who has no experience in politics.

Again, this experiment is gauging support for hypothetical Senate candidates, rather than presidential candidates, which may explain the parity in support observed between the two groups of candidates—the stricter criteria voters may have when considering candidates for the nation's highest office. Yet how candidates rank compared to one another is also a valuable indication of who Democrats' and Republicans' best bets may be when deciding who should run in 2020 or 2024. Remember also that prior work suggests voters are reluctant to admit that they would vote for celebrity candidates due to social desirability concerns. Despite this, these results indicate that Democrats would be much better off nominating Oprah Winfrey or Tom Hanks as their party's candidate for president than sitting U.S. Senator Cory Booker, former Pennsylvania Governor Deval Patrick, sitting U.S. Senator Tim Kaine, former Mayor and Cabinet Secretary Julian Castro, current New York Governor Andrew Cuomo, or Current California Governor Jerry Brown.

Similar results were recovered for Republicans, which are displayed in Figure 4.4. Republicans are only slightly less likely to support celebrity candidates than traditional politicians, with a mean of 48.6 out of 100 on the likelihood to vote scale, compared to 55 out of 100 for politicians. Contrary to what I found in the paired comparison experiment, Republicans also appear in this case to be statistically indistinguishable from Democrats when it comes to their support for celebrity candidates (the mean level of support for celebrity candidates of 48.6 out of 100 for Republicans versus 50 out of 100 for Democrats). This finding supports my expectation that Republican support for celebrity candidates is muted in polls that simply ask them whether they would support a celebrity candidate running for office or whether a celebrity might influence their voting decisions. These results, which show a much higher willingness among Republicans to vote for celebrities, are consistent with the interpretation of the earlier experiment that Republican voters associate celebrities with Hollywood liberalism unless explicitly reminded of the celebrity's Republican affiliation.

These results also contrast with recent polls in which Republicans report being less open to celebrity influence, and less supportive of the idea of celebrities getting involved in politics, than Democrats. For example, Morning Consult, a polling firm that recently announced a partnership with *The Hollywood Reporter* to conduct surveys on sports and entertainment in addition to politics, found that while 33% of Democrats said celebrity opinions are effective in influencing their midterm vote, only 18% of Republicans said the same. The same poll found that 28% of Americans said celebrities should be as vociferous regarding political and social issues as possible, while 29% said celebrities should not express their political opinions at all.[16] But as my results show, there are no discernable party-based differences in likelihood to vote for a celebrity. Republican voters merely need to be reminded that the celebrity under consideration is a Republican. When this reminder is present, interparty differences evaporate. Ratcheting down the stakes from a presidential election to one for U.S. Senate also appears to make Republicans more comfortable with the concept of a celebrity holding elective office. One reason might be that they are no longer imagining a candidate, celebrity or otherwise, running against President Trump when they answer the likelihood to vote question.

Figure 4.4 shows that, like Democratic candidates, the top Republican celebrities do just as well as the top Republican politicians when it comes to support in a hypothetical election. Mike Pence, Nikki Haley, and Condoleezza Rice are the most preferable politicians, with average support levels of 72 out of 100, 68 out of 100, and 66 out of 100, respectively. But Republican celebrities are nipping at their heels. Republican respondents in my survey were more likely to vote for Clint Eastwood (67 out of 100) than Condoleezza Rice (66 out of 100).[17] They are more likely to vote for actors Dwayne "The Rock" Johnson and Chuck Norris for U.S. Senate than they are to vote for established politicians Mitt Romney, Carly Fiorina, Paul Ryan, John Kasich, and Michael Bloomberg. Seasoned New York Mayor and media mogul Michael Bloomberg, who is considering a 2020 presidential run, scores only 41 out of 100 on the likelihood to vote scale, barely beating out Republican country singer Kellie Pickler at 40 out of 100—a dismal result for a national political figure.[18]

Still by far the lowest level of support belongs to Caitlyn Jenner, who achieved only an average of 28 out 100 on the likelihood to vote scale. While Jenner, a Republican, has specifically mentioned an interest in running for U.S. Senate in California where her experience as a transgender woman might be perceived as a political asset rather than a liability, her low standing among Republicans may be too much of an obstacle to overcome.

Gender Moderates Celebrity Electability

Jenner is also emblematic of another finding that is important for the future of Republican campaigns. As Figure 4.5 demonstrates, candidate gender plays an important role in how respondents evaluate celebrity candidates and traditional political candidates within the Republican Party. Overall, both Republicans and Democrats slightly prefer traditional politicians to celebrity candidates. Overall, both Republicans and Democrats prefer female traditional political candidates to male traditional political candidates. But in the Republican Party, this preference does not transfer to female celebrity candidates. There is a steep cost to being a female candidate if you are a celebrity running as a Republican, and a slight, barely detectable advantage to being a female candidate if you are a celebrity running as

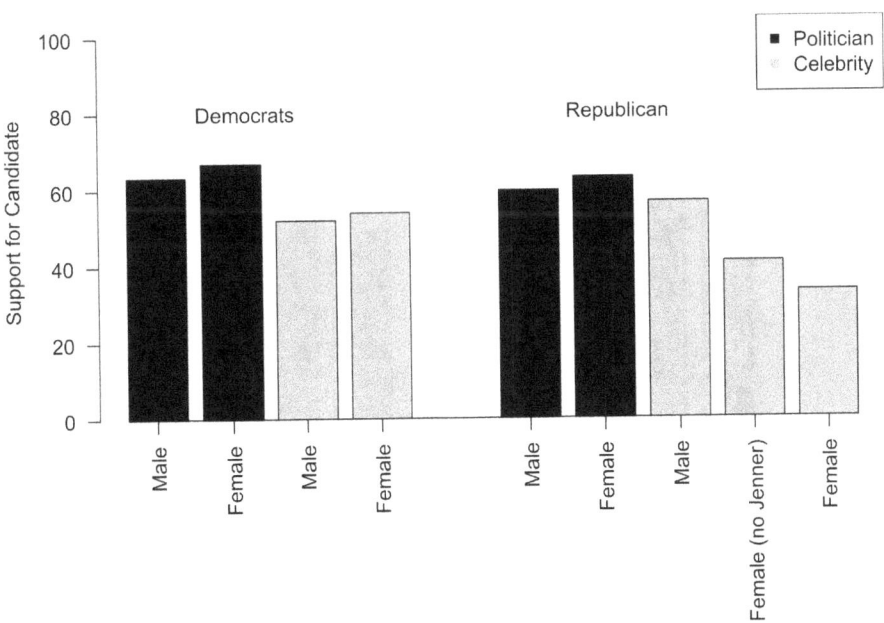

Figure 4.5 Candidate Support by Celebrity Status and Gender

a Democrat. This sharp difference endures even when Caitlyn Jenner is removed from the data. In addition, for male Republican candidates, there is barely any difference in likelihood to support celebrity candidates versus traditional politicians. But when female celebrities are introduced into the equation, the level of celebrity support drops off considerably.

The same trend, whereby Republican celebrity candidates are punished when they are female, is detectable among political Independents in the sample, voters who do not identify as Democrats or Republicans and do not "lean" toward the Democratic or Republican Party. Independents in the sample were randomly assigned to receive either a Democratic or Republican set of candidates. The results in Figure 4.6 are pooled treatment effects, meaning that the results represent average levels of support across the headshot, star and political treatment categories. As Figure 4.6 shows, there are virtually no meaningful differences between the likelihood of Independents to vote for male Democratic celebrities, female Democratic celebrities, male Democratic celebrities, or male Democratic politicians. Female Democratic politicians appear to have a slight edge on the other candidate categories, but this difference is not statistically significant.

However, there is much more variation when Independents are assigned to evaluate Republican candidates. Independents statistically significantly prefer Republican celebrities, giving them a 3-point boost (on a 0 to 100 scale) over

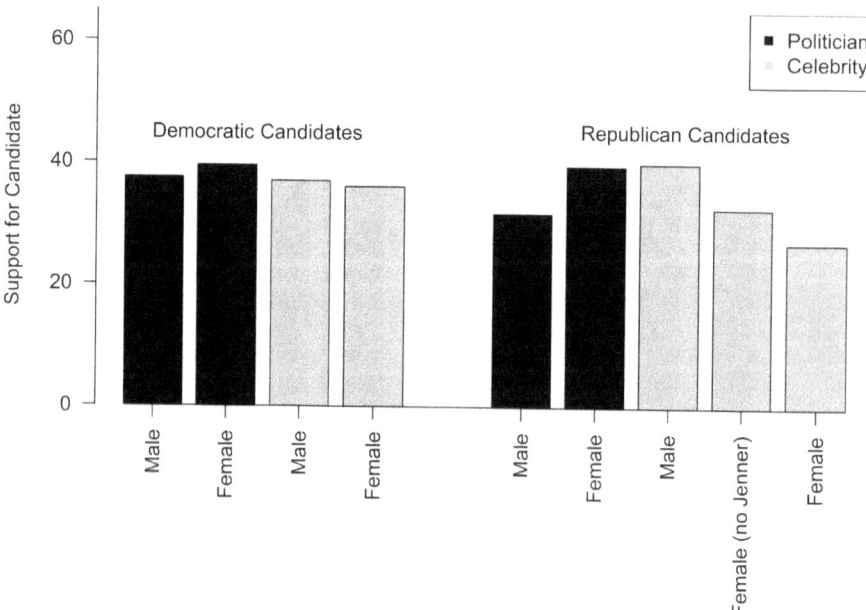

Figure 4.6 Candidate Support by Celebrity Status and Gender (Independents)

Republican politicians. However, things again get more complicated with candidate gender. Female Republican celebrity candidates are evaluated 12.6 points lower than female Republican politicians, whereas Republican male celebrities do 8 points better than female Republican politicians. All of these differences are statistically significant. The celebrity advantage appears to exist for Republican candidates among a key voting group, Independents, but only when the candidates are male.

The role of gender in these results is consistent with a burgeoning literature on women in Hollywood, which essentially finds what we have known in politics for a long time, but has almost disappeared on the campaign trail: there are important differences in the way the public perceives men and women in the entertainment industry. Research by Martha Lauzen at the Center for the Study of Women in Television and Film at San Diego State University found that less than 12% of protagonists in top-grossing films were women in 2014, a figure that has decreased since then. Furthermore, only 29% of major characters and 30% of speaking characters are women, and the majority of characters that are shown in the workplace, have identifiable jobs in the film, and are defined by their professional roles in the film, are men. This is true for only a sliver of women, 57% of whom are instead identified by their roles in relation to men, as wives and mothers, which is the case for only 31% of male characters. Stacy Smith et al. (2017) finds that men are 2.3 times more likely to have a speaking role in movies than women, and only 33 of the top grossing 100 films in 2017 depicted a female leading or co-leading character.[19] Things only get worse when age differences between men and women in TV and film are examined. According to research by Lauzen, most men are over 40 years of age, and most women are in their twenties and thirties. The effect of this underrepresentation and age gap, suggests Lauzen, is that men are seen as authority figures on screen and women are not. "When we keep [women] young, we keep them relatively powerless," said Lauzen in an interview with *Variety*.[20]

It makes sense that these effects could translate into politics, where the perceptions voters form of political novices are based heavily on what they did do before, such as roles they played in their acting careers. At the same time, women in politics and business are punished when they appear too ambitious or power-hungry and rewarded when they exhibit feminine qualities like warmth.[21] It cannot be ignored that the campaign trail, particularly at the level of the presidency, is a highly masculine space. Some scholars have gone so far as to say that presidential politics in and of itself is "the site of an ongoing struggle over the meaning of American manhood."[22] Leadership is closely associated in the minds of American voters with strength and power—even physical strength and power—with fatherhood rather than motherhood, and with aggression and conflict rather than amity and cooperation. President Trump made this clear on the campaign trail for the 2018 midterms when he praised a Republican congressman Greg Gianforte who body slammed a reporter in 2017, calling him "a tough cookie" and suggesting that the violent act helped the congressman win the election. "Any guy that can do a body slam," Trump said, making a body slam motion with his arms, "he's my kind of guy." Later in the speech Trump addressed Joe Biden's comments that he would "beat the hell" out of Trump if they were in high school. "He'd be down, faster than Greg would take him down."[23]

Female candidates must walk a tightrope between emphasizing their toughness and professional credentials and experience without appearing too masculine, and showing enough femininity not to spook voters. It is perhaps no surprise that voters have trouble imagining that women in entertainment, who are systematically placed in roles and contexts in which they are supportive of males or desirable to them or under male control, can be strong leaders. They do not even have the benefit that female politicians have of being seen often in the masculine political arena.

The fate of Republican female celebrity candidates in these experiments is precisely what Helen Douglas and Shirley Temple Black experienced firsthand on the campaign trail in the 1950s and 1960s. Women in politics were "looked on in many places as sufficiently odd to warrant a place in a zoo or museum," Douglas said in 1950.[24] And on top of running for U.S. Senate when only one woman, Margaret Chase Smith of Maine, held a seat, she was an actress. The jabs the press and her opponent Richard Nixon threw her way involved the worst stereotypes of women in show business. While Nixon joked behind closed doors that she was probably sleeping with Harry Truman, reporters called Douglas "gushy," "unqualified," a "bubble-blower," and a "fluttering satellite."[25]

While not a Republican race, sexist undertones were certainly at play in actress Cynthia Nixon's failed bid for the Democratic New York gubernatorial nomination in 2018. During his debate with Nixon, Governor Andrew Cuomo went out of his way to paint Cynthia Nixon as an unserious, unexperienced celebrity living a glamorous, out-of-touch life, to paint her as an unpragmatic dreamer, and to frame her ideas as fantasies. And he had anecdotes to help thread the needle—one alleging Nixon pulled a special favor from the New York City Mayor to stop helicopters from flying over performances of Shakespeare in the Park—and one claim that Nixon once forwarded an email to the Mayor's office from her former *Sex and the City* co-star, Sarah Jessica Parker, to help save a small business called "Tea and Sympathy." Cuomo simply referred to the latter as "the teahouse for Sarah Jessica Parker."[26] Even the temperature in the debate room was a point of contention between Nixon and Cuomo. Cuomo, like many male politicians, prefers ice-cold rooms for public appearances, but when Nixon's team demanded the thermostat be set to 76 degrees, her request backfired, only reinforcing the narrative of her as high-maintenance.[27]

While averaging evaluations of celebrities and politicians as groups in order to gain insight into voter preferences is a valuable and necessary exercise, it is important to acknowledge that there is substantial variation *within* these groups in addition to differences between them. No two celebrities are exactly alike.

Politicians are not all the same, either. The next chapter summarizes key qualitative and quantitative findings throughout this book, including insight into how gender can moderate support for celebrity candidates, especially when they are Republican women.

Notes

1. Barr, Jeremy. October 10, 2018. "When Stars Like Taylor Swift Get Political, Do Voters Listen?" *The Hollywood Reporter*.
2. Shaw, Jonathan. July-August 2017. "Votes for Celebrities Are Influenced by Electoral Rules." *Harvard Magazine*.
3. Klar, Samara et al. 2016. "Social Desirability Bias in the 2016 Presidential Election." *The Forum* 14(4): 433–443.
4. Ibid.
5. Coppock, Alexander. 2017. "Did Shy Trump Supporters Bias the 2016 Polls? Evidence From a Nationally-Representative List Experiment." *Statistics, Politics, and Policy* 8(1): 29–40.
6. Mummolo, Jonathan, and Clayton Nall. 2016. "Why Partisans Do Not Sort: The Restraints of Political Segregation." *Journal of Politics* 79(1): 45–59.
7. Kurrild-Klitgaard, Peter. December 15, 2016. "Trump, Condorcet, and Borda: Voting Paradoxes in the 2016 Republican Presidential Primaries." Munich Personal RePEc Archive, University of Copenhagen. Pages 7–8.
8. As I mentioned earlier, while random assignment is useful here, the possibility remains that it is not celebrity status, but some other attribute of the individual candidates, that is driving differential support. For example, we may see strong support for Meryl Streep not because she is a celebrity, but because of some unmeasured attribute she possesses that is not considered part of celebrity status. This is the tradeoff of using real-world candidates in experiments: while more realistic (and thus more externally valid) we run the risk that respondents are inferring an unintended treatment. However, the paired comparison design helps mitigate this concern. Because we present so many different celebrity candidates and average responses across them, we can relax concerns that an indiosyncratic feature of any one person, rather than celebrity status, is driving results.
9. Due to a branching irregularity in the survey that affected a small number of people, some respondents saw a mix of Republican and Democratic candidates. After examining the results among this group, the findings hold up. That is, even if a Republican respondent had Democratic choices mixed in, she was still statistically significantly more likely to choose the politician for president, and even if a Democratic respondent had Republican choices mixed in, she was still statistically significantly more likely to choose the celebrity for president. While these results are perhaps unsurprising given the strong draw of partisanship, they helpfully rule out the possibility that merely seeing candidates from a different party could change the way in which respondents evaluate the candidates.
10. Bump, Philip. June 4, 2018. "Trump Is a Wartime President—In a War Against His Political Opponents." *The Washington Post*.
11. Morning Consult National Tracking Poll. Conducted September 27 through October 1, 2018. Project number 180975.
12. Piacenza, Joanna. March 1, 2018. "Putting a Number on Hollywood's Perceived Liberalism." Morning Consult.
13. Shepard, Jack. January 20, 2017. "Donald Trump Inauguration Concert: Jon Voight Criticises 'Barrage of Propaganda' and Thanks God in Speech." *The Independent*.

14. Firozi, Paulina. December 22, 2016. "Trump: I Don't Need Celebrities at Inauguration, Just 'the People'." *The Hill*.

15. The results for Kanye West are not included here. A routing error in the survey caused respondents who received the Kanye West treatment to answer a question about how likely they would be to vote for him before the treatment was shown. Kanye West is an interesting case because he is a registered Democrat and he and his wife Kim Kardashian supported Hillary Clinton during the 2016 election. He also famously announced he was running for President of the United States in 2020, which many assumed would be against Donald Trump. Because of his party affiliation, West was included in the group of Democratic celebrities in the survey. However, West has recently become a vocal supporter of President Trump.

16. Press. October 10, 2018. "Morning Consult Joins Forces With The Hollywood Reporter For First-of-its-Kind Polling Partnership." Morning Consult.

17. Despite his brief tenure as Mayor of Carmel, California, Clint Eastwood is likely better known as an actor and filmmaker than a politician. For this reason he is included in the "celebrity" category of these results, deviating from my definition of a celebrity which includes that the candidate not have held prior elective office. Eastwood continues to be involved in filmmaking, but he was only Mayor of Carmel from 1986 to 1988. The town is so small that on Election Day, Eastwood won with only 2,166 votes out of a total 2,965.

18. Michael Bloomberg announced he was leaving the Republican party and re-registered as a Democrat shortly after this survey was conducted. Had this been the case before the survey he would have been included in the list of Democratic politicians. However, because of the way the question was hypothetically phrased, "Imagine Michael Bloomberg was running for the Republican nomination for U.S. Senate in your state. How likely would you be to vote for him?" the results are still meaningful.

19. Smith, Stacy and Marc Choueiti, Katherine Pieper, Ariana Case and Angel Choi. July 2018. "Inequality in 1,100 Popular Films: Examining Portrayals of Gender, Race/Ethnicity, LGBT & Disability From 2007 to 2017." Annenberg School of Communication, University of Southern California. Also cited in Lang, Brent. July 31, 2018. "Despite Diversity Push, Women and Minorities Aren't Getting Better Movie Roles (Study)." *Variety*.

20. Research by Martha Lauzen as cited in Lang, Brent. February 9, 2015. "Study Finds Fewer Lead Roles for Women in Hollywood." *Variety*.

21. Paquette, Danielle. November 3, 2016. "Why Ambitious Men Are Celebrated and Ambitious Women Are Scrutinized." *The Washington Post*.

22. Dittmar, Kelly. "Finding Gender in Election 2016." Published on the CAWP website by Barbara Lee Family Foundation and Center for American Women and Politics.

23. Miller, Zeke and Ashley Thomas. October 19, 2018. "Trump Praises Montana Congressman Who Body-Slammed Reporter." *AP*.

24. Mitchell, Greg. February 22, 1998. "The Subtle Use of Sexism to Bring Down Women Candidates." *The Los Angeles Times*.

25. Ibid.

26. McKinley, Jesse and Tyler Pager. August 29, 2018. "Fact Check on Cuomo-Nixon Debate: Who Stretched the Truth?" *The New York Times*.

27. Chiu, Allison. August 29, 2018. "Cold Rooms 'Notoriously Sexist'? Cynthia Nixon Seeks 76-Degree Setting for Cuomo Debate." *The New York Times*.

CHAPTER 5

THE DEATH OF U.S.?

Findings

I have devoted considerable space in this book to the non-zero possibility that the United States government could, one day, be full of democratically elected, inexperienced, unknowledgeable, self-aggrandizing entertainers. In the absence of evidence, clinical psychologists refer to thought exercises like this as 'catastrophizing.' Catastrophizing is twofold. First, the catastrophizer predicts a negative outcome with limited information—in this case, extrapolating Trump's election to the election of future celebrities. Second, the catastrophizer jumps to the conclusion that if the negative outcome does happen, a catastrophe would occur. That is, that if the government was indeed overrun with celebrities, chaos would ensue, and the Republic would crumble. Yet the empirical study undertaken herein suggests that neither of these scenarios—celebrities winning elections or becoming a detriment to democracy—is particularly outlandish.

Though it stops short of predicting the downfall of American democracy, this book demonstrates through survey experiments that when voters are presented the option of a celebrity candidate, they are very likely to choose them. As we discovered in Chapter 4, the average likelihood of Democrats to choose a celebrity candidate for United States Senate is 50 out of 100. When Democrats are asked to choose among randomly generated hypothetical candidates for the presidency, Democrats choose the celebrity candidate almost 50% of the time. Republicans choose the celebrity candidate for president only 25% of the time in the same survey experiment. However, when Republicans are provided the partisan affiliation of the candidate, they become much more comfortable with celebrity candidates. The average likelihood of Republicans to choose a celebrity candidate for United States Senate is 49 out of 100. We also learned in Chapter 4 that the most popular celebrity candidates are on par with mainstream politicians when it comes to electability, even when the mainstream politicians in question already have the jobs celebrities seek. On the Democratic side, Oprah Winfrey and Tom Hanks are within striking distance of several rumored 2020 presidential hopefuls, including Bernie Sanders, Kamala Harris, Joe Biden, and Elizabeth Warren. Winfrey and Hanks are more electable than Jerry Brown, Andrew Cuomo, and Deval Patrick—governors of several of the most populous states in the union—and Julian Castro and Tim Kaine, both well-known Democratic politicians. If Winfrey and Hanks do this well in surveys without spending any time on the campaign trail, imagine what the numbers might look like if serious time, effort and resources were invested into their candidacies and they garnered DNC support.

On the Republican side, Clint Eastwood, Dwayne 'The Rock' Johnson and Chuck Norris are only slightly less electable than Vice President Mike Pence, Nikki Haley and Condoleezza Rice. Like Winfrey and Hanks, Eastwood, Johnson and Norris are more electable than a large slate of presidential aspirants and top government representatives, including Carly Fiorina, Paul Ryan, Marco Rubio, Mitt Romney, John Kasich, and Michael Bloomberg. In the era of Donald Trump, neither Democratic nor Republican voters seem to be shying away from the prospect of celebrity candidates in the future. If Trump's inexperience and disregard for democratic norms has spooked the public, that unease with celebrity politicians is not evident in this book. It also was not evident in the 2018 midterm elections. The hyper-hyped "blue wave" looked more like a trickle. In their first chance since November 2016 to deliver a swift repudiation of a president Democrats have called a "tyrant" and a "traitor" and argue needs to be immediately impeached, American voters displayed trademark apathy on election day, and in doing so further normalized the Trump presidency and brought it closer to another term.[1] Trump continues to shine on the campaign trail while in office. Stumping for congressional and gubernatorial candidates gives him a chance to practice for his 2020 run. Trump's media toolkit is sharp, and he never struggles to attract news coverage and shape it to his benefit. With RNC, DNC and PAC support and a formal campaign organization, it is hard to imagine that any candidate as famous and skilled as Trump would not similarly dominate a large field of primary candidates like the reality show star and businessman did in 2016.

As Trump's whirlwind election also demonstrated in 2016, there is not much a traditional politician can do, even one as famous as Hillary Clinton, to compete with a serious celebrity contender on his or her own terms. The mere label of "politician" is used as a cudgel in American politics. Whereas politicians are expected to have a squeaky clean public image and a firm grasp of the issues they purport to know how to fix, celebrities are given many chances to make mistakes and learn on the job. When politicians call celebrity candidates out on their inexperience, they appear as elitists attacking the American public. Most Americans are not knowledgeable about politics or current events, but they do not like to be reminded of that. There are plenty of things politicians can do to hurt themselves on the campaign trail in addition to deploying self-aggrandizing tactics. There is some limited evidence in the survey experiments I conducted in Chapter 4 that politicians suffer disproportionately when they appear too political. Survey respondents were less likely to vote for politicians when they were shown giving speeches than when a plain headshot was shown, or when they appeared with supporters signing autographs or taking selfies. While the message here seems somewhat clear—get out from behind the podium and interact with real people— the finding only holds up among Democrats. There appears to be no equivalent way for Republican candidates to stage themselves that makes a difference in how survey respondents perceive them.

However, the finding that politicians appear more appealing in some contexts more than others is not without parallels in other areas of research, especially studies on gender and politics. My own research on effective communications strategies of presidential spouses come to mind here because first ladies of the United States occupy an almost unique space between politician and celebrity. In order to maintain and capitalize on their public appeal, which is mobilized to garner support for the president's policy agenda, first ladies must stay clear of the overtly political. Hillary Clinton learned this the hard way when she pitched the administration's health reform plan, the Health Security Act, to the American public in 1993. She proposed the plan as any male politician with years of experience in a certain policy area would have. Clinton testified before Congress, drawing on her success launching similar reforms in Arkansas when her husband was Governor, made speeches in and around Washington, DC, and met with countless experts at the White House, some of whom joined her on the Taskforce on National Healthcare Reform, which she chaired. But the highly politicized appearances made it too easy for Clinton opponents to scream overreach—Clinton, as first lady, appeared to be acting as an unelected, unappointed, unofficial government representative. First ladies are expected to arrange flowers and host the White House Easter Egg Roll and the Congressional Spouses Luncheon, not wade elbow deep into decades-long policy battles. In response, future first ladies provided their input on policy behind the scenes. Though they have consistently proven to be the most effective presidential policy messengers and campaign surrogates, first ladies now carry out their advocacy efforts in a covert manner. Healthcare policy is invoked in conversations about childhood obesity and preventative care on the set of *Top Chef* or while gardening with kids. The War on Terror is framed as a humanitarian effort to liberate women and girls from Taliban rule. The conversation about changing national education standards starts in a classroom with a former librarian emphasizing the importance of early childhood literacy.

Unfortunately these requirements, that women discuss serious political matters by first bringing up their credentials as a mother and a wife instead of their specific education or experience in an area, extend to women running for office for themselves. There are no systematic differences between male and female candidates across a range of variables closely associated with electability that I measured in Chapter 3. Female candidates—both celebrities and politicians—are just as recognizable as their male counterparts, just as likeable, just as relatable, and they have just as many social media followers and generate just as many internet search results as men. Female celebrities can capitalize on being outsiders just as easy as male celebrities can, and they are equally successful stumpers and fundraisers for other candidates. But there are different rules of engagement for women on the campaign trail than there are for men, and we may as well be tying women's arms behind their backs when we consider the lines and boundaries to which women must heed when they run for office. Female candidates, as I mentioned in previous chapters, must appear stoic but not overly stiff, compassionate but not too soft, and feminine without letting emotion show. The 2018 midterm elections featured plentiful examples of this tightrope walk. Stacey Abrams, a Yale-trained lawyer and businesswoman who ran for Governor of Georgia in 2018, was attacked relentlessly by her opponent Brian Kemp and President Trump, who called her "crime-loving" and "not qualified" for the post, yet Abrams refrained from shooting back, instead keeping her cool and focusing on campaign issues.[2] In Texas, House candidate MJ Hegar, an Air Force veteran and self-described "ass-kicking, motorcycle-riding, Texas Democrat" engaged her opponent, sitting Representative John Carter much more directly, for example, replying "you don't know sh** about war" to his statement that "It's a war . . . I will beat this lady."[3] However even Hegar's campaign ads, which were replete with pictures of her in uniform, helicopter rescue reenactments and Hegar riding a motorcycle to a biker bar, are careful to highlight her family and children. The first and most widely circulated of Hegar's ads, titled "Doors" begins with a shot of her at home feeding her kids.

Negotiating these difficult paradoxes is especially fraught for female celebrities running for office, who are trying to project authority and garner power after a career of unserious and powerless roles. It is much easier for Ronald Reagan or Clint Eastwood to convince the American public they can take charge and protect their constituents after playing dozens of rugged heroes in movies than it is for Cynthia Nixon or Stacey Dash. The programs that made these women famous were called *Sex and the City* and *Clueless*, respectively. This is not to say that Nixon and Dash are not woefully underqualified to hold a publically elected position. But they are not any less qualified than the countless male athletes and actors that have been elected to public office in the 20th and 21st centuries, riding the strong undercurrents of patriarchy that run through every major American industry.

The inherent bias that voters, particularly Republican voters, appear to have when it comes to female celebrities is one of the most disturbing and robust conclusions that can be drawn from this book. We are not just electing unqualified celebrities to represent us in government, we are electing unqualified male celebrities who have played the part of a strong responsible citizen on television. Those opportunities are not nearly as available to women in Hollywood as they are to men. But the inherent macho culture bias in Hollywood is not the only aspect of the entertainment industry that has a clear complement in Washington, DC. In other words, it is not difficult to understand why celebrities believe that if they could succeed in one world they can probably succeed in the other.

It is important to remember at this juncture that before the proliferation of visual media, especially television, for the most part, politicians *were* the only celebrities. Before mass communication, the most recognizable people were civic leaders and war heroes, which were often one and the same. But modernity, as Leo Braudy writes in *The Frenzy of Renown*, democratized fame.[4] With so many ways to become known, and so many media vehicles to consume information about people who are known, scholars of mass communication and fame argue that celebrities have become a central part of how people conceive of and construct their own social and political identities. Anthony Elliot says it more clearly when he explains John Thompson's theory of "mediated quasi-interaction" in his article about the influence of celebrity and the death of John Lennon:

> In this view, individuals reflexively draw on mediated symbolic forms-such as images of celebrity-in order to fashion their day-to-day lives, their conceptions of their own selves, understandings of others, and their broader relation to the social and political world. The reflexive organization of media communication becomes routinely internalized and acted on by lay individuals in the course of their own biographical self-framings.[5]

The identities of certain groups, it turns out, are more susceptible to being shaped by what celebrities do and say than others. One of these is young people. For example, two research studies reported by the *Telegraph* find that women under 25 years of age are influenced more by late singer Amy Winehouse than they were by politicians and teachers. In a similar survey of young people, musicians, actors, sports stars, reality television stars, and fashion models were the most frequently cited role models of the study group. Politicians were last on the list, and celebrities ranked higher than people the survey respondents personally knew.[6] Symptomatic of and possibly a contributing factor to this mess is the fact that most young people feel detached from their local communities and are unknowledgeable about what goes on in their surrounding neighborhood, politically or otherwise. For most people, the national community, where celebrities reside, is the most salient. Most voters do not know their local representatives and are not aware of what they can do for them. The detachment of people from their local communities and the harm that can come from it is the central thesis in Robert Putnam's famous book *Bowling Alone*: people have become increasingly disconnected from one another and the social structures that once bonded humans together (like bowling leagues and PTA committees and political parties) have disintegrated, ultimately preventing the formation of a safe, healthy, and happy society.[7] Now enter celebrities, who easily fill the void of detachment from family members, friends, and political organizations. As Lisa Respers France reported on CNN about the cultural phenomenon of the show *Survivor* on CBS in the summer of 2000, ". . . everyone was watching it, and if you weren't watching it, you were completely left out of the conversation that summer."[8] But people are not only vaguely interested in the lives of celebrities, they shape their own lives around them, whether consciously or not. At the extreme end of this spectrum is "celebrity worship" in which a fan has a personal preoccupation with a favorite celebrity and develops obsessive-compulsive tendencies surrounding that relationship, but "normal" levels of celebrity preoccupation, which France mentions, are extremely widespread in the West. Just as political science offers Putnam's theory, psychologists have pointed to their own "empty self theory" to explain what has happened surrounding Western culture, celebrity, materialism, and social disconnection since the 1800s. Reeves et al. describe Philip Cushan's theory as follows: "The contemporary empty self is characterized by strivings for self-contained individualism, autonomy, self-sufficiency, and attempts to master the environment for one's own needs."[9]

In addition to helping us understand why Americans are drawn to celebrities and influenced by them, empty self theory can help us understand why we let celebrity candidates get away with so much. On the 2016 presidential campaign trail, Donald Trump frequently made statements widely considered to be racist and sexist, which some believe were part of a targeted strategy to monger fear among white male voters, and some believe are indicative of genuine ignorance on these topics.[10] Either way, when a 2005 Access Hollywood tape surfaced in October 2016 on which Donald Trump bragged about sexually assaulting women, a large share of Americans thought his candidacy could not survive such an egregious discovery. But "Teflon Don" overcame that too. One factor that has always helped Donald Trump move on from scandals is the high-speed, short-memory media environment that we have today; new scandals are constantly eclipsing old ones, and Donald Trump seizes on this feature to redirect media attention. But it is also important to understand that one of the reasons we let stars off the hook—even stars that are running for the most powerful public offices in the world—is because celebrities are central to our fundamental understanding of morality. When stars disgrace themselves, their audiences grow larger, not smaller, which reinforces the idea that all press is good press. In other words, standards of moral and ethical acceptability are not imposed on celebrities, but instead defined by them. This cycle makes it especially difficult to hold celebrities to account. In an article about Kate Moss's 2005 cocaine scandal, Ilana Hanukov illustrates that the media coverage surrounding the incident benefitted Moss's career rather than halted it. "By creating and disseminating star personas and dominant moralities," Hanukov says, "the press mediates the "icon" and imbues it with a distinctive aura to be presented to the public. Behind this lies the central element of celebrity production and consumption: the star's value lies in the attention they can generate and their ability to attract an audience. This, ultimately, is the commodity being sold."[11]

Hanukov appropriately uses the term celebrity "addiction" here, which I have mostly avoided in this book. As a political scientist, calling the shots on what does and does not constitute a cultural addiction is not my specialty. Yet after immersing myself in the psychology literature on fame and celebrity I believe the term is entirely appropriate. James Houran asserts celebrities are "like a drug . . . They're around us everywhere. They're an easy fix."[12] We depend on celebrities for entertainment, direction, and self-identification; they are the yardstick against which Americans measure themselves. Celebrity scandals, in particular, appear to trigger a sequence of reward and destruction among the public. When a powerful and popular person engages in shameful or dishonest behavior, we get to feel better about ourselves. As Barbara Goldsmith wrote in 1983, we form an attachment to celebrities because they "vicariously act out our noblest and basest desires."[13] The moral compass as which celebrities tend to serve puts most of us on top. This may be an agreeable process when it comes to the entertainment industry, but when celebrities enter the White House, there are real costs associated with elevating someone with poor moral character. This last point will be discussed later in the chapter.

Finally, the way in which voters make the cognitive leap necessary to elect a celebrity to public office is not that surprising. We are disconnected and rely on celebrities to help form our perceptions of ourselves and to give us fundamental social and political cues. But American politics has also become about identity, not about issues. Voters do not make rational decisions in the voting booth. In their book *Democracy for Realists*, Christopher Achen and Larry Bartels argue that this "folk theory of democracy" (in which voters seek information and weigh evidence to choose good policies, and then vote for government representatives who will champion those policies) is antithetical to how American politics actually work. Instead:

> most people possess almost no useful information about policies and their implications, have little desire to improve their state of knowledge, and have a deep aversion to political disagreement. We base our political decisions on who we are rather than what we think. In other words, we act politically—not as individual, rational beings but as members of social groups, expressing a social identity.[14]

Those social identities have become central to partisan polarization in the United States. Particularly problematic is affective polarization, the formal term political scientists Sean Westwood and Shanto Iyengar use to describe "the tendency of people identifying as Republicans or Democrats to view opposing partisans negatively and copartisans positively."[15] The stability of group identities, and the constant opportunities frequent elections offer to reinforce those identities, contribute to our negative political climate. The outcome of the presidential election of 2016, according to political scientists Lynn Vavreck, John Sides, and Michael Tesler, can be traced to this precise construction of identity and Donald Trump's ability to exploit it. According to the authors, "Trump's victory was foreshadowed by changes in the Democratic and Republican coalitions that were driven by people's racial and ethnic identities. The campaign then reinforced and exacerbated those cleavages as it focused on issues related to race, immigration, and religion."[16]

Celebrity candidates are central to this equation not only because they play a role in the identity formation processes of Americans, but because they have a particular skillset that allows them to tap into the irrational and emotional proclivities of voters. To build a loyal fan base (the kind that forgives you no matter how poor your personal conduct is), celebrities foster parasocial relationships with fans. The stability of these depends on several factors, according to psychologist Donna Rockwell. Chief among them is projecting a reliable character. Reliable characters are strengthened by the degree of reality approximation of the persona and the media, the frequency and consistency of appearance by the persona, stylized behavior and conversational manner of the persona, and effective use of the formal features of television.[17] As I have said many times in this book, the entire job of an entertainer is to elicit emotional responses from fans and audiences. Politicians, by contrast, are rarely inherently skilled in this area, and they are not afforded the same leeway when it comes to their public conduct. That does not mean that they have not tried to adopt some of the postures and skills of celebrities.

Recent presidents have turned to alternative media outlets to expand their audience and showcase their personality and sense of humor. They seek to make themselves more relatable. Barack Obama appeared on the Hanoi episode of *Parts Unknown* on CNN in 2016 where he chatted with Anthony Bourdain about his childhood and politics over noodles and beer. But he also took bigger risks, appearing on comedians Zach Galifianakis's and Jerry Seinfeld's web series, *Between Two Ferns*, and *Comedians in Cars Getting Coffee*, respectively. Perhaps one of the most outrageous examples of politicians attempting to appeal to voters on a personal, apolitical level is the episode of *Rival Survival* that aired in 2014 on Discovery Channel which featured Senators Jeff Flake (R-AZ) and Martin Heinrich (D-NM) stranded on a remote island in the Marshall Islands with no natural sources of fresh water. The lawmakers fished, collected debris from a nearby island, built a shelter and tried to start a fire, all the while making partisan cracks at one another. As viewers noted, the fact that the senators had to spend a week on a remote island to demonstrate that they can work together in a bipartisan manner is nothing if not tragic. Drastic efforts like these make evident how aware politicians are of the need to humanize themselves and how in tune celebrities are with what they perceive to be a ripe political environment for their career changes. We have a serious problem on the voter side of the equation—we are voting with our hearts rather than our minds—but the pipeline of celebrity candidates is problematic too.

Celebrities, as most scholars who study these issues concur, are often deeply flawed individuals despite their apparent knack for campaigning. As we observed in Chapter 2, the celebrities who succeed most often on the campaign trail are those that are the most recognized by voters, receive the most media attention, and that take the process seriously by enlisting the help of experienced experts. But even the most effective celebrities run for office for the wrong reasons. These range from the classic claim that they were asked or recruited to run or that they want to help people to outright admitting that they were bored with Hollywood, wanted to try a new career or prove their detractors wrong, or that they wanted to distinguish themselves from other entertainers. It is probably quite obvious to the reader why these are not good reasons to run for public office, but I should point out that they are especially inexcusable for celebrities.

Most of these reasons are obviously self-centered in nature, but the "want to help people" trope is the most misleading. Celebrities succeed on the campaign trail because they already have immense public influence. They do not need a political platform to help people. They are already in the best possible position as wealthy and famous individuals to do so. And one of the avenues in which they have succeeded at influencing outcomes is by becoming involved in politics as issue advocates and campaign surrogates. Kim Kardashian, Kanye West, Jim Brown, and Kid Rock all recently visited the Trump White House, for example. Kardashian was successful in persuading the president to commute Alice Johnson's lifetime prison sentence for a nonviolent drug offense, while Kid Rock lent his support to Trump as he signed a bill that modernizes music royalties. Merely spending time with politicians is another frequent reason celebrities cite when explaining why they wanted to run. Celebrities are prone to the belief that "if they can do it, I can do it."

There is some research on the way in which the entertainment industry attracts precisely the kinds of people we should eschew as government leaders. Psychologists like Rockwell, and David Giles have completed extensive interviews with celebrities. Others, like Charles Figley, have sent questionnaires to hundreds of celebrities and analyzed their responses. There are several themes that emerge from analyses like these. First, fame makes people particularly prone to magical thinking. Celebrities often believe they are immune to the normal laws of humankind and that their personal hopes and desires can have an effect on the way the world works. They overestimate their ability to influence large-scale outcomes. They are extremely focused on approval, which depends on public recognition and acclaim, but rather than be applauded for their actions, they seek to be applauded for their personal attributes. Celebrities want to be beloved. Most of all, celebrities who win the attention of the public worry incessantly about losing it, writes Christopher Lasch in his book *The Culture of Narcissism*.

This makes celebrities extremely vulnerable to the personal evaluations of other people.[18] Perhaps to protect their egos, psychologists also note, celebrities surround themselves with sycophants, people who constantly praise them in order to gain approval from the celebrity. Finally, the extreme self-consciousness of celebrities can approach paranoia.[19] While this is not specific to entertainers—Richard Nixon comes to mind—the constant fear that you are being undermined or wronged or that people are coming after you can be a distraction from governing at best, and can cause the destruction of a presidency or even lead to international conflict, at worst. James David Barber's classic work on presidential character places Richard Nixon in a category Barber defines as "active-negative" personality. Presidents in this category are compulsive; for them, power is an avenue to self-realization, they are preoccupied with whether they are failing or succeeding and public perceptions of such, and have low self-esteem.[20] It is important to take typologies like Barber's with a grain of salt. While meticulously crafted and helpful tools for understanding what sorts of forces may have motivated presidential decision-making, typologies are not based on empirical evidence, the categories are not mutually exclusive, and the theory is unfalsifiable. Yet the characteristics that scholars like Barber, and his contemporaries who study the personal presidency mark as problematic seem to be almost universal in their applications to celebrities.

The research in this book strongly supports my contention that electing celebrities to public office is bad for democracy. Many of the problems Trump currently faces as president, some of which threaten his removal him from office, are related to his celebrity status. Trump rose to prominence in 2011 and 2012 by circulating a conspiracy theory about President Barack Obama's birthplace. He continues to divide the country with hyperbolic rhetoric that stokes fear and resentment among Americans while satisfying his personal need for acceptance and adoration from his base. He personally castigates people on an almost daily basis, which cheapens the office of the presidency and lowers the bar for moral authority. Running for president, winning, and governing should not be a publicity stunt. Whether you agree that the focus of Robert Mueller and the Russia investigation and media scrutiny of the president's possible illegal behavior is warranted, self-imposed, or not, it is harmful for the United States to have the legitimacy of its leader questioned. It makes foreign leaders distrustful of our intentions and less willing to concede our interest. It is bad for presidents, who have their hands on nuclear weapons, to be distracted with scandals and investigations. When presidents are impeached it disrupts the normal business of government and international affairs. These are extremely destructive occurrences. They should be rare, not part of the regular fabric of presidential administrations. James Q. Wilson predicts in his 1962 book *The Amateur Democrat* that when political professionals (i.e., traditional politicians) who are willing to make deals and compromise are replaced by amateurs (e.g., celebrity candidates), who are unyielding in their righteousness, "Political conflict will be intensified, social cleavages will be exaggerated, party leaders will tend to be men skilled in the rhetorical arts, and the party's ability to produce agreement by trading issue-free resources will be reduced."[21]

The founders agreed that the biggest threats to American democracy were indeed factions led by charismatic and selfish leaders, particularly those with rhetorical talents and popularity. Madison writes in Federalist 10, "Men of factious tempers, of local prejudices, or of sinister designs, may, by intrigue, by corruption, or by other means, first obtain the suffrages, and then betray the interests, of the people." Hamilton concurs that it is possible that "the great interests of society are sacrificed to the vanity, to the conceit, and to the obstinacy of individuals, who have credit enough to make their passions and their caprices interesting to mankind" in Federalist 70. But both Madison and Hamilton assume that the public will recognize these "unfit characters" and hold them accountable in the next election. And with a large enough population, they argue, voters will have enough men of "attractive merit and the most effusive and established characters" from which to choose.[22] Like the folk theorists and populists of today that Wilson, Achen and Bartels critique, Hamilton and Madison conceived of a rational and informed voter when they designed American government. They were worried about human nature and the corrupting influence of ambition, but mostly to the extent that empowering individual leaders and centralizing power in the executive branch could lead to tyranny. The predilection of voters to make bad choices was a secondary concern, and the founders were overconfident in the ability of elites (such as the electoral college) to keep these poor choices in check. Electors are, after all, humans.

It is important to note that there are accomplished scholars on the "Do Not Panic" side of this argument. The overarching assertion of researchers in this camp is that once elected, political amateurs such as celebrities do not behave very differently than traditional politicians. Reeves, for instance, who I cited earlier, finds that it makes no discernable difference for constituents whether they fill a legislative seat in Japan with a celebrity or an experienced politician. David Canon's study of political amateurs in the United States Congress approaches the topic from a similar perspective. According to Canon, political amateurs have always made up a large portion of Congress. About 25% of the seats in the United States House of Representatives have been occupied by political amateurs since 1930, Canon finds, and many of them have been "actors, athletes, and astronauts." While amateurs may be more ideologically extreme and behaviorally unorthodox—they have not been steeped in the norms and processes that moderate interactions in Congress—the ambitious and policy-interested amateurs eventually assimilate into the role of a normal politician. They raise money and try to get reelected, they vie for powerful committee positions, and their legislative records are virtually indistinguishable from more politically experienced co-partisans. The amateurs that do not assimilate (he "hopeless" ones, in Canon's view), do not stick around for very long anyway.[23] Some scholars have gone even further, suggesting that the filling of congressional seats by political amateurs is the natural state of democracy; the only way to prevent political machines of the likes of Tammany Hall from reemerging.

What We Know About Celebrity Politicians

The debate over whether celebrity candidates are good or bad for American democracy clearly remains unresolved. Many of the postulations surrounding it are speculative and untestable. The successes and failures of politicians are rarely specific to the individuals in question; political forces beyond individual control dictate most outcomes in American politics. But this book has minimized several existing gaps in the celebrity studies literature. What have we learned?

A New Definition of Celebrity

As I discussed in the introduction, too many theories surrounding celebrity studies rely on vague and contradictory definitions of celebrity that are difficult to measure. Words like "aura," "ether" and "icon" are commonly used to describe the special qualities celebrities have, but they do not help us identify generalizable traits shared by celebrities that are required to empirically study their electability. I define *celebrity* as a person who attains fame through some form of entertainment. Sports, music, movies and TV shows are all forms of entertainment. Politics is not. Journalism is not, although I distinguish between journalists who report the news and television personalities who discuss news reports (see Chapter 1 for more on this). "Celebrity candidates" in this book are candidates who have *not* held elective office before. "Traditional politicians" *have* held elective office before. Next, celebrity status is assessed according to seven observable criteria: name recognition, favorability, outsider status, relatability, social media following or fan base, fundraising ability, and ability to garner media attention. I speculated that there would be a great degree of variance in the way that celebrity candidates and traditional political candidates score on these measures as distinct groups. For example, I expected celebrity candidates to have higher name recognition than traditional politicians. I also expected them to be more likable, more relatable, and to generate more media interest.

Fame Is Not Binary

There are indeed considerable differences in the way that survey respondents evaluate celebrities and politicians across a variety of criteria. Celebrities, on average, have much higher name recognition, receive much more media attention, and have more social media followers than traditional politicians. They are also slightly more relatable and slightly more likable. However, there is a tremendous amount of variation within these categories. Oprah Winfrey, Dwayne "The Rock" Johnson, and Tom Hanks are significantly more well-known and well-liked than Mark Cuban and Caitlyn Jenner. Joe Biden and Elizabeth Warren are better known and liked than Tim Scott and Michael Bloomberg. These are important differences to note. Not only do measurable components of celebrity allow us to place celebrities on a continuous scale of star power, but they also help us understand why election outcomes might be so different for some celebrities than others. For instance, Cynthia Nixon and Arnold Schwarzenegger are both celebrities who ran for Governor of their respective states, but Schwarzenegger's name recognition has been estimated as high as 100% in some surveys, while Nixon's was just 40% in New York six months before the election.[24] Schwarzenegger won the California gubernatorial election in 2003 handily while Nixon suffered a big loss in the 2018 New York gubernatorial primary.

Celebrity Politicians Are Not a New Phenomenon

We also learned that even though the media environment has changed immensely over the last 200 years, there have always been celebrity politicians in the United States. P.T. Barnum first ran for public office in 1865 as a Republican in Connecticut. Many of the advertising strategies he used to promote his museums and circuses were used in his political campaigns to draw positive attention to his candidacy and remain classic tactics of political persuasion today. Simple slogans, large colorful signs, and "leaking" information to the press are hallmarks of most modern political campaigns, including that of our current president, who is also a businessman-turned-entertainer. The roots of celebrity, though, trace back at least to Alexander the Great and Julius Caesar. There is even an argument to be made that as long as humans and social hierarchies have existed so has celebrity. Several scholars have attributed the fall of Rome to the rise of forces we now recognize as adjacent to celebrity culture; a loss of civic and moral virtues, weakening public reputation of leaders, and increasing internal conflicts (e.g., polarization) and corruption.[25] There is not sufficient evidence to make a conclusive determination about these theories. But they do show that celebrity has been a constant component of conversations about political outcomes throughout history. It is central to understanding human nature and it is central to understanding how humans govern themselves, particularly with regard to democracies. Plato and Aristotle debated the qualifications of government leaders; should knowledgeable elites, Plato's "philosopher kings" rule the Republic, or should the unfit "mob" be allowed to make decisions? Hamilton, Madison and Jay did not use the word celebrity but it is a ubiquitous theme throughout The Federalist Papers. The problem with letting the people choose their own leaders is that from time to time they will be persuaded to choose badly. The structure of the United States government is based on safeguards that prevent one branch led by one unfit leader from making precipitous decisions. Ambition must be made to counteract ambition. While Appendix Table A.1. is surely not a complete representation of every celebrity that has run for public office throughout United States history, it does reflect several of the empirical findings in this book. According to this table, of the celebrities that ran for office, 58% of them won their first race. 44% are Republicans, 39% are Democrats, and the remaining percentage ran as Independents, Libertarians, Green Party, or Reform candidates. The vast majority, 83%, are male. And they hail from a variety of states, although California and New York account for the largest share of political campaigns.

We Still Have a Gender Problem

It may not be long until America has its first woman president, but it will probably take much longer for a female *celebrity* candidate to win. While Republicans, Democrats, and Independents demonstrated a slight preference for traditional female political candidates over traditional male political candidates, this advantage did not extend to female celebrity candidates, most notably among Independents and Republicans. Female celebrities appear to suffer from a perception issue. The double-bind of fame and femininity is a topic that deserves much more academic consideration in the future, both by political communication and gender scholars.

Voters Do Not Prefer Celebrities to Traditional Politicians, but They Are About as Likely to Elect Them

I am often asked what kind of celebrity candidate could beat Donald Trump in 2020 and my answer is frequently the same: I think it might have to be a comedian. Because of the way media coverage of political contests has evolved, one of the most important attributes candidates must have is an ability to campaign through soundbites. Americans' attention spans are too short and their political knowledge is too limited for political candidates to wade deeply into policy debates. But even uneducated voters tend to know if a candidate did something shocking or funny or if one candidate insulted another. Campaign events, too, have become organized in a way that favors the quickest-witted candidate. Televised presidential debates are not policy discussions—they are roasts. Campaign speeches are not educational opportunities for voters—they are improvised spectacles. We have come to expect the current president to speak extemporaneously and derogatorily about his political rivals when he takes the podium. At the early stages of the debates Trump often trolled his Republican opponents, for example, castigating CNN debate moderator Hugh Hewitt for only asking the other candidates questions revolving around him. "Mr. Trump said this, Mr. Trump said that, Mr. Trump . . . these poor guys," said Trump of the other candidates. Later in the same debate Trump directly mocked Jeb Bush. "Oh yeah you're a tough guy Jeb," Trump said, contorting his face for added effect. "You're never going to be President of the United States by insulting your way to the presidency," Bush responded. "Well let's see I'm at 42 and you're at 3," said Trump, "so so far I'm doing better . . . You know you started off over here Jeb," Trump continued, motioning to the podium next to him at the center of the stage. "You're moving over further and further. Pretty soon you're gonna be off the end."[26] Trump's nicknames for his opponents remain memorable today: "Low Energy Jeb Bush," "Lyin' Ted Cruz," "Crooked Hillary," "Crazy Bernie Sanders," and "Little Marco Rubio." The surveys in Chapter 4 suggest that as of September 2018 the best positioned Republican candidates to win an election (against Trump or otherwise) are Mike Pence, Nikki Haley, Condoleezza Rice, Clint Eastwood, Dwayne "The Rock" Johnson, and Chuck Norris. The best positioned Democrats are Bernie Sanders, Kamala Harris, Joe Biden, Elizabeth Warren, Kirsten Gillibrand, Oprah Winfrey, and Tom Hanks. The bottom line is that when famous and popular celebrities run for elective office, they tend to perform about as well as experienced politicians. The time in which we could laugh off the political ambitions of entertainers has long passed.

Conclusion: A Slow Boil

When it comes to public affairs, Americans are by and large politically uninformed, myopic and unmotivated. Their partisan identification mostly informs their political preferences (rather than the other way around). These traits create a favorable environment for celebrity candidates. Inattentive voters are more likely to know who they are even if they never consume political news. Because these candidates rise to prominence in industries which monetize popularity, those same uninformed voters are also likely to think highly of them, and be largely unaware of the skills necessary to govern.

Is the rise of celebrity candidates cause for concern? The charitable view of political amateurs such as celebrities is that they are a breath of fresh air for democracy. People who vote for political amateurs, as Former House Majority Leader Eric Cantor once described, believe that they will "go to Washington, take Washington by the lapels, shake it up and then return it back to what we need to be doing."[27] One might even argue celebrity candidates are manifestations of populism in its purest form—antidotes to the machines, big money, and backroom deals that political realists maintain are necessary evils to keep government running smoothly.[28]

But existing research casts a cloud over this sunny evaluation. Political amateurs are, on average, more ideologically extreme, less willing to work in a bipartisan manner, and inferior when it comes to the essential political skill of bargaining compared to experienced elected officials. A survey of the psychological literature on celebrities and a close examination of political memoirs in this book lend further support to the notion that celebrities appear to be almost uniquely ill-equipped to successfully govern. They have selfish motivations for running, serious personality anomalies that make the grisly and unglamorous work of policymaking more difficult, and are more likely to surround themselves with fearful sycophants than teams of rivals. Lack of interpersonal trust, insecurity, and a constant need for public adoration play a similarly foreboding role.

This is a deeply unsettling combination of qualities for world leaders, one that cost the founders sleep. Hamilton and Madison all but equate fame with ineptitude and poor character throughout The Federalist Papers. They designed slow, rigid government institutions and ensured frequent elections, partly to ensure that if an unfit celebrity was swept into office by an undiscerning and uneducated public, voters could remedy their error a short time later before too much damage was sustained. But because the effects of government policy and administration can take so long to manifest, the founders' institutional fail-safes may not function as intended. The decisions our leaders impose on us often exert lagged effects on social conditions. Americans are routinely reminded of this fact when it comes to social progress. President Obama frequently uses a Martin Luther King Jr. quote to bring Americans hope and assuage their fears about the future of the United States: "The arc of the moral universe is long," King famously said, "but it bends toward justice."[29] Supreme Court Justice Ruth Bader Ginsburg has a similar way of putting this. "Progress is slow, but we have traveled a considerable distance," she said recently at George Washington University.[30]

Voters are less often reminded that deterioration, like progress, can also occur slowly. It happens when nobody is paying attention, when our daily lives are undisturbed for extended periods of time. Both the GOP and Democrats have consistently strengthened the executive when their party is in power and Congress has been lethargic and weak with regard to preserving its Article I powers. The "legislature's unexercised muscles" have atrophied, wrote George Will in a rebuke of congressional Republicans who have followed President Trump's lead, "because of people like them, who have been too weak to use their Article I powers against the current wielder of Article II powers."[31] And so far, the effects of expanded executive power have been relatively muted, perhaps because those powers have mostly been vested in presidents with ample experience and at least a modicum of moral integrity in recent decades. But now we have a president who has publicly considered pardoning himself and his political allies if found guilty of illegal behavior, who has fired and punished his political enemies, unilaterally withdrawn from international agreements, levied tariffs against allies, censored the press, threatened nuclear war, befriended and praised dictators and tyrants, sowed doubt in the integrity of elections and flirted with the idea of staying in office for life.

While Trump's erosion of democratic norms is shocking to the most astute political observers, many Americans cannot yet perceive any material consequence. But we should not make the mistake of assuming these actions will not wreak havoc down the road. The economy performed well in the first two years of Trump's presidency, but continued trade wars may one day bring it to its knees. Straining European alliances may not inspire alarm during peacetime, but if a global conflict erupts America could find itself dangerously isolated and vulnerable. If such a crisis occurs in the near future, Americans may learn their lesson, and think twice before again electing an inexperienced candidate bereft of relevant talents save for the "little art of popularity." But if the event that reveals the danger of impulsive, uninformed policymaking is sufficiently delayed, Americans may wrongly infer that skill and experience are orthogonal to sound stewardship of the state. If enough voters accept such a fallacy, we can expect the nation's public stage to be increasingly lit by the flash bulbs that surround crowd-pleasing neophytes, while our brightest political stars are one by one extinguished.

Notes

1. See Luce, Edward. July 19, 2018. "The Risk of Calling Trump a Traitor." *Financial Times*, and Hanson, Victor Davis. July 5, 2018. "Why the Left Keeps Saying Trump Is a Nazi, Facist, Tyrant or Buffoon." *The Mercury News.*

2. See Sonmez, Felicia. November 4, 2018. "Stacey Abrams on Trump's 'Not Qualified' Remark: Republicans Are 'Getting Scared.'" *The Washington Post.* Also see Bluestein, Greg. August 6, 2018. "Opening Maneuvers: Kemp Attacks, Abrams Avoids 'Fisticuffs'." *AJC.*

3. Gstalter, Morgan. November 2, 2018. "Combat Veteran after GOP Opponent Says Campaign 'Is a War': 'You Don't Know s—About War.'" *The Hill.*

4. Leo Braudy as quoted in Elliott, Anthony. 1998. "Celebrity and Political Psychology: Remembering Lennon." *Political Psychology* 19(4): 833–852. Page 834.

5. Ibid.

6. See both Beckford, Martin. June 6, 2008. "Amy Winehouse More Influential than Teachers and Politicians for Modern Girls." *The Telegraph*, and "Teenagers Most Influenced by Celebrities" published with no author in the *Telegraph* on August 12, 2009.

7. Description of Robert Putnam's book on Simon & Schuster's website. Putnam, Robert. 2000. *Bowling Alone: The Collapse and Revival of American Community.* New York, NY: Simon & Schuster.

8. Shwarz, Hunter. July 12, 2018. "How Reality TV Took Over Politics." *CNN.*

9. Reeves, Robert and Gary Baker and Chris Truluck. 2012. "Celebrity Worship, Materialism, Compulsive Buying, and the Empty Self." *Psychology and Marketing* 29(9): 674–679. Page 675.

10. See Leonhardt, David, and Ian Philbrick. January 15, 2018. "Donald Trump's Racism: The Definitive List. *The New York Times.* Also see Cohen, Claire. July 14, 2017. "Donald Trump Sexism Tracker: Every Offensive Comment in One Place." *The Telegraph.*

11. Hanukov, Ilana. 2015. "The "Cocaine Kate" Scandal: Celebrity Addiction or Public Addiction to Celebrity?" *The Journal of Popular Culture* 48(4): 652–661. Page 653.

12. Pappas, Stephanie. February 24, 2012. "Oscar Psychology: Why Celebrities Fascinate Us." *Live Science.*

13. Goldsmith, Barbara. December 4, 1983. "The Meaning of Celebrity." *The New York Times.*

14. Monbiot, George. October 4, 2016. "Lies, Fearmongering and Fables: That's Our Democracy." *The Guardian*.

15. Iyengar et al. April 23, 2018. "The Origins and Consequences of Affective Political Polarization in the United States." Annual Review of Political Science, 1–36. Accessed online. Page 3.

16. Sides, John et al. 2018. *Identity Crisis: The 2016 Presidential Campaign and the Battle for America*. Princeton, NJ: Princeton University Press.

17. Rockwell, Donna. January 9, 2017. "Celebrity Worship and The American Mind." *The Huffington Post*.

18. Loftus, Mary. June 9, 2016. "The Other Side of Fame." *Psychology Today*.

19. Rockwell, Donna and David Giles. 2009. "Being a Celebrity: A Phenomenology of Fame." *Journal of Phenomenological Psychology* 40(1): 178–210.

20. Barber, James David. 1985. *The Presidential Character*. New York, NY: Prentice Hall.

21. Wilson, James Q. as quoted in Rauch, Jonathan. May 2015. "Political Realism: How Hacks, Machines, Big Money, and Back-Room Deals Can Strengthen American Democracy." *Brookings*.

22. Federalist 10 and Federalist 70 accessed online through The Avalon Project at Yale Law School.

23. Canon, David T. 1990. *Actors, Athletes, and Astronauts: Political Amateurs in the United States Congress*. Chicago, IL: University of Chicago Press. Pages 113, 116 and 117.

24. Wright, Lauren. March 27, 2018. "Cynthia Nixon Is No Donald Trump." *The Hill*, and Evans, Michael. 2016. *Seeking Good Debate*. Berkeley, CA: University of California Press. Page 112.

25. Schnee, Christian. 2016. "Images of Weakness and the Fall of Rome;—An Analysis of Reputation Management's Impact on Political History." *Management and Organizational History* 11(1): 1–18.

26. Real Clear Politics Video Archive. Clip Posted December 15, 2015. "Trump to Jeb Bush: "I'm at 42 And You're At 3," "Pretty Soon You're Going To Be On The End.""

27. Eric Cantor, as quoted in a transcript of an episode of PBS Frontline titled "Trump's Takeover." April 10, 2018.

28. Rauch, Jonathan. May 2015. "Political Realism: How Hacks, Machines, Big Money, and Back-room Deals Can Strengthen American Democracy." *Brookings*.

29. Lewis, Matt. January 16, 2017. "Obama Loves Martin Luther King's Great Quote—But He Uses it Incorrectly." *The Daily Beast*.

30. Steinhardt, Ruth. July 25, 2017. "Ruth Bader Ginsburg: 'We Are Far From Perfection.'" GWToday. Justice Ruth Bader Ginsburg speaking at George Washington University.

31. Canon 1990, Page 115.

Appendix

Table A.1 provides a list of celebrities who ran for elective office from 1865 through 2018. While likely not comprehensive, it is a useful tool to begin to draw parallels across celebrity candidacies based on party, level of office, and states in which celebrities frequently run. All of the celebrities listed here filed official paperwork to run for the indicated office in the indicated state, and their names eventually appeared on an election ballot. Things get much more complicated when we consider celebrities who are not listed, or who were recruited by parties to run for office, but declined to do so, such as George Clooney, Brooks Robinson, Roger Staubach, Burt Reynolds, Shailene Woodley, Warren Beatty, and Ashley Judd. Also not listed are celebrities who ran for office and dropped out before election day. These include Stacey Dash (CA U.S. House 2018), Melissa Gilbert (MI U.S. House 2016), Howard Stern (NY Governor 1994), Krist Novoselic (Wahkiakum WA County Clerk 2009), Gary Kroeger (IA U.S. House 2016), Ron White (President 2016), Doug Stanhope (President 2008), Dick Gregory (President 1968 and a Chicago Mayor write-in candidate in 1966), and Dan Blizerain (President 2012). Celebrities who became famous outside of the entertainment industry and launched successful bids for federal office are not included either, such as American astronaut and Senator John Glenn, or Edward M. Davis, who served as Los Angeles Police Chief and was made famous by his television appearances surrounding the Charles Mason killings before consulting on movie sets and becoming a California State Senator. Finally, celebrities who have entered politics through appointed positions are not listed here, such as Reagan and Nixon speechwriter Ben Stein, Reagan-appointed Ambassador John Gavin, and White House and State Department staffer under Reagan Morgan Mason.

Table A.1 Celebrity Runs for Elective Office

Name	Year	Profession	Won?	First Office Pursued	Party	State
P.T. Barnum	1865	Businessman	Yes	State House	Republican	CT
Upton Sinclair	1934	Author	No	Governor	Democrat	CA
Will Rodgers	1942	Actor	Yes	U.S. House	Democrat	CA
Albert Dekker	1944	Actor	Yes	State House	Democrat	CA
Helen Douglas	1945	Actor	Yes	U.S. House	Democrat	CA
John Lodge	1947	Actor	Yes	U.S. House	Republican	CT
Roy Acuff	1948	Musician	No	Governor	Republican	TN
Rex Bell	1955	Actor	Yes	Lt. Governor	Republican	NV
Gore Vidal	1960	Author/TV Personality	No	U.S. House	Democrat	NY
Norman Mailer	1960	Author	No	Mayor	Democrat	NY
George Murphy	1965	Actor	Yes	U.S. Senate	Republican	CA
Wendell Corey	1965	Actor	Yes	City Council	Republican	CA
William F. Buckley	1965	Author/TV Personality	No	Mayor	Republican	NY
Bob Mathias	1967	Athlete	Yes	U.S. House	Republican	CA
Ronald Reagan	1967	Actor	Yes	Governor	Republican	CA
Shirley Temple Black	1967	Actor	No	U.S. House	Republican	CA
Pat Paulsen	1968	Comedian	No	President	Independent	WA*
Willmer Mizell	1969	Athlete	Yes	U.S. House	Republican	NC
Jack Kemp	1971	Athlete	Yes	U.S. House	Republican	NY
Ralph Metcalfe	1971	Athlete	Yes	U.S. House	Democrat	IL
George Takei	1973	Actor	No	City Council	Democrat	CA
Bob Dornan	1977	Actor	Yes	U.S. House	Republican	CA
Jerry Springer	1977	TV Personality	Yes	Mayor	Democrat	OH
Bill Bradley	1978	Athlete	Yes	U.S. Senate	Democrat	NJ
Jello Biafra	1979	Musician	No	Mayor	Green Party	CA
Steven Zirnkilton	1982	Actor	Yes	State House	Republican	ME
Jack Kelly	1983	Actor	Yes	City Council	Republican	CA
Nancy Jane Kulp	1984	Actor	No	U.S. House	Democrat	PA
Jerry Butler	1985	Musician	Yes	County Commissioner	Democrat	IL
Ben Knighthorse Campbell	1986	Athlete	Yes	U.S. House	Democrat	CO
Clint Eastwood	1986	Actor	Yes	Mayor	Republican	CA
Russell Means	1987	Actor	No	President	Libertarian	SD*
Tom McMillen	1987	Athlete	Yes	U.S. House	Democrat	MD
Sonny Bono	1988	Musician	Yes	Mayor	Republican	CA
Ben Jones	1989	Actor	Yes	U.S. House	Democrat	GA
Jason Lewis	1990	Author/Radio Personality	No	U.S. House	Republican	CO

Name	Year	Profession	Won?	First Office Pursued	Party	State
Ralph Waite	1990	Actor	No	U.S. House	Democrat	CA
Tom Laughlin	1992	Actor	No	President	Democrat	WI*
Fred Grandy	1993	Actor	Yes	U.S. House	Republican	IA
Fred Thompson	1994	Actor	Yes	U.S. Senate	Republican	TN
Shiela Kuehl	1994	Actor	Yes	State House	Democrat	CA
Steve Largent	1994	Athlete	Yes	U.S. House	Republican	OK
J.C. Watts	1995	Athlete	Yes	U.S. House	Republican	OK
Jim Ryun	1996	Athlete	Yes	U.S. House	Republican	KS
Al Lewis	1998	Actor	No	Governor	Green Party	NY
Barry Gordon	1998	Actor	No	U.S. House	Democrat	CA
Jesse Ventura	1998	Athlete	Yes	Mayor	Reform	MN
Jim Bunning	1998	Athlete	Yes	U.S. Senate	Republican	KY
Alan Autry	2000	Athlete	Yes	Mayor	Republican	CA
Jerry Doyle	2000	Actor/TV Personality	No	U.S. House	Republican	CA
Tom Osborne	2000	Athlete	Yes	U.S. House	Republican	NE
Arnold Schwarzenegger	2003	Athlete	Yes	Governor	Republican	CA
Gary Coleman	2003	Actor	No	Governor	Independent	CA
Leo Gallagher	2003	Comedian	No	Governor	Independent	CA
Marilyn Chambers	2003	Actor	No	Governor	Libertarian	CA
Mary Carey	2003	Actor	No	Governor	Independent	CA
Ronia Tamar Goldberg (Angelyne)	2003	Actor	No	Governor	Independent	CA
Sonny Landham	2003	Actor	No	Governor	Republican	KY
Justin Jeffre	2005	Musician	No	Mayor	Independent	OH
Martha Reeves	2005	Musician	Yes	City Council	Democrat	MI
Heath Shuler	2006	Athlete	Yes	U.S. House	Democrat	NC
John Hall	2006	Musician	Yes	U.S. House	Democrat	NY
Lynn Swann	2006	Athlete	No	Governor	Republican	PA
Melody Damayo (Mimi Miyagi)	2006	Actor	No	Governor	Republican	NV
Al Franken	2008	Comedian	Yes	U.S. Senate	Democrat	MN
Kevin Johnson	2008	Athlete	Yes	Mayor	Democrat	CA
Matthew Lindland	2008	Athlete	Yes	State House	Republican	OR
Sam Wyche	2008	Athlete	Yes	City Council	Republican	SC
Craig X. Rubin	2009	Actor	No	Mayor	Independent	CA
Dave Bing	2009	Athlete	Yes	Mayor	Democrat	MI
Linda McMahon	2010	TV Personality	No	U.S. Senate	Republican	CT
Che Smith (Rhymefest)	2010	Musician	No	City Council	Democrat	IL
Sean Duffy	2010	TV Personality	Yes	U.S. House	Republican	WI
Luther Campbell	2011	Musician	No	Mayor	Democrat	FL

(Continued)

Table A.1 (Continued)

Name	Year	Profession	Won?	First Office Pursued	Party	State
Park Overall	2012	Actor	No	U.S. Senate	Democrat	TN
Roseanne Barr	2012	Actor	No	President	Green Party	UT*
Clay Aiken	2014	Musician	No	U.S. House	Democrat	NC
J.G. Hertzler	2014	Actor	Yes	City Council	Independent	NY
Marianne Williamson	2014	Author/TV Personality	No	U.S. House	Democrat	CA
Donald Trump	2016	Businessman/TV Personality	Yes	President	Republican	NY*
Colin Allred	2018	Athlete	Yes	U.S. House	Democrat	TX
Antonio Sabato Jr.	2018	Actor	No	U.S. House	Republican	CA
Cynthia Nixon	2018	Actor	No	Governor	Democrat	NY
Diane Neal	2018	Actor	No	U.S. House	Independent	NY
Glenn Jacobs	2018	Athlete	Yes	Mayor	Republican	KY
Steven Michael Quezada	2018	Actor	Yes	County Commissioner	Democrat	NM

Fields in which the "*" symbol appears correspond to presidential candidates who, obviously, did not run in a particular state. Instead, the state in which the candidate was born is provided.

Index

Note: Page numbers in italics indicate figures, and page numbers in bold indicate tables on the corresponding pages.

ABC 16, 33, 49; ABC News/Washington Post poll 77
Abramowitz, Alan 70
Abrams, Stacey 122
Access Hollywood tape 124
Achen, Christopher 125, 129
achieved celebrity 13, 14
Acuff, Roy 31, 46, 48, 51–52, **138**
Adkins, Trace 108, *110*
Aiken, Clay **140**
Alexander III of Macedonia 23
Alexander the Great 23, 131
Al Franken: Giant of the Senate (Franken) 54
Allen, Mike 16
Allred, Colin **140**
Allred, Kevin 7
Amateur Democrat, The (Wilson) 128
American Association of Physicians and Surgeons v. Hillary Rodham Clinton 11
American Life, An (Reagan) 51
American Museum 47
American National Election Studies 74
American Voter Revisited, The (Lewis-Beck) 74
Amos, Clinton 21
Annenberg Public Policy Survey 94
Anzia, Sarah 46
Apprentice, The (television show) 4, 89, 94, 107
Aristotle 131
ascribed celebrity 13
Athearn, Forden 59
athletes *see* celebrity athletes
Austin, Erica 19
Autry, Alan **139**
Ayotte, Kelly 46

Baby Boomers 18
Baker, Peter 17
Baldwin, Alec 108, *110*, 111
Banks, Elizabeth 108, *110*
Barber, James David 128
Barnum, P.T. 24, 31, 46, 46–48, 51, 53, 70, 131, **138**
Barnum, William H. 47
Barr, Roseanne 98n26, **140**
Bartels, Larry 70, 125, 129
Baum, Matthew 15, 16
Bauman, Zygmund 12
Beatty, Warren 137
Bell, Rex **138**
Bennet, Stephen 18
Berlin, Irving 66
Berry, Christopher 46
Best Man, The (Vidal) 49
Between Two Ferns (Galifianakis) 126
Biafra, Jello **138**
Biden, Joe 72, *73*, 74, *78*, 81, *82*, 87, 94, 103, 108, *110*, 116, 120, 131, 133
Bieber, Justin 55, 86
Biel, Jessica 90
Bilello, Joseph 79
Bing, Dave **139**
Biswas, Somdutta 21
Blake, David Haven 66
Blizerain, Dan 137
Bloomberg, Michael 72, *73*, *78*, *82*, 87, 98n26, 104, 108, *110*, 112, 118n18, 120, 131
Bloomberg poll 77
Blumenthal, Sidney 3, 7
Board, Elizabeth 57
Bogart, Frank 55

Bono 90
Bono, Sonny 31, 52–54, 55, **138**
Booker, Cory 72, 73, 74, 78, 82, 87, 103, 108, *110*, 111
Bourdain, Anthony 126
Bowling Alone (Putnam) 123
Bradford, Lamed G. 50
Bradley, Bill 31, 34, 35, 39, 41, 42, 45, 57, **138**
Braudy, Leo 23, 24, 123
Brayboy, Stacy 68
Breslin, Jimmy 50, 51
Broockman, David 71
Brooklyn Daily Eagle (newspaper) 47–48
Brown, Jerry 108, *110*, 111, 120
Brown, Jim 127
Buckley, John 39
Buckley, William F. 48–49, **138**
Bunning, Jim **139**
Bush, George H. W. 77
Bush, George W. 7, 10, 15, 60, 76, 79, 105
Bush, Jeb 2, 45, 92, 133
Bush, Laura 10, 14
Bustamante, Cruz 38
Bustos, Cheri 46

cable news 16
Caesar: A Life in Western Culture (Wyke) 23
Caesar, Julius 23–24, 131
California: Sinclair running for Governor 31–34; California Democratic Party 31
Campbell, Ben Nighthorse 34, 36, 40, 42, 43, **138**
Campbell, Luther **139**
candidates: hipness of 19; *see also* voter preference for candidates
Cannon, Lou 55
Canon, David 96, 129
Cantor, Eric 133
Carey, Mary **139**
Carson, Ben 3, 51
Carter, John 122
Carville, James 13
Case, Clifford 39
Castro, Julian 108, *110*, 111, 120
CBS 16, 56, 124
Cecil B. DeMille Award 6
celebrities in politics: fame and 130–131; favorability of 75–78; fundraising by 88–91; gender problem in 132; large and passionate following 85–88, *87*; likelihood by party 119–120; media attention for 91–95; name recognition 69–75; new definition of celebrity 130; outsider status of 82–85; phenomenon of 131–132; relatability of 79–81, *82*; research findings 133–135; runs for elective office 137, **138–140**; theory and expectations of 95–97; voter preferences and 132–133
celebrity: bucking the status quo 65–69; definition of 11; description of 12–15; first ladies 10, 11; levels of 13; new definition of 130; phenomenon of 22–25; political endorsements 18–22; public opinion and voting behavior 17–22; term 12
celebrity athletes in politics: candidacy of 41–42; with friends in high places 43–44; irresistible challenge of 40–41; macho culture of 44–46; pressure to perform 39–40; rehearsal in politics 38–39; rigors of politicking and 34–46
Chambers, Marilyn **139**
Cher 53
Christie, Chris 10, 92
Clines, Francis 56
Clinton, Bill 60
Clinton, Hillary 14, 30, 45, 68, 77, 79–80, 92, 120, 121; fundraising 90; media attention 92, 94–95; social media 86
Clooney, Amal 90
Clooney, George 90, 103, 108, *110*, 111, 137
CNN 16, 94, 124, 126, 132
Coleman, Gary **139**
Coleman, Norm 53–54, 103
Collateral Damage (film) 45
Comedians in Cars Getting Coffee (Seinfeld) 70, 126
Coppock, Alexander 102
Corey, Wendell **138**
Cruz, Ted 92, 103, 133
Cuban, Mark 72, 73, 78, 82, 87, 108, *110*, 131
cultural divide 6–8
Culture of Narcissism, The (Lasch) 127
Cuomo, Andrew 108, *110*, 111, 116, 120
Cushan, Philip 124

Damayo, Melody (Mimi Miyagi) **139**
Dash, Stacey 98n26, 122, 137
Davis, Edward M. 137
Davis, Gray 40
Dawkins, Richard 7
de Borda, Jean-Charles 103

DeBusschere, Dave 42
de Condorcet, Nicolas 103
Dekker, Albert **138**
Democracy for Realists (Achen and Bartels) 125
Dickerson, John 89
Dionne, E. J. 18
Dole, Bob 37, 38
Dooley, Vince 35
Dornan, Bob **138**
Douglas, Helen 116, **138**
Downs, Anthony 80
Doyle, Jerry **139**
Draper, Robert 68
Dr. Oz Show, The 94
Duffy, Sean **139**
Dunning-Kruger effect 94

Eastwood, Clint 55, *72, 73, 78, 82,* 87, 104, *110,* 112, 118n17, 120, 133, **138**
Eisenhower, Dwight 57–58, 66–67
elections 8–11
Elliot, Anthony 123
Eversole, Ed 41

Facebook 4, 71, 85, 87, 92
fame: celebrities and 130–131; term 12
favorability: celebrities in politics 75–78; celebrities *vs* politicians *78;* media coverage and 76–77
Federalist Papers, The 24, 25, 129, 131
Ferrell, Will 98n26
Figley, Charles 127
Fiorina, Carly 2, *72, 73,* 74, *78, 82, 87,* 104, 108, *110,* 112, 120
Fire and Fury (Wolff) 8, 27n28
first ladies 10, 11
Flaherty, Joe 50
Flake, Jeff 126
Flynn, Errol 56
following: celebrities in politics 85–88; celebrities *vs* politicians *87*
Fonda, Jane 13
Forsyth, Justin 90
Fox & Friends (Fox News) 91
Fox News 16, 17, 48–49, 91
France, Lisa Respers 124
Franken, Al 25, 31, 53, 54–57, 65, **139**
Franklin, Benjamin 25
Freeman, Ira 49, 58
Frenzy of Renown, The (Braudy) 123
Fresno Bee, The (newspaper) 32
Fukumoto, Kentaro 70
fundraising, celebrities in politics 88–91

Gahagan Douglas, Helen 58–59
Galifianakis, Zach 126
Gallagher, Leo **139**
Gallup 77
Gamson, Joshua 22, 24
Garthwaite, Craig 19, 20
Gavin, John 137
gender: celebrity electability and 113–117; celebrity politicians and 132
Gianforte, Greg 115–116
Gilbert, Melissa 137
Giles, David 23, 127
Gillibrand Kirsten 46, 103–104, 108, *110,* 133
Ginsburg, Ruth Bader 134
Gipp, George 56
Glenn, John 13, 137
Goldberg, Ronia Tamar (Angelyne) **139**
Goldsmith, Barbara 125
Gomez, Selena 86
Google 92, 102
Gordon, Barry **139**
Gore, Al 79
GOTV campaigns 19
Grandy, Fred **139**
Green, Donald 71
Gregory, Dick 137
Griffey, Ken Jr. 14
Griffey, Ken Sr. 14
Gulati, Jeff 89
Gunn, Anton 68
Gunter, Barrie 15

Haidt, Jonathan 80
Haley, Nikki 108, *110,* 112, 120, 133
Hall, John **139**
Hamilton, Alexander 9, 24–25, 129, 131, 134
Hammond, Johnny 56
Hanks, Tom 1, 2, *72, 73,* 74, *78,* 81, *82, 87,* 103, 108, *110,* 111, 120, 131, 133
Hannity, Sean 17
Hanukov, Ilana 124
Harris, John 16
Harris, Kamala *72, 73,* 74, *78, 82, 87,* 103, 108, *110,* 120, 133
Harvey, Mark 15, 17
Hastert, Dennis 45
HBO 16
Health Security Act 121
Hegar, MJ 122
Heinrich, Martin 126
Herbst, Kenneth 19
Hertzler, J. G. **140**

Heston, Charlton 13
Heth, Joice 24, 46–47
Hewitt, Hugh 132
Hill, The (newspaper) 3
Hinich, Melvin 83
Hollywood Reporter, The (magazine) 112
Holmes, Gary 21
Holt, Lester 17
Houran, James 125
Huckabee, Mike 2
Huffington, Arianna 38, 45
Humphrey, Skip 103
Hunston, Susan 84

I Ain't Got Time to Bleed (Ventura) 35, 45
I Candidate for Governor (Sinclair) 32
Illusions of Immortality (Giles) 23
Ingraham, Laura 17
Instagram 5, 85, 86
Internet 97n9
Iyengar, Shanto 125

Jack the Ripper 23
Jacobs, Glenn **140**
James, LeBron 98n26, 108, *110*
Jarrett, Valerie 68, 69
Jay, John 24
Jeffre, Justin **139**
Jenner, Bruce 13
Jenner, Caitlyn 13, *72, 73, 78, 82, 87,* 104, 108, *110,* 113, 131
Johnson, Alice 127
Johnson, Dwayne "The Rock" 1, 2, 14, *72, 73,* 74, 77, *78,* 81, *82, 87,* 93, 104, 108, *110,* 112, 120, 131, 133
Johnson, Kevin **139**
Jones, Alex 17
Jones, Ben **138**
journalists, famous 15–17
Judd, Ashley 137
Jungle, The (Sinclair) 32

Kaine, Tim 108, *110,* 111, 120
Kam, Cindy 70
Kardashian, Kim 14, 86, 118n15, 127
Kardashian, Robert 13
Kasich, John 2, *72, 73,* 74, *78, 82, 87,* 92, 103, 104, 108, *110,* 112, 120
Kelly, Jack **138**
Kemp, Brian 122
Kemp, Jack 31, 35, 37, 38, 39, 40, 43–44, 67, **138**

Kemp, Jeff 44
Kennedy, Bobby 56, 57
Kennedy, Jack 49
Kennedy, John F. 59, 68
Kennedy, Ted 43
Kerry, John 79
Kibby Ed 53
Kid Rock 1, 127
King, Larry 42
King, Martin Luther, Jr. 134
Kings Row (film) 56
Klar, Samara 102
Knute Rockne, All American (film) 56
Kopelson, Gene 56, 57
Kroeger, Gary 137
Krupnikov, Yanna 102
Kuehl, Shiela **139**
Kulp, Nancy Jane **138**

Lamont, Michele 85
Landham, Sonny **139**
Lane, Ken 42
Lapham, Lewis 23
Largent, Steve **139**
Lasch, Christopher 127
Laughlin, Tom **139**
Lauzen, Martha 115
Lee, Dwight 80
Lemon, Don 1
Lennon, John 123
Leno, Jay 42
Letterman, David 42
Lewandowski, Cory 50
Lewis, Al **139**
Lewis, Jason **138**
Lewis, Joseph 57
Liking Ike (Blake) 66
Lindland, Matthew **139**
Lodge, John **138**
Longoria, Eva 90, 108, *110*

McCain, John 76, 83
McCloskey, Peter 58
McConnell, Mitch 1, 65–66
MacFarlane, Seth 90
McGhee, Bob 44
McHugh, Drake 56
McMahon, Linda **139**
McMillen, Tom **138**
Maddow, Rachel 17
Madison, James 9, 24–25, 129, 131, 134
Mailer, Norman 50, 51, **138**

"Make America Great Again" Trump slogan 92
Manafort, Paul 50
Manigault Newman, Omarosa 94
Manning, Archie 14
Manning, Eli 14
Manning, Peyton 14, 104, *110*
Mansbridge, Jane 81
Marquette poll 77
Mason, Morgan 137
Mathias, Bob 31, 34, 37, 43–44, **138**
Mathias, Jim 37
Mayer, Louis 67–68
Means, Russell **138**
Mechanical Turk 72, 74, 81, 94
media attention: celebrities in politics 91–95; celebrities *vs* politicians 93
mediated quasi-interaction 123
Metcalfe, Ralph **138**
Millennials 18
Miller, Warren 70
Mitchell, George 59
Miwa, Hirofumi 70
Mizell, Willmer **138**
Modesto Bee, The (newspaper) 32
Moe, Terry 9
Moore, Timothy 19, 20
Morning Consult poll 106, 112
Morning Joe (MSNBC) 91
Moss, Kate 124
MSNBC 16, 17, 91
Mueller, Robert 37, 128
Murphy, George **138**
Murphy, Ryan 80
Murray, Patty 45
My Day (Roosevelt) 49

name recognition 14; celebrities in politics 69–75; celebrities *vs* politicians 72–75; multiple choice responses *73*; open-ended responses *72*
National Rifle Association 65
NBC 16, 17, 43
Neal, Diane **140**
New Bedford Standard Times (newspaper) 67
Newman, Paul 48
New York Times (newspaper) 49, 68
Nighthorse Campbell, Ben *see* Campbell, Ben Nighthorse
Nixon, Cynthia 1, 8, 59, 116, 122, 131, **140**
Nixon, Richard 59, 116, 128

No Child Left Behind 10
Norris, Chuck 108, *110*, 112, 120, 133
Novoselic, Krist 137
Nugent, Ted 98n26

Obama, Barack 5, 7, 20, 33, 60, 68, 70, 76, 83, 128; fundraising 89–90; social media followers 86
Obama, Michelle 69
Oprah effect 20; *see also* Winfrey, Oprah
O'Reilly, Bill 48–49, 54
Osborne, Tom 35, 36, 40–41, 44, 44–45, 45, **139**
outsider status 3, 82–85
Overall, Park **140**

Palimpsest (Vidal) 48
Palin, Sarah 83
Parker, Sarah Jessica 116
Pataki, George 2
Patrick, Deval 108, *110*, 111, 120
Paul, Rand 2
Paulsen, Pat **138**
Pence, Mike 10, *104*, 108, *110*, 112, 120, 133
Pennock, Roland 81
Perry, Katy 86
Perry, Rick 2, 75
Phillips, Busy 90
Pickler, Kellie 108, *110*, 112
Pitkin, Hanna 81
Plato 131
politicians: celebrity athletes and rigors of politicking 34–46; memoirs of 30–31; term 12
Politico 16, 77
politics: American democracy and celebrities 128–130; bias of voters 122–123; celebrities in 130–133; celebrity endorsements 18–22; celebrity involvement in 119–130; different rules for women 58–61; elections 8–11; entertainment industry and 127–128; female candidates in 121–123; loveable roles in 54–58; as show business 46–61; visual media and celebrity identity 123–127; *see also* celebrities in politics; celebrity athletes in politics
Pound, Ezra 51
preference of voters *see* voter preference for candidates
Priestly, Joseph 25

Prior, Markus 16
public opinion 17–22
Putnam, Robert 123, 124

Quezada, Steven Michael **140**

Reagan, Nancy 56
Reagan, Ronald 3, 13, 25, 31, 46, 51, 55–58, 65, 67, **138**
Real Time with Bill Maher (HBO show) 16
Reece, B. Carroll 52
Reeves, Justin 71, 129
Reeves, Martha **139**
relatability 4; celebrities in politics 79–81; celebrities *vs* politicians *82*
Reuther, Walter 49
Reynolds, Burt 137
Rice, Condoleezza 40, 104, *110*, 112, 120, 133
Rihanna 55
Ringling Bros. and Barnum & Bailey Circus 47
Ringmaster! (Springer) 52
Robinson, Brooks 137
Rockwell, Donna 126, 127
Rodgers, Will **138**
Rojek, Chris 13, 22, 24
Roll Call (website) 54
Rollins, Ed 39
Romney, Mitt 79, 89, 108, *110*, 112, 120
Ronaldo, Christiano 87
Roosevelt, Eleanor 48, 49
Ross, Steve 67
Rove, Karl 40
Rubin, Craig X. **139**
Rubio, Marco 2, 92, 103, 108, *110*, 120, 133
Rush Limbaugh is a Big Fat Idiot and Other Observations (Franken) 54
Ryan, Paul 3, 108, *110*, 112, 120
Ryun, Jim 31, 34, 35, 38, 41, 43, 44, **139**

Sabato, Antonio, Jr. **140**
Sabato, Larry 7
Sacramento Bee, The (newspaper) 32
Sanders, Bernie 86, 92, 108, *110*, 120, 133
San Diego State University 115
San Francisco Chronicle, The (newspaper) 49
Santorum, Rick 89
Schlesinger, Arthur 66

Schmid, David 12
scholarship, celebrities public opinion and voting behavior 17–22
Schuessler, Alexander 80
Schwarzenegger, Arnold 25, 31, 35, 38, 39, 40, 41, 43, 45, 48, 57, 65, 67, 69, 131, **139**
Scott, Tim *72*, *73*, *78*, *82*, *87*, 131
Seinfeld, Jerry 70, 126
She (film) 59
show business: politics as 46–61; *see also* celebrities in politics
Shriver, Maria 43
Shuler, Heath **139**
Sides, John 126
Sinclair, Upton 31–34, 47, 48, 49, **138**
Smith, Che (Rhymefest) **139**
Smith, Margaret Chase 116
Smith, Stacy 115
Snow White and the Seven Dwarfs (film) 59
social media 4, 12, 15, 22, 85–88, 93, 96, 101, 122, 130–131
Society of Professional Journalists (SPJ) Ethics Committee 16
Sokolsky, George 66
Sowell, Thomas 7
Spector, Phil 52
Spielberg, Steven 90
Springer, Jerry 52, **138**
Springsteen, Bruce 108, *110*
Stabenow, Debbie 1
Stanhope, Doug 137
stardom 12
Staubach, Roger 137
Stein, Ben *110*, 137
Stephanopoulos, George 13
Stern, Howard 137
Stevenson, Adlai 49
Stevenson, Seth 79
Stewart, Jon 48–49
Stokes, Donald 70
Streep, Meryl *72*, *73*, *78*, *82*, 87, 103, 104, *104*, 108, *110*, 111, 117n8
Strutton, David 21
Sullenberger, Sully 13
Sully (film) 14
Swann, Lynn **139**
Swift, Taylor 5, 98n26

Takei, George **138**
Talk, The (television show) 16
Taskforce on National Healthcare Reform 121

Tea Party 83
Teigen, Chrissy 86
Temple Black, Shirley 31, 58, **138**
Tesler, Michael 126
Thompson, Fred 67, **139**
Thompson, John 123
Timberlake, Justin 90
Time Present, Time Past (Bradley) 34
Tonight Show with Jimmy Fallon, The (television show) 16
Truman, Harry 48, 59, 116
Trump, Donald 1–4, 7, 8, 10, 14, 25, 31, 45, 47, 50, 51, 60, 61, 115–116, 120, **140**; bucking the status quo 65, 69; favorability 77–78; following of 86; fundraising 88–90; media attention 91–95; name recognition 74; outsider status 83–85, *85*; preference for 102–103, 105–107; relatability 79–80; "Teflon Don" 124
Trump, Ivanka 10
Trump, Melania 10
Twitter 65, 66, 86, 87, 92, 94, 96, 102

University of Birmingham 84
Upgrove, Mark D. 2
USA Today (newspaper) 2
U.S. Constitution 9, 24
U.S. government *see* politics
US Weekly (magazine) 86

Van Horne, Harriet 68
Vanity Fair (magazine) 2
Variety (magazine) 115
Vavreck, Lynn 126
Veer, Ekant 20
Ventura, Jesse 25, 31, 35, 41, 45, 54, 67, 69, 103, **139**
Vidal, Gore 31, 48, 49–50, **138**
View, The (television show) 16
Voight, Jon 104, *104*, 106, 108, *110*
Von Furstenberg, Diane 90
Vote.org 5
voter preference for candidates: candidate support by celebrity status (Democrats) *110*; candidate support by celebrity status (Republicans) *110*; candidate support by celebrity status and gender *113*, *114*; celebrities and 132–133; evidence from priming experiment 107–109; gender moderating celebrity electability 113–117; paired comparison experiment for 101–107; results of priming experiment 109, *110*, *111*–113; selection rates by party and status *105*
voting behavior 17–22
Vox Populi Polling 74

Wade, Rick 68
Waite, Ralph **139**
Wallace, Chris 17
Walsh, Kenneth 2
Walton, Bill 14
Walton, Luke 14
War on Terror 121
Warren, Elizabeth *72*, *73*, 74, 77, *78*, 81, *82*, *87*, 93, 103, *104*, 108, *110*, 120, 131, 133
Washington, George 24, 47
Washington Post, The (newspaper) 8
Watts, J. C. **139**
Weber, Christopher 102
Wellstone, Paul 53–54, 55, 57
West, Kanye *72*, *73*, *78*, *82*, *87*, 103, 108, 118n15, 127
Westwood, Sean 125
White, Ron 137
Wilde, Oscar 70
Will, George 134
Williams, Christine 89
Williamson, Marianne **140**
Wilson, James Q. 128
Winehouse, Amy 123
Winfrey, Oprah 5, 6, 20, 42, *72*, *73*, 74, *78*, 81, *82*, *87*, 103, 104, 108, *110*, 111, 120, 131, 133
Wintour, Anna 90
Wolff, Michael 8, 27n28
Wolff, Sherrie 42
Wood, Natalie 19
Woodley, Shailene 137
Woodward, Joanne 48
Wyche, Sam **139**
Wyke, Maria 23

YouTube 85

Zechmeister, Elizabeth 70
Zirnkilton, Steven **138**

For Product Safety Concerns and Information please contact our EU representative GPSR@taylorandfrancis.com
Taylor & Francis Verlag GmbH, Kaufingerstraße 24, 80331 München, Germany

www.ingramcontent.com/pod-product-compliance
Lightning Source LLC
Chambersburg PA
CBHW071411300426
44114CB00016B/2269